AF206980

Women across Time / *Mujeres a Través del Tiempo*

THE TEXAS EXPERIENCE
Books made possible by
Sarah '84 and Mark '77 Philpy

Women across Time
Mujeres a Través del Tiempo

Sixteen Influential South Texas Women

EDITED BY SUSAN L. ROBERSON

Texas A&M University Press   *College Station*

♾ This paper meets the requirements of ANSI/NISO Z39.48–1992
(Permanence of Paper).
Binding materials have been chosen for durability.
Manufactured in the United States of America

Library of Congress Cataloging-in-Publication Data

Names: Roberson, Susan L., 1950– editor, author, writer of introduction,
    writer of epilogue. | Roberson, Susan L., 1950– Frances Tarlton "Sissy"
    Farenthold.
Title: Women across time / Mujeres a través del tiempo : sixteen
    influential South Texas women / edited by Susan L. Roberson.
Other titles: Mujeres a través del tiempo | Texas experience (Texas A & M
    University. Press)
Description: First edition. | College Station : Texas A&M University Press,
    [2022] | Series: The Texas Experience (Books made possible by Sarah '84
    and Mark '77 Philpy) | Includes index.
Identifiers: LCCN 2022015963 | ISBN 9781648430855 (cloth) | ISBN
    9781648430862 (ebook)
Subjects: LCSH: Mexican American women—Texas, South—Biography. | Mexican
    Americans—Texas, South—Biography. | Mexican American civic
    leaders—Texas, South—Biography. | Leadership in women—Texas, South. |
    Hispanic American leadership—Texas, South. | Transformational
    leadership—Texas, South. | Mexican American mural painting and
    decoration—Texas—San Antonio. | Texas, South—Biography. | LCGFT:
    Biographies.
Classification: LCC E184.M5 W64 2022 | DDC
    976.4/0046872073—dc23/eng/20220506
LC record available at https://lccn.loc.gov/2022015963

Cover and title page: *Mujeres a Través del Tiempo*, by Arnold Gonzáles Sr.

To
Arnold Gonzáles Sr. and
Charles "Chuck" Wissinger,
for their vision

Contents

Acknowledgments   ix

Introduction: The Art of Biography / Art as Biography
SUSAN L. ROBERSON   1

Part I: The Unnamed Women   9

Chapter 1. Breaking Past Borders:
Las Soldaderas during the Mexican Revolution
VERONICA NOHEMI DURÁN AND SHANNON L. BAKER   11

Part II: The Ranchers   21

Chapter 2. Henrietta King
LARRY KNIGHT   23

Chapter 3. Petra Vela de Kenedy
HOMERO S. VERA   42

Chapter 4. Sarita Kenedy East
DAVID SABRIO   53

Chapter 5. Helen Kleberg
SANDRA REXROAT   69

Part III: The Educators   77

Chapter 6. Jovita González Mireles
MICHELLE JOHNSON VELA   79

Chapter 7. Mary Alice Berlanga Gonzáles
ADRIANA GARZA-FLORES   91

Chapter 8. Dr. Juliet V. García
MANUEL FLORES   101

Part IV: The Politicians   111

Chapter 9. Frances Tarlton "Sissy" Farenthold
SUSAN L. ROBERSON   113

Chapter 10. Anne Legendre Armstrong
MARY LEE GRANT AND NIRMAL GOSWAMI   125

Chapter 11. Irma Lerma Rangel
MANUEL FLORES   134

Part V: The Artists   151

Chapter 12. Carmen Lomas Garza
MARY JANE GARZA AND SANTA CONTRERAS BARRAZA   153

Chapter 13. Selena Quintanilla Pérez
OCTAVIO QUINTANILLA   165

Part VI: Women of Service   177

Chapter 14. Dr. Clotilde P. García
PAMELA WRIGHT   179

Chapter 15. Merideth L. Howard
JENNI VINSON AND RICHARD P. SPAINHOUR   192

Chapter 16. Paving the Way for the Next Generation
JODY A. MARÍN   202

Epilogue
SUSAN L. ROBERSON   221

Contributors   225

Index   229

Acknowledgments

We wish to thank Arnold González Sr. for permission to reproduce his mural *Women across Time:* Mujeres a Través del Tiempo. It is the inspiration for this book of essays.

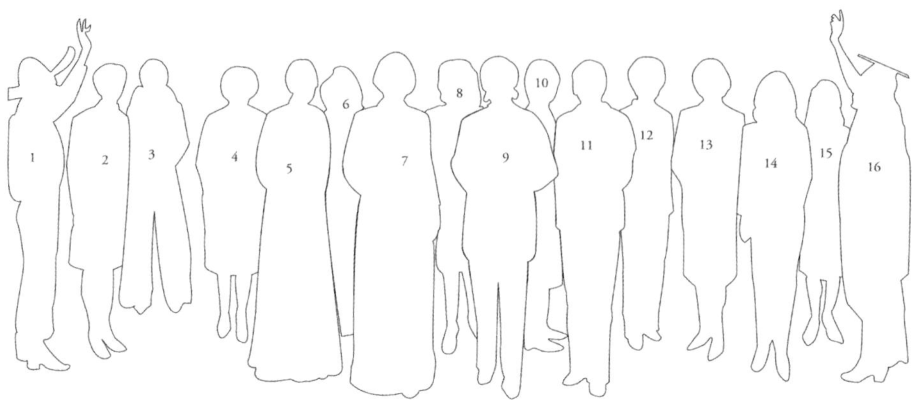

Women across Time or *Mujeres a Través del Tiempo* is a historical mural by alumnus Arnold Gonzáles of Corpus Christi, Texas. On the far left is a photo of a young woman in the nineteenth century waving to a young woman (far right) of the twenty-first century. This connection would not have been possible without the hard work of many influential women in South Texas, including those portrayed in the mural. In the background is a depiction of the Spanish architecture of Texas A&M University–Kingsville, also a key player in the progress made by women and everyone in South Texas. The mountains represent the tie to Mexico, the nuns are reminiscent of the impact of the Catholic Church in South Texas, and the other figures represent a link to the past.

1. Nineteenth-Century Woman
2. Merideth Leigh Howard
3. Helen Campbell Kleberg
4. Dr. Clotilde P. García
5. Henrietta Maria Morse Chamberlain King
6. Sarita Kenedy East
7. Petra Vela de Vidal Kenedy
8. Frances Tarlton "Sissy" Farenthold
9. Irma Lerma Rangel
10. Jovita Gonzáles Mireles
11. Juliet V. García
12. Mary Alice Gonzáles
13. Anne Armstrong
14. Selena Quintanilla Pérez
15. Carmen Lomas Garza
16. Twenty-First-Century Woman

Women across Time / *Mujeres a Través del Tiempo*

Introduction

The Art of Biography / Art as Biography

SUSAN L. ROBERSON

When Arnold Gonzáles was asked to paint a mural for Texas A&M University–Kingsville, he turned to the women of South Texas for his inspiration. In them he found stories of endurance, grit, and love, stories not always celebrated when one thinks of the harsh South Texas terrain and its history of cattle, oil, and rough-and-tumble politics. He wanted to show the important role of women in the area and their impact in the fields of ranching, education, politics, the military, and the arts. And he wanted to contribute to a revision and reimagining of the history of this part of Texas. As he was thinking about his project, he asked himself, "Where are the women? Everything you read is about how the men did it; why not the women?" Discovering the story of Petra Vela Kenedy, wife of rancher Mifflin Kenedy, he wondered, "Why don't I know who this lady is?" Surprised that he had spent most of his life in South Texas and yet did not know about Petra Kenedy, Arnold decided to do something to recover women's history and supplant pervasive stereotypes about women. To help fill the gap, to complete the picture of the development of South Texas, he decided to celebrate the lives of some of the strong and influential women who come from this area. So, he chose to paint the figures of Frances "Sissy" Farenthold, Anne Armstrong, and Selena Quintanilla, whose impact was felt beyond our corner of Texas, as well as women locally known, like Henrietta King, Sarita Kenedy East, Clotilde García, and Irma Rangel, who changed the political and cultural landscapes of South Texas. A politician, artist, and husband to a longtime educator, Arnold also chose to paint the artists, educators, and philanthropists who contributed to the lives of South Texans and devoted themselves to the betterment of others. But he also decided to paint representations of the unnamed women who contributed to the development of South Texas—the Native women, the Catholic nuns, the *soldaderas* who helped pave the way for the young women of tomorrow, represented by the college coed who stands waving *a través del tiempo*, across time, to *la soldadera* who greets her. In this way, the mural represents women across time and class who have contributed to the making of South Texas. It also aims at revising history by focusing on women and their accomplishments instead of on the usual stories of *patrones* and cattle barons.

In the introduction to her book *Telling Women's Lives*, biographer Linda Wagner-Martin enumerates some of the problems associated with telling women's lives. Not only has "history . . . sometimes prevented women from telling stories" and from having their stories told, but there are difficulties in the telling. One of these difficulties is "being recognized as someone's daughter, someone's wife, or someone's mother" instead of as a woman with her own story. How does one tell the story of Henrietta King without submerging her biography in that of her husband, Captain King, who founded the King Ranch, or tell the story of Dr. Clotilde García apart from that of her brother Dr. Hector García, both physicians and civil rights advocates? To complicate matters, the documents from which to construct a woman's biography are often lost or subsumed in the biographies of the men in their lives, or simply unwritten. Another challenge to writing women's biography that Wagner-Martin points to is "society's reaction to a woman's ambition" and the way it shapes women's lives. Women of talent and energy, like those featured in the mural, had to learn how to handle their ambition, perhaps tempering it against social and familial pressures, the "demands of loved ones against her individual needs." As well, the ways to represent that ambition in the face of gendered expectations for women's lives figure into the ways women's stories are told, sometimes in more oblique ways than those of famous men whose youthful adventures seem to have foretold their later achievements. How does one tell of Selena Quintanilla, the Tejana singer who quickly rose from the working class to fame before she was killed? Merideth Howard, who found careers in firefighting and the military, certainly must have strained against expectations about the ways a woman's life "should" unfold. How does one figure the political ambitions of "Sissy" Farenthold, Irma Rangel, and Anne Armstrong, the latter a political figure who was also the charming wife of a strong and influential man, against gender and class expectations for the arc of a woman's life? A further challenge that Wagner-Martin outlines arises when the biographical subjects, like the unnamed women in the mural, have no voice, have left no documents by which to reconstruct a life. What are the untold events, aspirations, and fears of women who left no record behind? How does one reconstruct an individual story from the collective? Part of the adventure in constructing these brief biographies has consisted in finding the archives, digging through the newspapers, interviewing the subjects, or visiting their museums. These are some of the challenges that the authors of the biographical sketches have confronted as they have tried to bring to life, if briefly, the lives of the famous, the nonfamous, and the unnamed women of the mural. In doing so, they contribute to a rewriting of biography and history. As Ralph Waldo Emerson recognized, "There is no history: There is only biography." For Emerson, history was made by the great men whose lives changed the course of nations and eras. By writing biographies of the women who shaped an area and an era, we also rewrite history, making room for a fuller, more nuanced vision of the past and prospects for the future.[1]

To some extent, Arnold Gonzáles, the artist, has avoided several of the pitfalls of telling women's stories that Wagner-Martin outlined by painting the women all together, collectively, standing in formal poses with fixed facial features that do not betray the joys and vicissitudes of their individual lives. The task of the biographers, in even these quick sketches, has been to fill in the stories suggested by the portraits with details that give a sense of "fullness and a perspective" missing in the mural. The English essayist and critic William Hazlitt once remarked, "Portrait-painting is the biography of the pencil." The impulses that lie behind the two art forms, portraiture and biography, their methods and effects, Richard Wendorf argues, "are often strikingly similar." Both art forms seek to celebrate the subject, as do the visual and verbal sketches of *Women across Time*. One of the reasons for biography's popularity has been its celebration of the great and famous, in part to inspire readers to similar achievements and to shape an ethos of greatness for a particular time, an ethos that for the women in the mural included moral, social, and economic philanthropy. Both art and biography seek to give a sense of the character of the individual, her identity, and importance. In doing so, portrait and biography, the mural and the sketches contained here, illustrate "the relations between visual and verbal portraiture." Portraits show the figure in a framed historical or social context—the home, the business, the landscape. Likewise, the biography sets the individual in context, showing the figure as a product of the multiple environments that shape her character. For the women of these sketches, the unique South Texas geographic, demographic, and political landscapes shaped an ethos, a world view that guided their lives, possibilities, and choices. But where fully developed biographies of women might seek to uncover the "hidden, more interior self," the essays in this collection, really a "multibiography," seek to quickly place each figure within her historical context and to indicate what made each woman exceptional.[2] In this way they perform some of the work of traditional biographies of women—to entertain, educate, and inspire—even if they avoid some of the dangers often associated with *fully* telling women's lives.

Even as the women featured in the mural and this book span more than 150 years and come from a variety of economic and ethnic backgrounds, and even though they chose different life paths, their life stories exemplify some common themes. Ambition, talent, and energy consistently describe the likes of Carmen Lomas Garza, Clotilde García, Anne Armstrong, and Selena Quintanilla. Generosity and concern for others frame the lives of Henrietta King, Petra de Vela Kenedy, and Sarita Kenedy East, philanthropists who gave time and money to help others less fortunate than they. The women who went into politics did so with an eye to helping their constituents, often against the existing political machines. And so, the stories of Irma Rangel, "Sissy" Farenthold, and to some extent Anne Armstrong demonstrate the struggles of women going into politics in the mid-twentieth century. Certainly, educators like Jovita González Mireles, Mary Alice Berlanga Gonzáles, and Juliet García devoted their lives to helping others achieve their dreams. While some women like Frances Farenthold were born into prestigious families, others like Irma, Carmen, and Selena came up the ranks from the working classes. All the women, however, had to struggle against stereotypes for women's lives and resistance from a patriarchal society to find the space in which to realize their calling and vocation. Situated on the borderlands between Mexico and Texas, the women featured in this collection navigated more than geographic borders as they tested the place of women in economic, political, and artistic arenas long recognized as male domains. They are the trailblazers, the border crossers, who forged new identities for themselves and the women who follow in their footsteps, the women who wave back to their foremothers in the painting.

As an accompaniment to the mural, the book also makes the case for the need not only for biography but for public art as ways to depict and celebrate, to inspire and teach. As artist Chuck Wissinger of Texas A&M University–Kingsville put it in an interview, public art is an important part of a mature culture because it helps enrich, enlighten, and enhance the quality of life for a community. The mural tells us that not only are the lives of women important to our understanding of history, but art that is accessible to the public is important to enhancing the lives of all people. In the spirit of Selena and Carmen Lomas Garza, who found inspiration for their art in the life around them, the mural touches the community, becomes a part of a community that is as diverse as the women depicted in it.

The essays in this collection are organized around defining attributes, like ranching and art, rather than a strict chronology to give a sense of the contributions of the women to South Texas history. Many of the women could—indeed, should—have been placed in more than one category because their lives were so rich with accomplishment and personality. Jovita González Mireles was both an educator and a writer; Anne Armstrong was connected to the Armstrong Ranch but was also a political figure. Readers will also see how many of the lives intersected with each other, how the Kenedy, King, and Armstrong women knew each other and were related by marriage, and the ways many of the women experienced a shared historical moment—the Mexican War, and the political and social turmoil of the mid-twentieth century.

The first essay frames the collection by examining the unnamed woman on the edge of the mural who represents *las soldaderas*, both the collective groups of women fighters and individuals like Leonor Villegas de Magnón who served in the Cruz Blanca (White Cross) during the Mexican Revolution. Like the many anonymous women who worked hard and served others, her presence haunts the history and the picture of South Texas.

The following section chronicles the lives of the ranching women, the matriarchs of the King and Kenedy dynasties that sprang up in the mid-nineteenth century. Their stories tell of a love for the land and ranch life, for the vaqueros who worked the ranches that were to become some of the largest in Texas. Despite the mythic images we have of cowboys and ranch life, these women quietly maintained their families, their religion, and their homes. They left behind legacies of philanthropy, of care and concern not only for those within their family and ranch circle but also for others in need. These women, as stewards of great fortune, used their money to extend and enrich the lives of others.

The theme of concern for others runs through the next section, which considers some of the women who led educational reform in South Texas, particularly for children of Mexican or Tejano backgrounds. Ensuring that all children had access to a first-rate education, these women led initiatives in bilingual education, an interdisciplinary approach to education, and access to higher education. At a time when careers for women were limited, Jovita González Mireles, Mary Alice Berlanga Gonzáles, and Juliet García approached a field open to them—teaching—with intelligence, care, and gusto, demonstrating their determination to contribute to their communities.

The women who stepped into politics at a time when opportunities for women were rare faced not only the challenges of balancing private and public lives, of advocating for their constituents, but also sexism from their male colleagues. Frances "Sissy" Farenthold, Anne Armstrong, and Irma Rangel, all brilliant and determined women, became foremothers for later generations of women who wanted to use the political realm to better the lives of others. They were "firsts" in many things: the first woman Mexican American state legislator; the first female ambassador to Great Britain and the first woman to speak on the floor of a national party convention; the first serious woman candidate for Texas governor and founding member and chair of the National Women's Political Caucus.

Giving voice to the working classes and depicting everyday life, Selena Quintanilla and Carmen Lomas Garza evince the determination of talented women to express themselves and to speak for others. Selena's particular brand of Tejano music still resonates with listeners not only from South Texas but from around the world. And Carmen Lomas Garza's paintings illustrate scenes of everyday life that speak to viewers of their own experiences in the Mexican American community.

Concern for others, a willingness to commit their lives to the service of others, runs through the lives of the women featured in this book. This commitment is clearly represented in the lives of Clotilde García, physician and activist, and Merideth Howard, who broke gender stereotypes to serve her communities and her nation as firefighter and soldier. Intimate stories of Dr. García's care for her patients and Merideth Howard's community projects and ultimate sacrifice in battle attest to their devotion to others.

The concluding essay provides the other frame for the collection by recognizing the women who answered the salute of the soldadera and instilled a call to service in students at South Texas State Teachers College (and its successive names). Sketching the contributions of female students at Texas A&M University–Kingsville, this final essay brings the collection to the present and forecasts a future in which opportunities for women are broadened. As Jody Marín puts it at the conclusion of her essay, "As the soldadera and millennial South Texas woman salute each other's evolutionary accomplishments, they too wave in the next generation of women revolutionaries, pioneers, educators, politicians, artists—all future leaders of South Texas and all called on to serve their communities."

Notes

1. Linda Wagner-Martin, *Telling Women's Lives: The New Biography* (New Brunswick, NJ: Rutgers University Press, 1994), x–xi; Ralph Waldo Emerson, *The Journals and Miscellaneous Notebooks of Ralph Waldo Emerson*, ed. William H. Gilman, Alfred R. Ferguson, George P. Clark, Merrell R. Davis, Harrison Hayford, Ralph Orth, J. E. Parsons, Merton M. Sealts, and A. W. Plumstead (Cambridge, MA: Harvard University Press, 1960–1982), 7:202.

2. Richard Wendorf, *The Elements of Life: Biography and Portrait-Painting in Stuart and Georgian England* (Oxford: Clarendon Press, 1990), 5–7, 13; Wagner-Martin, *Telling Women's Lives*, 8; Alison Booth, *How to Make It as a Woman: Collective Biographical History from Victoria to the Present* (Chicago: University of Chicago Press, 2004), 2.

I

The Unnamed Women

1

Breaking Past Borders

Las Soldaderas during the Mexican Revolution

VERONICA NOHEMI DURÁN
AND SHANNON L. BAKER

Throughout Mexico's often-violent history, women have participated on or near the field of battle. While many took on this role out of necessity, others voluntarily stepped into the fray. Poor women often found themselves with no other option but to follow their husbands into war, children in tow. Some women of means made a conscious decision to participate in military life, offering their services as journalists, spies, soldiers, or nurses. These women often not only supported the political cause of the day but also consciously pushed gender boundaries as they did so. During the Mexican Revolution (1910–1920), both poor and wealthy women participated in a variety of ways. Not even the international border between Texas and Mexico stood in the way as women in the United States who identified themselves as Mexicanas became involved in the revolution, publishing persuasive articles in the region's newspapers and providing nursing care to wounded soldiers from Mexico.[1]

Throughout the lengthy and violent conflict, many women decided to follow the troops as they supported a range of revolutionary leaders, including Francisco Madero, Victoriano Huerta, Venustiano Carranza, and Emiliano Zapata. Some of these women had voiced their opinions even before the revolution began, speaking out for gender equality in the male-dominated Mexican and border cultures. Jovita Idar, a border activist, used journalism and politics to further the agenda of women. With the advent of the revolution, female activists hoped that the idealistic promises of the revolution would create a fertile space in which they could continue their quest for women's rights.[2] Even so, not all women concerned themselves with gender issues as they crossed traditional gender lines to become *soldaderas*. Many joined because they truly believed in the causes espoused by various leaders. They supported issues such as the restoration of democracy or land reform. Some revolutionary leaders, including Pancho Villa, did not support the presence of women in the battlefield, claiming that they would prove a distraction. Such opinions, however, did not stop women from joining. They ran guns, served as spies, cared for the wounded, cooked, buried soldiers, and fought in the battlefields.[3] The women who joined the revolution, motivated by broader political concerns, unwittingly advanced notions of gender equality by inserting themselves into a traditionally male environment for the purpose of engendering change.

The majority of women who joined the revolution, however, did so neither because they desired to promote gender equality nor because they sought to support a political or military leader. Most did so out of necessity. They followed the troops into the revolution in order to remain with their husbands, who they hoped would provide physical and economic protection. Many single, impoverished women—some abandoned or widowed—also followed the troops and earned money by cooking and cleaning for the soldiers.[4] Soldaderas faced many challenges. Besides the expected perils of war, women soldiers also had to manage their own challenges such as gender biases in the military, sexual misconduct, and the lack of support and recognition of them as soldiers.[5]

One of the soldaderas was Leonor Villegas de Magnón, a native of Nuevo Laredo, who wrote about her unusual experiences in her memoir *The Rebel.* Her life provides a lens through which one can gain an idea about the general sentiment of women directly and indirectly linked to the war. Although Leonor Villegas de Magnón provides an example of the life and actions of soldaderas in the Mexican Revolution, it is important to understand that her position was unique. She was an educated woman whose family had wealth and influence on both sides of the Rio Grande, which allowed her greater influence and success. Indeed, the story of Villegas de Magnón illustrates the profound influence that a woman of means could have when she decided to become an active participant in the revolution. The typical soldaderas did not enjoy Leonor's affluence and influence; their prosaic roles were often undervalued and unappreciated. Even so, the life and subsequent memoir of Leonor Villegas de Magnón brought recognition to all soldaderas, regardless of class.

Leonor Villegas de Magnón: An Auspicious Beginning

Leonor Villegas de Magnón was born on the night of June 12, 1876, when the Rio Grande was threatening to overflow because of an impending storm. Authorities warned the inhabitants of Laredo and Nuevo Laredo of the dangerous situation, and many fled to higher ground to seek escape from the flooding river, carrying what animals and supplies they could. In Nuevo Laredo, on the Mexican side of the Rio Grande, one family did not abandon their home in search of protection. Don Joaquin Villegas, a wealthy landowner and merchant, decided to stay behind on this stormy night because his wife, Valerianna, was in labor. Throughout that night authorities had warned that thieves and rebels could take advantage of the storm and the abandoned towns to sack homes. Thus, when he heard a knock at his door followed by persistent demands, Don Joaquin decided to act as prudently as possible. He opened the door, despite the warning of his servant Pancho, and found a group of rebels. He led them in, showed them the house and warehouse, and offered them some of his best wines. The rebels then demanded to search the house and quickly grew suspicious of a room with a closed door from which voices could be heard. Don Joaquin hesitantly opened the door to reveal his newborn baby girl. The rebels apologized for the intrusion and then started back toward the warehouse.[6]

Just then he again heard knocking and shouting at the main gate. It was a group of *Federales* in search of rebels and thieves. As the rebels heard them, they quickly fled, climbing over a back wall. When Don Joaquin led the Federales in, they too quickly grew suspicious of the closed room and demanded to know whether Don Joaquin was hiding rebels. Don Joaquin opened the door to the room and said, "I am hiding one rebel." Again he revealed to his visitors his newborn child; the Federales apologized and, after toasting the health of the new arrival, left Don Joaquin's home. It was on that night that Don Joaquin unknowingly gave his daughter, Leonor, a moniker, "The Rebel," that would follow her throughout her life.[7]

The Rebel's family spent the next two years at her father's ranch, Rancho San Francisco. Don Joaquin's business and wealth increased and Leonor grew up surrounded by the love and attention of her parents and older brother, Leopoldo. The children were often intrigued by ranch activities such as the branding of animals with a letter *V*; Leonor did not like it but understood it was a way of marking the Villegases' property.[8]

As a result of her father's growing business interests, Leonor and her family went on a long business trip. On the trip they were accompanied by Damiana, Valerianna's mother, as well as the family doctor and his family, because Valerianna was pregnant again. After traveling for some months and with some difficulties, they finally arrived in Cuatro Ciénegas, Coahuila. Here Valerianna gave birth to Lorenzo on a night that would hold unexpected symbolic significance for little Leonor. On that night Leopoldo and Leonor, along with Pepito, the doctor's son, were being entertained by Isabelita, the doctor's wife. Tired of playing, Leonor climbed on the woman's lap. Pepito, upon seeing this, asked his distracted father to borrow his pocketknife. He held the knife over the fireplace until it was red hot and then walked toward Leonor and his mother. He then pressed the red-hot iron against Leonor's left hand, branding her with an everlasting V-shaped scar.[9]

It so happened that on that same night, after having delivered the Villegases' third child, the doctor was called to another emergency, this time at the house of Colonel Jesús Carranza. When he arrived at the house he found a young man injured with a burn similar to Leonor's on his left hand. The young man was Venustiano Carranza, to whom the doctor remarked about the great coincidence. Carranza then purportedly said softly, "We will be in the same movement. I see many people around us. All of us in red flames."[10] The rest of Leonor's childhood would prepare her to fulfill Carranza's prophecy years later.

Political Awakening

After a childhood in San Antonio, Leonor married Adolpho Magnón on January 10, 1901. The couple relocated to Mexico City, where Adolpho worked. Here the Rebel first began taking a more active role in politics. Porfirio Díaz, who had come to power the year of her birth, still governed Mexico. Because Adolpho was involved in politics and economics and her father was well respected thanks to his business, Leonor had easy access to information and to like-minded individuals who began to voice their discontent with the Díaz dictatorship. The Rebel's home was, in fact, close to the Hotel Colón, where the nascent revolutionary Francisco I. Madero often went to dine and converse with his followers about political reform. Both Leonor and Adolpho supported Madero.

From the start of his political career, Madero advocated for effective suffrage and honest elections, opposing in particular the notion that Díaz could be reelected indefinitely.[11] During the Mexican presidential election of 1910, Madero contested for the presidency against Porfirio Díaz, who was running for yet another term. Although Díaz at first welcomed Madero, he soon realized that there was strong popular support for Madero and had him arrested and jailed in order to win the election once more. Madero escaped to San Antonio, where he began plotting a rebellion against Díaz.[12] Much of his support came from the working class, who opposed Díaz not only for political reasons but also because they wanted social and economic reforms.[13]

Leonor began her early work as a journalist during this contentious time. She bravely wrote articles against Díaz, jeopardizing her family's reputation. After her father's death in 1910, Leonor settled in Laredo, where she joined the revolutionary struggle and became a member of the opposition group Junta Revolucionaria. She also joined community leader Jovita Idar in writing for *La Crónica*, a newspaper owned by the Idar family. She contributed to other revolutionary newspapers like *El Radical* and helped establish *El Progreso*, a Spanish-language daily newspaper for border readers that reported on events occurring in Mexico and the United States.[14]

In Mexico, Díaz surrendered on May 26, 1911, to the forces led by Madero and resigned his post as president of the Republic of Mexico, which he had held for thirty-six years. Two months after Díaz left Mexico for France, Francisco de la Barra, interim president of Mexico, received Madero at the Palacio Nacional, where he was ultimately elected president. Madero was able to serve only two years as various political factions fought to achieve different goals for Mexico. At the end of a violent siege that began on February 12, 1913, General Victoriano Huerta had Madero assassinated on February 22 and assumed control of Mexico. Venustiano Carranza, the young man who had burned his hand on the same day as Leonor, was serving as the governor of Coahuila. Protesting Huerta's questionable rise to power, he organized troops against the new president. The violence in Mexico thus continued, and Leonor Villegas de Magnón had a new leader to follow in Carranza, who advocated a return to constitutional order.[15]

The Cruz Blanca

Leonor inserted herself into the movement directly on March 17, 1913, after a brief skirmish between Federalist troops (supporting Huerta) and rebel forces led by General Jesús Carranza in Nuevo Laredo. Upon hearing the shots in her Laredo home, Leonor recruited the help of her friend Jovita Idar and four other young women. Together, they drove across the bridge into Mexico in a car displaying a red cross to take care of wounded soldiers. They soon transformed their emblem from a red cross to a white cross in a field of red to differentiate themselves from the American Red Cross. The Cruz Blanca was born. Nine months later, after another battle in Nuevo Laredo, she set up an impromptu hospital in Laredo and recruited the help of women to care for the wounded Carrancistas with financial support from her brother Leopoldo and donations from citizens. Within a few hours of being established, the hospital was serving more than a hundred people with various degrees of injury.[16]

Soon Leonor put her writing and administrative skills to use. At the request of General Pablo Gonzáles, Leonor, her secretary Lily Honeycutt Long, and a small group of twenty-six Cruz Blanca members traveled to El Paso on April 5, 1914, intending to continue with the Carrancistas into Torreón, Coahuila. Leonor met with first chief Venustiano Carranza, who commended her on her work with the Carrancistas and for the establishment of hospitals. They reminisced about the night on which they were both scarred on their left hands. At the conclusion of the meeting, the first chief asked her to write about the war and his involvement in it. Leonor thus became part of the Carrancista revolutionary movement as president of the Cruz Blanca Constitucional, with the knowledge that once she and her organization crossed into Mexico the repercussions for her actions could be much greater. Nonetheless, she followed Carrancista forces to Mexico, where she founded new Cruz Blanca brigades and hospitals in Durango and Chihuahua.[17]

During her travels, Leonor met with Francisco Villa, who at the time was working with Carranza to depose Huerta.[18] Although Villa distrusted Leonor at first, over time she gained his respect. Leonor's organization not only tended to the wounded and ill but also gathered information for the Carrancistas, documenting and photographing soldiers, serving as spies, and providing aid when needed. As president of the Cruz Blanca, Leonor had frequent contact with first chief Carranza and some of the most prominent leaders of the movement; she traveled alongside them constantly as they made their way into the Mexican Republic. After Carranza finally took power, he officially recognized the Cruz Blanca Constitucional in Saltillo. The Cruz Blanca Constitucional, or Constitutional White Cross, now became the Cruz Blanca Nacional, or National White Cross. The Rebel was recognized for her work as president of the Cruz Blanca.[19]

This alliance with Carranza signified two great trials for Leonor. First, her commitment to the Cruz Blanca and the revolution required her to part with her husband and children. At a time when men were the head of the family and expected to support and guide women, a decision such as this was not taken lightly. Separating from Adolpho implied a great challenge to traditional social, religious, and marital guidelines. Many soldaderas did not have this option; instead, they followed the troops into the revolution in order to remain with their husbands, for protection and economic gain and to serve alongside the men.[20]

Second, by crossing into Mexico she was formally announcing her support for Carranza. This act was significant and daring since doing so made her an enemy of Huerta and the Federalists. In Leonor's case it proved even more noteworthy because she was a woman publicly voicing her opinion on political matters. In addition, crossing into Mexico at the side of Carranza placed her and her organization in great peril. As she became part of Carranza's forces, she was often at or near places of armed conflict. Yet Leonor and her followers believed enough in Carranza and the revolution that they followed him despite the dangers.[21]

The Memoirs

After ten years of conflict and war, Leonor began leading a quiet life. Although the conflict in Mexico was not concluded, Leonor excused herself from it and remained in Laredo with her husband. She used her time and energy to write a memoir in Spanish, *La Rebelde*, in the hope of recognizing all the men and women who had participated and died in support of Carranza and the Cruz Blanca.[22] She spent the rest of her life unsuccessfully attempting to have her memoir published.

After the revolution, she had time and peace to think about her actions and those of other soldaderas during the war. Carranza had once asked her to write about the war when it was over, but Leonor knew that her objective in writing a memoir was not just to depict the actions of male leaders. Throughout her participation in the conflict, Leonor and her staff had collected documents, photographs, and stories about the people involved; many of them became the basis for her narrative. Primarily, however, she wanted to make sure that the bravery and participation of women in the Mexican Revolution did not go unnoticed. She wanted the deaths and sacrifices of women to be immortalized in some small way and to serve as an example for the country.[23] As history minimized the importance of soldaderas and nurses who participated in the Mexican Revolution—especially those in the Texas-Mexico border area and those who established the Cruz Blanca—she determined to leave both a written account and a pictorial documentation of the women involved.[24]

Although the Rebel did not publish her memoir during her lifetime, her storytelling is of great importance. Not much history is written on the involvement of soldaderas in the Mexican Revolution or the Cruz Blanca, but her writing eventually helped remind people that soldaderas played a key role in the Mexican Revolution. They fought alongside men, performed various tasks in aid of the soldiers, and supported the overall goals of the revolution. Although their actions and bravery are seldom recognized, their presence helped propel the development of the revolution and its end results. While most soldaderas had a less influential position than Leonor Villegas de Magnón, her life story brings to light the importance of all soldaderas in the war. With their actions, the Rebel Leonor, members of the Cruz Blanca, and other soldaderas both intentionally and inadvertently helped initiate many of the gender changes that came after the revolution.

Notes

1. Teresa Palomo Acosta and Ruthe Winegarten, *Las Tejanas: 300 Years of History* (Austin: University of Texas Press, 2003), 70–87.

2. Clara Lomas, "Transborder Discourse: The Articulation of Gender in the Borderlands in the Early Twentieth Century," in *Gender on the Borderlands: The Frontiers Reader*, ed. Antonia Castañeda with Susan H. Armitage, Patricia Hart, and Karen Weathermon (Lincoln: University of Nebraska Press, 2007), 51–52.

3. Acosta and Winegarten, *Las Tejanas*, 81.

4. Elizabeth Salas, *Soldaderas in the Mexican Military: Myth and History* (Austin: University of Texas Press, 1990), 75–76.

5. Acosta and Winegarten, *Las Tejanas*, 82–83.

6. Leonor Villegas de Magnón, *The Rebel*, ed. Clara Lomas (Houston: Arte Público Press, 1994), 3–7.

7. Villegas de Magnón, 8–13.

8. Villegas de Magnón, 27–28.

9. Villegas de Magnón, 28.

10. Villegas de Magnón, 28.

11. Ward S. Albro, *Always a Rebel: Ricardo Flores Magón and the Mexican Revolution* (Fort Worth: Texas Christian University Press, 1992), 1:122.

12. Linda B. Hall and Don M. Coerver, *Revolution on the Border: The United States and Mexico, 1910–1920* (Albuquerque: University of New Mexico Press, 1988), 18–19.

13. Alan Knight, *The Mexican Revolution: Porfirians, Liberals and Peasants* (Lincoln: University of Nebraska Press, 1986), 1:62–63.

14. Acosta and Winegarten, *Las Tejanas*, 77; Villegas de Magnón, *The Rebel*, 75; Leonor Villegas de Magnón, *La Rebelde* (Houston: Arte Público Press, 2004), 55.

15. Villegas de Magnón, *La Rebelde*, 79–86.

16. Villegas de Magnón, *The Rebel*, 85–86, 96–97.

17. Villegas de Magnón, *The Rebel*, 105, 110–12, 238–39.

18. Knight, *Mexican Revolution*, 1:115–29.

19. Villegas de Magnón, *The Rebel*, 121, 167.

20. Salas, *Soldaderas in the Mexican Military*, 75–76.

21. Villegas de Magnón, *The Rebel*, 104–8.

22. Lomas, "Transborder Discourse," 66.

23. Villegas de Magnón, *The Rebel*, 198; Lomas, "Transborder Discourse," 67.

24. Clara Lomas, "In Search of an Autobiography: On Mapping Women's Intellectual History of the Borderlands," introduction to *The Rebel*, by Leonor Villegas de Magnón, ed. Clara Lomas (Houston: Arte Público Press, 1994), viii.

II

The Ranchers

2

Henrietta King

LARRY KNIGHT

When Henrietta King became a widow, she inherited the King Ranch, 500,000 acres of land. With the land, she also inherited $500,000 in debt, or one dollar of debt for every acre of land, about what the land was worth. When Henrietta died, she left 997,444 acres, not including land she had already given to her daughter, Alice, or other Kleberg land. Unlike with the estate she inherited, however, Henrietta did not leave her heirs in debt. Instead, she left ranch lands worth $4,784,324, city lands worth $73,555, and a personal estate worth $2,243,593. Her total real and personal estate upon her death was worth $7,101,473, and her total liabilities were $1,695,531. After the death of her husband, Henrietta almost doubled her land holdings, and, in 2012 dollars, after liabilities were subtracted from assets, she left her heirs $70,800,000. Richard King is noted, and rightly so, as the founder of the King Ranch, but much of the legacy of the ranch is thanks to the abilities of Henrietta, her upbringing, her father's influence, and her deep religious convictions.[1]

Henrietta's Other Inheritance

Certainly Henrietta's upbringing was instrumental in her success on the King Ranch. Ironically, though she became rich, powerful, and even famous, Henrietta's childhood was not one to be envied. In fact, one could say that she was a vagabond until she married Richard King, but that story will come later. Henrietta was born in Boonville, Missouri, on July 21, 1832. Her mother, Maria Morse Chamberlain, herself born in Vermont, named Henrietta after her good friend Henrietta Jackson. Henrietta, called Netta by the mother she never knew, was left motherless when Maria and her infant son died in March 1835. Henrietta did not stay motherless for long. On April 19, 1836, her father, Hiram Chamberlain, married Sarah H. Wardlaw of Rockbridge County, Virginia. Sarah was the mother Henrietta knew as a young, impressionable child, and while little is known of the relationship between Sarah and Henrietta, it was probably close since the marriage between Hiram and Sarah produced no children who would have competed with Henrietta for Sarah's affection. If stepdaughter and stepmother were close, Sarah's death in May 1840 would have been exceptionally hard on Henrietta. Again, Henrietta was not motherless for long. Hiram married Henrietta's third mother on August 16, 1842, at Pinckney, Missouri. For a second time he married a New Englander, Anna Adelia Griswold from Wethersfield, Connecticut. Nor would Henrietta be lacking in sibling companionship for long. Hiram and Anna had eight children, their first, Hiram Jr., born in 1843, and their last, Edwin, in 1857.[2]

The relationship between Henrietta and Anna was probably both close and affectionate—the few letters between them seem to indicate so. It was the only adult constant in her life, Hiram, however, with whom Henrietta was closest as a child and from whom she learned the lessons of life. In fact, Hiram and Henrietta lived close to each other until his death in 1866, and she named the cemetery she was later buried in Chamberlain Park in honor of her father. To understand Henrietta, it is necessary to know a bit about Hiram.[3]

Hiram was a New Englander, born in Monkton, Vermont, on April 1, 1797. He was also brought up in the Old School Presbyterian Calvinist faith, a faith that underwent significant changes during Hiram's life because of the teachings of Reverend Charles Grandison Finney. Steering a somewhat neutral course between Old School and New School, he favored the Old School teachings of predestination but, somewhat incongruously, believed that salvation was a personal choice and responsibility and that each person must accept or reject Christ. Those choices and responsibilities included his belief in "a life favoring constructive activity rather than idle enjoyment. . . . Art, music, literature, and recreation were approved only if edifying." The Sabbath he celebrated was also Calvinist. It was a day set aside for the Lord.[4]

For Hiram, Calvinism was not just a form of religion, but the true religion. Hiram believed he was called not only to follow Christ but also to preach to the mission field, and as a good Calvinist, he needed to be armed with a good education. For that education, he attended Princeton Theological Seminary and Andover Theological Seminary, where he helped establish the American Home Missionary Society, whose mission was to evangelize the American West, which at that time included Missouri. After his graduation in 1825, Hiram dedicated himself to going west as a Home Missionary.[5]

Not wanting to go to the American frontier alone, Hiram asked Maria Morse to go with him. His letter to her, written to convince her that the life of a missionary's wife was worthwhile, contained the same advice he later inculcated in Henrietta. "I have often wondered that there was self denial enough in any female's heart to lead her to become the companion of a stranger in a strange land. . . . Yes, Maria, the wife of a Missionary should confide her whole heart in the bosom of her companion and he, in return, with equal fidelity, should watch over her comfort, and her happiness with feelings of untenable tenderness." Maria, to Hiram's delight, accepted his proposal.[6]

Henrietta's Education

Little is known of Henrietta's early childhood except that Hiram was the only permanent presence in her life and her primary teacher. The first lesson he taught her was love, his love for her. He expressed this love to his father-in-law, Alpheus Morse, shortly after Henrietta's birth: "Your daughter presented me with this precious little treasure from the Lord . . . after four hours of anxiety and painful suspense. I must tell you what her foolish, doting parents now think about her. . . . They really think she is as pretty a child as was ever born into the world. As *wise*, as *sweet*, as *lovely* and *quiet*. Her eyes are perfect brilliants. Her skin is exceedingly fair. She looked around the room and on every object and thought—for her eyes told her thoughts—that she was in a *New World*."[7] Despite the staid picture we have of the Puritans' descendants, Hiram's letter indicates the abiding love he had for his first child.

After her mother's death, Henrietta and her father moved to St. Charles, Missouri, and lived there for six years. There he married and buried Sarah Wardlaw. In 1842, having married Anna Adelia Griswold, Hiram moved the family to St. Louis, Missouri, where he became the editor of the *Herald of Religious Liberty.* He believed his job was "to wake up the attention of the Protestants of the State of Missouri to the errors and evils of Roman Catholicism."[8]

In the summer of 1846, fourteen-year-old Henrietta experienced one of the most traumatic events of her childhood when she was shipped off to a boarding school, the Female Institute in Holly Springs, Mississippi. Founded in 1837, it was a Protestant school whose philosophy of education noted that its students were educated by "the inculcation of a high tone of Christian ethics. Christian morals shall be the prominent feature of instruction."[9] One can only imagine how lonely Henrietta was, with two mothers in the grave and now forced by her father to leave home. Henrietta may have felt abandoned; of course she was not. Hiram firmly believed Henrietta needed both to further her education and to live without the security of her family for a time. Though he would be absent from her in body, Hiram could never abandon Henrietta. He wrote faithfully to her until her schooling was over. In fact, he continued to write to Henrietta throughout his life except when they lived together or near each other. Being a deeply religious Calvinist, Hiram did not send letters to assuage the feelings of his daughter, though he never hid his love for her. Rather, his were letters of instruction.[10]

As he often did, he reminded Henrietta of his love for her and of their special bond: "Your father has loved you very much from your earliest childhood, and more especially since your own dear Mother, *Maria,* impressed upon your infant cheek her last kiss, saying, with a smile, *'sweet child'* as she turned her eyes from yours and *died.*" Love for her was a constant topic in his letters. "We all love you and speak of you often"; "All send much love to you"; and "All send love to you. Pray for us as we do for you" were not uncommon sentiments in Hiram's letters to Henrietta. Hiram adjured Henrietta to keep all his letters, as they would convey his love and counsel for her. And though he did not say so, he was giving her another lesson: death was ever present and could claim anyone at any time.[11]

The transient nature of life was, of course, nothing new to Henrietta, who had buried two mothers. If, however, she needed reminding of the transiency of life, Hiram willingly did so, but not without also reminding her of the hope of the resurrection. When he wrote to inform her of the deaths of two of her brothers—Milton, whom she knew, and Daniel, whom she had never met—he pressed the point with news of other local deaths. Death, of course, was not the end; Hiram's philosophy of a sovereign God and the resurrection made the acceptance of death possible: "The Lord had done it, and we must all bow with sweet submission to his will. It is best for us to have no will of our own . . . we are his people and the sheep of his pasture."[12]

Next to his love for Henrietta, Hiram's primary teachings were about God and her purpose in God's world. Henrietta was placed on the earth to glorify God, not to satisfy herself. This life, Hiram instructed, was not made for perfect happiness: "If we desired nothing but what was right, and had all we desired, Earth is not the place to enjoy [perfect happiness]. God has reserved that for a better world. We must wait till we get to Heaven for that. We are here to glorify Him." Henrietta's duty to God included a duty to society: "Do all the good and get all the good you can and may the Lord preserve and bless you."[13] Such admonitions were followed by practical advice about self-denial and sacrifice.

Though Hiram was sending Henrietta away to be educated, he noted that "the very best knowledge in the world is that which is derived from the Bible." The Bible was God's knowledge revealed and "sealed . . . with the Blood of his Son." The Bible had practical lessons in Proverbs, provided emotional support in Psalms, and revealed the evil in the world that attempted to "ruin the soul." "For these, and many other reasons, I wish you, my dear child, *to read some portion of the Bible every day*."[14]

Hiram also warned her against self-pity. This advice became especially important when he informed Henrietta that she would not be coming home for Christmas that first year away. He wrote, "You must not lie awake nights to think of home . . . you must be a good girl, and not mourn about it." As it turned out, Henrietta had something to mourn about. Not only did she spend Christmas away from her family for the first time in her life, but she received neither letters nor Christmas gifts nor greetings from her family; these were either lost en route or stolen. Having endured a lonely Christmas, she then faced a delayed reopening of school until February because of severe winter storms. Hiram's advice to his daughter was to befriend good books—"this is one great advantage of an Education,"—and to overcome self-pity through gratitude.[15]

He also admonished her to "sanctify all your studies with daily prayer." His religious instruction was best summed up in a letter he sent in her second year in school. "I hope you will live such a Christian life of prayer and humble dependency on God for his gracious assistance in all things that you do and say . . . that God will love you and cause others to love you, and to take knowledge of you, that you have been with Jesus."[16]

Hiram noted that Henrietta's obedience to his advice would be "his richest reward," and apparently Henrietta took her father's advice. After her third letter, Hiram wrote, "I am much pleased that you seem to be improving in your studies, and at the same time, not unmindful of our religious obligations." Henrietta had written to Hiram about a large revival meeting she had attended at the First Presbyterian Church of Holly Springs. The following year, Henrietta dedicated herself "to God and to Society as a meek and humble follower of Christ."[17] Though Henrietta did not know it, her education, both academic and spiritual, had prepared her for her next step—meeting Richard King and starting a ranching empire.

Brownsville Days

Henrietta stayed at school for two years and then returned to her father and the growing family. In 1849, the family left for Texas, arriving in the frontier town of Brownsville in February 1850. Hiram came to Brownsville to continue the work he had begun in Missouri, to establish a Protestant church on the Rio Grande. Henrietta was actively involved in the mission: she taught at the Rio Grande Female Academy, sang in the choir, and attended church meetings. At the same time, she avoided many of the activities available in what was largely a military town; Brownsville was named for Fort Brown, established in 1846. Because of the number of young, single soldiers, an attractive, single woman was a rarity; young men and women could mingle at social gatherings at Fort Brown and dances at "Gem, the principal café at Brownsville." Those activities did not interest Henrietta. In a fictional life some dashing young man would have met Henrietta in church and the two would have been married and lived happily ever after. Instead, Henrietta met Richard King.[18]

The meeting was accidental and certainly not church related. Lacking a house to live in, Hiram and family lived on a sailboat, the *Whiteville.* The *Whiteville* was tied at a slip where Richard King docked one of his steamboats. Ending a rough, upstream voyage as captain of an old steamship, the *Colonel Cross*, Richard found his accustomed slip blocked by the *Whiteville.* He managed to get his boat into its berth, cursing all the while and demanding to know who had blocked his way. When King was told the offending boat housed the new reverend, he declared the *Whiteville* a rattrap, which was the nicest thing he said. Seventeen-year-old Henrietta came out and offered a scathing rebuttal. Her rebuke, far more educated than Richard's tirade, noted that his "indecent tongue [was] unfit for decent ears" and assured him that any rats in the area were on his boat and not on the *Whiteville.*[19]

Whether Richard caught her reference to him as a rat is uncertain. He probably did not. The sight of this seventeen-year-old missionary struck him speechless. He was so taken with Henrietta that he asked his partner Mifflin Kenedy, a devout Quaker, about the new parson. Richard found that Kenedy approved of Reverend Chamberlain and his efforts to establish a Protestant church in Brownsville. Richard, of course, was not really interested in the new parson. He wanted to know about Henrietta and how he could meet her. Kenedy informed the profane Richard King that the only way he could meet Henrietta was to attend church on the *Whiteville.* King did so, repeatedly.[20]

While Hiram most likely welcomed Richard to services, he did not take kindly to his advances toward Henrietta. He had another type of suitor in mind, one he wrote about shortly after Henrietta had left for Holly Springs. "I would not be surprised if you should fall in Love with him, when you see him. . . . You have my full consent to receive very special attention from this youth, when you come home if he should think proper to bestow them." Hiram did not feel the same way about Richard King, and for perhaps the only time in their lives, father and daughter "seriously clashed." King, however, was not to be denied. He attended services on a regular basis and a four-year, proper courtship began. Richard and Henrietta had chaperoned visits, walks through Brownsville, and, of course, time together at church, though she sat in the choir. Apparently Richard won Henrietta over quickly. Hiram was another matter, but over time Captain Richard King, the homeless stowaway from New York, gained the approval of the Calvinist preacher from New England. Hiram "grew to admire this young captain's sterling qualities and strong personality."[21]

Married Life

Captain Richard King and Miss Henrietta Chamberlain became husband and wife on December 10, 1854. Reverend Hiram Chamberlain performed the ceremony at the First Presbyterian Church of Brownsville. Rather than a big wedding (Captain Richard King was already a man of some means), the marriage was merely an addendum to a regular Sunday evening worship service. As with most things concerning Henrietta, Hiram offered advice about marriage: "And first let me say to you, divest your mind of all romantic and foolish notions in regard to the married life, and view it as it really is, as a serious and solemn relationship, instituted by our great and good Father in heaven for very wise and beneficent purposes, and involving it in the most weighty responsibilities. Responsibilities that connect with both worlds—the present and future."[22]

While the wedding was without glamour, the honeymoon was not. For the first time, Henrietta saw the ranch that would be her home for over seven decades. The journey from Brownsville to the Santa Gertrudis—it was not yet called the King Ranch—was a 120-mile trip through the wilderness via stagecoach escorted by armed guards. The trip took four days. Henrietta arrived to "a cluster of earth-brown wattled huts, a gray tangle of shaggy mesquite corrals, a thatch-roofed commissary, a gaunt-faced blockhouse and stockade garnished with a brass cannon." The ranch was populated by the *Kineños*, who had followed King from Mexico when he purchased all their livestock. Like the vaqueros and their families, Henrietta lived in a jacal, a hut made of upright poles chinked with mud and topped by a thatched roof. But of course she was not just another woman on the ranch; she was Richard King's wife and was treated as royalty by the ranch workers and given the title La Patrona or La Madama. Both the stowaway boy who became a riverboat captain and the itinerant missionary now had a home, though until 1858 they mostly stayed in their house on Elizabeth Street in Brownsville.[23] Sixty years after her honeymoon, Henrietta wrote of her first time on the ranch: "When I came as a bride in 1854, the little ranch home then—a mere jacal as Mexicans would call it—was our abode for many months until our main ranch dwelling was completed. But I doubt if it falls to the lot of any bride to have had so happy a honeymoon. On horseback we roamed the broad prairies. When I grew tired my husband would spread a Mexican blanket for me and then I would take my siesta under the shade of the mesquite tree. . . . At first our cattle were long horns from Mexico. We had no fences and branding was hard work."[24] Perhaps the romantic notions of which Hiram had warned her were not so foolish after all. A letter from her grandfather Alpheus Morse, dated November 29, 1855, speaks to her bliss: "You speak of your conjugal union as very blissful. I rejoice that it is so. In this dark world, full of evils consequent upon the introduction of sin, life is often embittered by 'unequal yoking,' and if you have found a mate of congenial tastes and sympathies with your own, you have abundant reason for gratitude to Him."[25]

Early Ranch Life

Certainly the ranch changed Henrietta, but she also changed the ranch. Though enchanted by the ranch and its people, Henrietta remained a missionary and the daughter of a missionary. She read from her Bible each day. She also banished whiskey and mescal from the ranch, though the ban was probably honored more in the breach than in the observance, even by her husband. Apparently her presence was so daunting that when Richard was away and Henrietta was left to run the ranch, outlaws and other disreputable characters waited until Richard returned to approach the house.[26]

While disreputable characters may have been afraid of Henrietta, others, apparently reputable, were not. "RIP" Ford noted that Henrietta brought a woman's touch to a bachelor's world. Many men in South Texas, even married ones, were essentially bachelors in that their wives did not accompany them. An example was Robert E. Lee, who visited the ranch on many occasions between 1856 and 1861. Years later, Henrietta reminisced about the hospitality of life on the ranch. "In those days the houses were few and far between and owing to this I can recall with pleasure the many distinguished guests I entertained. Among them I recall General Lee, then Lieutenant Colonel. I am sure if General Lee were here to recall those days, he would say that a dinner served off our tin plates on this old ranch was more appetizing than many a banquet accorded him in later years." Lee and others did not dine in Henrietta's original jacal; they dined in the house built in 1858, the site of the present ranch house. According to legend, Lee suggested the site for the house to Richard.[27]

Though Richard remained in the steamboat business on the Rio Grande until 1874, his love was the ranch, and Henrietta and the children were thoroughly involved in its business. When Henrietta "Nettie" King was a babe in arms, Richard surprised Henrietta by presenting her with her own brand (HK, with the *H* and *K* sharing the second vertical). Hers was the first King Ranch brand registered in Nueces County, Kleberg County not yet having been formed. Shortly thereafter, on June 28, 1859, King bought land in Henrietta's name, "a one-half undivided interest in the twelve leagues of the de la Garza Santa Gertrudis grant." At that point, Henrietta owned more land than her husband, who showed his trust in her because under Texas law "all property of the wife [was] under her absolute control."[28]

Henrietta also made it clear that she wanted to be involved in the everyday workings of the ranch. Rather than stay at the house during roundups, Henrietta brought the children for picnics with Richard and the vaqueros. The cattle were rounded up "at the dam of the Tranquitas," the present site of the Kleberg County courthouse. While Henrietta's involvement in the ranch continued, her majority ownership did not last long. What is now known as the King Ranch (R. King & Company) was born on December 5, 1860. The ranch included a great deal of land, cattle, and some cash. The holdings were divided so that three-eighths belonged to Richard King, three-eighths to Mifflin Kenedy, and two-eighths to James Walworth—all steamboat captains. With the forming of the ranch, Richard and Henrietta made what they thought would be a permanent move. On December 3, 1860, the family—Richard, Henrietta, Nettie, Ella Morse, and Richard II—moved to the ranch. Though it is probably not true, Richard II claimed he was born on the stagecoach in transit from Brownsville to the ranch.[29]

During the Civil War, Richard, as both a ranch holder on the cotton route and a steamboat owner, was instrumental in transporting the primary economic asset of the Confederacy, cotton. He also raised a company of Confederate home guards to protect things locally. All of this made King, his property, and even his family a target of the Union forces. It was not Richard, however, whom the Union forces met when they raided the ranch, but Henrietta. Having been warned of an impending Union raid, Richard fled the ranch, believing it was safer for Henrietta, now seven months pregnant, and the children to face the Union soldiers rather than be on the run in the winter.[30]

Richard did not leave his family defenseless. He left them in the care of those he trusted most, the Kineños. He chose Francisco Alvarado to care for the family, telling him, "Francisco, you go and sleep at my house and take care of my family. I have to leave now, and I don't know when I can return." Alvarado did as he was asked, placing himself in the hall so he would be between the family and any intruders who came to the door. Henrietta made him a cot, and he bedded down for the night. Richard had been accurately warned; Union soldiers, many of them Tejanos, arrived that night. The soldiers wasted no time asking questions but simply began firing at the house. In an attempt to save the family, Alvarado rushed to the door to tell the soldiers that Richard was not at home. The soldiers, seeing the movement of his shadow and believing they were firing on Richard King, shot him dead. Having failed in their attempt to kill Richard, the soldiers looted the house, destroyed much of what they did not take, and put the men of the ranch in a prison pen. However, fearing they would be attacked, the soldiers left the ranch, not even bothering to take its most valuable asset, the numerous bales of cotton. The following day, Christmas, Henrietta and family left the ranch via coach, accompanied by guards. She traveled to San Patricio and stayed with friends until after the birth of her second son. Perhaps in response to the raid on the ranch, the baby, born on February 22, 1864, was named Robert E. Lee King. Shortly thereafter, Henrietta and family traveled by coach to the safety of San Antonio.[31]

Postwar Years

After the war, the family was back in Brownsville on Elizabeth Street. Rather than worry about the ranch, King, along with his partner Kenedy, spent his time rebuilding the steamboat business, which had been especially good to Richard during the war since he carried cotton. At Brownsville cotton prices had risen from $0.16 cents a pound in 1862 to $1.25 a pound in 1865, payable in gold. War gold allowed Richard to expand the ranch. On May 6, 1865, June Walworth sold her inherited part in the King Ranch for $50,000, or $727,000 in 2012 dollars.[32] Unlike many Texans, Richard and Henrietta were not left poor after the war. Shortly after Hiram's death on November 1, the family moved back to the ranch in December 1866.

Despite Hiram's death, the years following the war were probably the best of Henrietta's life. By 1867 the house had been remodeled and a second story added to provide rooms for the children: Nettie, born in 1856; Ella, born in 1858; Richard II, born in 1860; Alice Gertrudis, born in 1862; and Robert E. Lee, born in 1864. After her father's death some of Henrietta's kin came to live on the ranch.[33] Two years after the war, the family began a tradition of traveling during the summer. Some years they accompanied Richard on business and some years they met him on his business trips. They visited Galveston, San Antonio, New Orleans, and St. Louis, but their first trip, in 1867, may have been the most memorable. They first traveled to Kentucky so Richard could buy thoroughbred stallions for the ranch. That was followed by a visit to Lexington, Virginia, in the Shenandoah Valley, to visit Robert E. Lee, then president of Washington College. President Lee and his namesake were photographed together.[34]

When old enough, the children were sent off to school, much as Henrietta had been. Nettie, the oldest, was the first to leave. She headed to the Henderson Female Institute, a Presbyterian seminary in Danville, Kentucky, in 1870. She was soon joined by Ella and in 1874 by Alice. When Nettie finished school in 1875, Ella and Alice spent the summer at home and then transferred to Mrs. Cuthbert's Seminary in St. Louis. With the two youngest daughters in St. Louis, Henrietta and Nettie began to take long stays in St. Louis to visit them. Richard came as often as he could, bearing expensive gifts for Henrietta and the girls.[35]

Just as Nettie was finishing her time in Danville, Richard II arrived to attend Centre College—the male counterpart to the Female Institute. Richard II finished his schooling in 1878 and was followed to Danville by Robert Lee. The younger King, however, wanted to garner skills that would help him manage the ranch, so he transferred to St. Louis to take courses in business. It was in St. Louis that the world the Kings seemed to have so fully mastered came tumbling down. Robert contracted pneumonia in February 1883 and died on March 1. Though Henrietta and Richard II left the ranch for St. Louis as soon as they received news of the illness, there was nothing they could do to aid the stricken youth. Robert Lee, who with Alice seemed to most love the ranch, died far from it and was buried in St. Louis.[36]

For Henrietta, it must have seemed that she had come full circle. Her life, which had been so filled with death when she was a child, was filled with death again. Worse, Henrietta and Richard drew apart for the first time in their marriage. Henrietta became ill following the death of Robert Lee and remained in St. Louis. Richard returned to the ranch so heartsick that for the only time in his life he attempted to sell the ranch; he also returned to drinking. Henrietta remained in St. Louis for a time, but even when she returned to Texas she mostly absented herself from the ranch. During the crises, Alice held the family together. She had returned with her father to the ranch and took care of him on the many nights of hard drinking. It is not surprising that the death of Robert Lee, seemingly the favorite child, caused such a disruption in the lives of Henrietta and Richard. Perhaps, given time, Henrietta and Richard would have returned to wedded bliss, and perhaps they did; in any case, their marriage was almost over. Richard became ill, was finally convinced by Henrietta and Alice to see a doctor in San Antonio, and discovered that he had stomach cancer. He died at the Menger Hotel in San Antonio on April 14, 1885, surviving Robert Lee by just over two years.[37]

Whatever passed between Henrietta and Richard, it affected neither her devotion to his memory nor his absolute trust in her ability to run the ranch. Richard left everything to Henrietta "to be used and disposed of precisely the same as I myself might do were I living." Richard left three executors of the estate: Henrietta, Mifflin Kenedy, and Perry Doddridge, but the latter two surrendered their parts, leaving Henrietta the sole executrix.[38]

The Matriarch

Henrietta, who had been married to Richard for over thirty years, was his widow for almost forty. During her widowhood she almost always wore black. The rooms she most used contained large portraits of Richard, the ranch letterhead had Richard's picture on it, and she wore a brooch pinned to her collar with Richard's likeness, even as life on the ranch moved on. Nothing revealed the new life of the ranch as much as the three King daughters' marriages. Most important for the ranch was the marriage of Alice to Robert Kleberg. Richard had hired Robert Kleberg as the ranch's lawyer after Kleberg had won a case against the ranch. The wedding of Robert and Alice at the ranch on June 17, 1886, was a clear sign that life had returned to the ranch. Henrietta's presence on their honeymoon proved that she was a part of that new life. Her presence also defined the future leadership of the ranch: Henrietta, Robert, and Alice.[39]

Robert Kleberg is rightly given credit for building the King Ranch following the death of Richard King. He developed the ranch by fencing pastures, finding water, and improving the livestock. He did not manage the ranch, however, without Henrietta. For the rest of her life after Richard's death, Henrietta maintained not only ownership of the ranch, but control as well. Her control is best seen when then ranch manager Sam Ragland fired an old vaquero who had worked on the ranch for many years. Though Robert Kleberg disagreed with Ragland, he felt it better for the vaquero to be fired than for Ragland to lose his authority with the ranch hands. Henrietta heard of the firing and reinstated the vaquero, and the matter was closed. In other ways, she let Robert run the operation, including hiring architects and workers to build the new ranch house after the original was destroyed in a fire in the early hours of January 4, 1912. Henrietta had only one demand for the new home: "Build a house that anyone could walk in in boots."[40]

Most events on the ranch were not as dramatic as firings and fires, and Henrietta gave Robert "full and complete Power of Attorney for the handling of all legal and financial matters" concerning her property. Between 1885 and 1889, Henrietta and Robert bought and sold land in an attempt to make the ranch holding more rational. Even when Henrietta built a home overlooking the bay in Corpus Christi in 1893, she spent much of the year living on the ranch, and she visited all ranch holdings twice each year—during the spring and fall roundups—to see for herself how things were going so she could make decisions on the running of the ranch. Henrietta and Robert also diversified the ranch by building a ranch town, Kingsville, a milling company, a cotton gin, and a cotton oil mill. To tie the ranch to the national economy, they secured a railroad to run through the ranch on its way from Corpus Christi to Brownsville, and in 1907 they built an icehouse in Kingsville to provide ice for the railroads to foster the shipment of South Texas vegetables to the nation.[41]

While Henrietta and Robert ran the ranch, Henrietta and Alice ran the ranch family. Alice, Robert, and their children lived in the ranch house with Henrietta; in fact, her bedroom was right across the hall from theirs. And they moved with her to the house in Corpus Christi for the winters. As she grew older, Henrietta walked to the front gate of the ranch house and back with Alice's help. Henrietta watched her grandchildren play on the porch, told them stories, gave them candy when they were good, and whacked their little ankles with her cane when they were not. Through the many years following King's death, Alice "supervised and maintained [a home that was] never allowed to seem quite her own." According to Tom Lea, Alice was never disturbed by her subservient role. "All the home life [Alice] achieved was pervaded by the senior personality and presence of her mother. There is not a scintilla of evidence that Alice resented this." The architect for the new ranch house, Carleton Adams of San Antonio, who was at the ranch for eighteen months, reinforced the notion that Henrietta ran the home when he noted that Henrietta, who was a bit over eighty, "was able and kindly, of great religious faith, [and] keenly interested in both the family and business affairs that surrounded her. In quiet dignity she easily maintained her rightful position in the household." Henrietta's rightful position was the head of everything.[42]

Though Alice, Robert, and family lived on the ranch and spent the winters with Henrietta at her home in Corpus Christi, Henrietta liked spending time with all of her family and friends. Both the ranch and her home in Corpus Christi were often filled with people. Either house was a bit of a marvel for the time. The house in Corpus Christi contained twenty rooms and had turrets and gingerbread trim. It stood on the site of the present Corpus Christi Cathedral on the bluff overlooking the bay.

The new ranch house, finished in 1913, cost \$350,000, or \$8,370,000 in 2012 dollars, and took two years to build. Robert Kleberg, knowing firsthand of Henrietta's desire to be a good hostess, called the ranch house "a monument to Mrs. King's hospitality." The same could certainly be said for the house in Corpus Christi. But while Henrietta spent a lot of money on her houses, she was not attached to them. When the original ranch house burned in 1912, she told Sam Ragland, who was attempting to move a piano out of the burning house, to leave it. "Let nobody get hurt. We can build a new home. We can't replace life." She calmly carried a few things from the house, then "turned and threw a kiss at the burning house" and walked away. To Henrietta, houses were made for people, not people for houses.[43]

Her houses often saw famous visitors, as when President William Howard Taft visited Corpus Christi in 1909, and Henrietta King held a dinner for him in the mansion. While she was not known for her humor, she must have been smiling when, knowing the president's reputation as a man of enormous appetite, she had a sixty-pound turkey for the main course. On most occasions visitors were provided with numerous forms of entertainment, which included horseback riding, if on the ranch. In either location the night often ended with singing around the piano. Henrietta, always devout, sat in her chair holding her Bible throughout the singing, and the last song of the night was always "Rock of Ages," her favorite.[44]

The Kineños

While her family was important to Henrietta, she also had another, even larger *familia*, the Kineños. She was concerned with their education and in the early 1860s had a one-room school built for the Kineño children. The school was for both boys and girls since Henrietta believed in education for both. Later she had the Texas-Mexican Industrial Institute built in Kingsville to train Mexican American students for jobs. Each year on Christmas Eve, she also held a big party on the ranch for the Kineños. The event, held in the commissary because the school could not hold the crowd, included presents for all, food, and a big dance with music provided sometimes by an orchestra, sometimes by accordions. The dancing was quite a compromise on the part of Henrietta; the Christmas party was the only event on the ranch at which dancing occurred. The party began at 4:00 p.m. with Henrietta handing out presents: "candy for the children, sweaters for children and women, [and] coats for the men." The party lasted until the early hours of the morning, as late as 3:00 a.m., but by that time Henrietta was long since in bed, letting the Kineños celebrate in their own way.[45]

Nothing shows the attachment to and respect for Henrietta by the Kineños more clearly than her death and funeral. Henrietta, appropriately, died at the ranch house on March 25, 1925. The Kineños were informed of La Patrona's death within minutes of the event and were asked to be as silent as possible in respect for Henrietta's passing. Later, when her body was prepared, the Kineños had their last view of Henrietta as they passed through the living room to view her body. One Kineña noted that Mrs. King was "very well-liked because she helped the people on the ranch." The last look the Kineños had of Henrietta must have also been surprising. Henrietta was laid out in a lilac pink dress.[46]

The greatest sign of respect from the Kineños, though, was reserved for the funeral, which of course was a huge affair for the ranch and the town of Kingsville. While the funeral crowd included Manhattan bankers, state and town officials, South Texas cotton farmers, merchants, and ranch owners, the honor of accompanying Henrietta's body was given to the vaqueros of the ranch, almost two hundred of them, on horseback. "When the casket was lowered into the earth, there was a stir at the edge of the crowd where the bare-headed horsemen stood. They came reining forward in single file, unbidden and uncommanded save by their hearts, to canter . . . once around the open grave, their hats down at side salute to Henrietta King."[47] For Henrietta Chamberlain King, daughter of an itinerant missionary who had become La Patrona, the final salute of the Kineños was a fitting end.

Notes

1. Tom Lea, *The King Ranch* (Boston: Little, Brown, 1957), 606–7; "Measuring Wealth," accessed July 1, 2013, www.measuringwealth.com/uscompare.php.

2. Bruce S. Cheeseman, ed., *My Dear Henrietta: Hiram Chamberlain's Letters to His Daughter, 1846–1866* (Kingsville, TX: King Ranch, 1993), 10, 22, 26, 27, 48n69, 78; Lea, *King Ranch*, 65; Bruce S. Cheeseman, "Chamberlain, Hiram (1797–1866)," *Handbook of Texas Online*, Texas State Historical Association,

accessed June 30, 2013, http://www.tshaonline.org/handbook/online/articles/fch05.

3. Cheeseman, *My Dear Henrietta*, 82; Lea, *King Ranch*, 323; Jane Clements Monday and Betty Bailey Colley, *Voices from the Wild Horse Desert: The Vaquero Families of the King and Kenedy Ranches* (Austin: University of Texas Press, 1997), 199.

4. Cheeseman, *My Dear Henrietta*, 10, 16, 29; Cheeseman, "Chamberlain, Hiram."

5. Cheeseman, *My Dear Henrietta*, 17–18, 83n198.

6. Cheeseman, 18, 19.

7. Cheeseman, 26–27 (italics in the original).

8. Cheeseman, 27–29.

9. Cheeseman, 70.

10. Cheeseman, 71.

11. Cheeseman, 71, 78, 80, 90 (italics in the original).

12. Cheeseman, 75, 90, 93.

13. Cheeseman, 75, 82, 85.

14. Cheeseman, 77–78 (italics in the original).

15. Cheeseman, 83, 78, 80, 89.

16. Cheeseman, 96.

17. Cheeseman, 78, 76, 74n184, 11.

18. Mary Dodson Wade, *Henrietta King: Loving the Land* (Houston: Bright Sky Press, 2011), 6–7; Ann Fears Crawford and Crystal Sasse Ragsdale, "La Patrona," in *Women in Texas: Their Lives, Their Experiences, Their Accomplishments*, ed. Ann Fears Crawford and Crystal Sasse Ragsdale (Austin: Eakin Press, 1982), 98; Lea, *King Ranch*, 62, 126.

19. Lea, *King Ranch*, 60–62.

20. Lea, 62.

21. Cheeseman, *My Dear Henrietta*, 92; Crawford and Ragsdale, "La Patrona," 99; Lea, *King Ranch*, 437n21.

22. Lea, *King Ranch*, 127; Cheeseman, *My Dear Henrietta*, 98.

23. Lea, *King Ranch*, 127–28, 131; Crawford and Ragsdale, "La Patrona," 99–100.

24. Lea, *King Ranch*, 128–29, 438n26.

25. Lea, 129, 438n27.

26. Crawford and Ragsdale, "La Patrona," 100; Lea, *King Ranch*, 129, 131.

27. Crawford and Ragsdale, "La Patrona," 100; Lea, *King Ranch*, 144, 147.

28. Lea, *King Ranch*, 150, 173; *San Antonio Herald*, February 7, 1857.

29. Lea, *King Ranch*, 149–50, 439–40n25, 173–74.

30. Lea, 216–17.

31. Lea, 216–17; Monday and Colley, *Voices*, 71–73.

32. Lea, *King Ranch*, 242–43; "Measuring Wealth," accessed July 1, 2013, www.measuringwealth.com/uscompare.php.

33. Lea, *King Ranch*, 322; Wade, *Henrietta King*, 9; Cheeseman, *My Dear Henrietta*, 104n335.

34. Lea, *King Ranch*, 323–24.

35. Lea, 324–25.

36. Lea, 325.

37. Monday and Colley, *Voices*, 103; Lea, *King Ranch*, 359; Darrin R. Lehman, Camille Wortman, and Allan F. Williams, "Long-Term Effects of Losing a Spouse or Child in a Motor Vehicle Crash," *Journal of Personality and Social Psychology* 52, no. 1 (January 1987): 218–31; Crawford and Ragsdale, "La Patrona," 103.

38. Lea, *King Ranch*, 470, 471.

39. Lea, 470, 512; Monday and Colley, *Voices*, 102; Crawford and Ragsdale, "La Patrona," 103.

40. Crawford and Ragsdale, "La Patrona," Lea, *King Ranch*, 513–14, 569, 571.

41. Lea, *King Ranch*, 496–98, 515; Murphy Givens, "Cattle Barons Build Mansions on Bluff," *Corpus Christi Caller-Times*, June 9, 2010; Crawford and Ragsdale, "La Patrona," 105; Monday and Colley, *Voices*, 103.

42. Crawford and Ragsdale, "La Patrona," 104; Givens, "Cattle Barons"; Jane Clements Monday and Frances Brannen Vick, eds., *Letters to Alice: Birth of the Kleberg-King Ranch Dynasty* (College Station: Texas A&M University Press, 2012), 128; Lea, *King Ranch*, 512–13, 571, 786n106.

43. Givens, "Cattle Barons"; Lea, *King Ranch*, 569, 570, 572.

44. Murphy Givens, "President Taft's Visit Was Big Event for Corpus Christi," *Corpus Christi Caller-Times*, October 21, 2009; Monday and Vick, *Letters to Alice*, 137.

45. Monday and Colley, *Voices*, 110, 112; Crawford and Ragsdale, "La Patrona," 105.

46. Monday and Colley, *Voices*, 157.

47. Monday and Colley, 199.

3

Petra Vela de Kenedy

HOMERO S. VERA

Petra Vela de Kenedy was a caring and independent Mexican woman living in a turbulent era throughout most of her life on the northern Mexican frontier and the US–Mexican border. Through all the turmoil, this woman of faith managed to raise a large family, survive many family tragedies, and marry a white, Anglo Protestant who supported her giving nature, both to others and to her beloved Catholic faith.

Background

To know what Petra Vela de Kenedy lived through we have to understand the history of her family and this area. Petra came from landed family with extensive ties to cattle and sheep ranching. The Velas trace their ancestry to Francisco Vela, who came to the new kingdom of Nuevo León from Cuencamé, Nueva Vizcaya (present-day Durango, Mexico), around 1645 during the Spanish Colonial period of Mexico. On May 25, 1685, he applied for a land grant in which he mentioned that he had been in this area for almost forty years and in the service of the king as a lieutenant in the military.[1]

Doña Petra descends from Lázaro Vela, a great-grandson of Francisco. Lázaro and his wife, María Antonia García, and their children moved from Cerralvo, Nuevo León, to Ciudad Mier and were one of the original families when the new province of Nuevo Santander was officially established by Spanish count and military governor José de Escandón in 1753. When Spanish dragoon Captain José Tienda de Cuervo came to record the census and report on the citizens of the newly established villas of Nuevo Santander in 1757, Lázaro, María Antonia, and seven children were counted along with four horses and no arms. In 1767, during the Auto de la General Visita (Acts of the Visit of the Royal Commissioners), Lázaro was granted *porción* 57 on the eastern bank of the Rio Grande. These *porciones* were long, narrow tracts of land with access to water.[2] Lázaro and María Antonia's ranch was named Rancho La Gloria.

During this period Petra's grandparents Gregorio Vela and Gertrudis Ramírez had been living with Gertrudis's parents, Antonio Ramírez and Catarina Vela, on their ranch, Rancho de Sabanitos or Small Cypress Ranch. Antonio had been granted *porción* 67, about ten to twelve miles downriver from Lázaro's. They also were originally from the Cerralvo area in Nuevo León. Much like his father, Lázaro, Nicodemus wanted his own ranch and was given a land grant on December 4, 1807. Located in present-day Live Oak County on the west bank of the Nueces River, the ranch was known as Veleño. Nicodemus and Gertrudis had two sons, Gregorio and José María, the latter of whom died as a young boy. Like his father and grandfather before him, Nicodemus wanted his own ranchlands, and on March 25, 1836, he denounced two leagues of land in Ciudad Victoria, Tamaulipas, and was granted title to the tract of land known as the *agostadero* Santa Teresa.[3]

Even though the Velas had always been land rich, there had not been much more proof to show any other type of net worth. While on a research trip to Ciudad Mier, I ran across an interesting two-page document concerning Gregorio Vela that indicates family assets. It was a petition by Gregorio to the Supreme Court of Tamaulipas signed on May 24, 1826, asking the court to intervene on his behalf so that his father, Nicodemus Vela, could give him the inheritance that his mother had left him from an asset list compiled after 1822, shortly after her death. The petition was approved by the magistrate of the Supreme Court, José Feliciano Ortiz, who ordered the mayor of Ciudad Mier to distribute the assets to Gregorio according to the list. Nicodemus had since remarried and now, at the age of around seventy years, had another son. Gregorio, who was now around fifty, wanted to make sure that he received his fair portion of his mother's inheritance without having to share it with his new three-year-old sibling. Gertrudis Ramírez de Vela was originally from Cerralvo, Nuevo León. Not much is known about her family except that they had come to the Mier area from Cerralvo. Apparently, they had means to support themselves and were people of culture, as noted from the list compiled by Nicodemus after Gertrudis's death on December 23, 1821, at the age of sixty years. Nicodemus first compiled the list of assets on February 14, 1822, and then he and Gregorio agreed on two guarantors to appraise the list, Don Antonio Montalvo and Don Prudencio Salinas, the first named by Nicodemus and the second by Gregorio. They inventoried and valued the list on December 14, 1822.[4]

Doña Gertrudis had a *sillar* (stone) house located on a straight line north of the city jail with the front of the house facing east, next to the corner of the main plaza of the villa and the Immaculate Conception Catholic church. Besides the usual items one finds in homes such as beds, tables, and kitchen utensils, Doña Gertrudis had silver table service and silver plates. She had a small amount of *ganado mayor*, or major livestock such as horses, cattle, bulls, and mules, but most of her livestock was *ganado menor*, minor livestock such as sheep and goats. Besides her breeding stock of a few thousand head of ganado menor, which were pastured on their ranches along the Rio Grande and Nueces River, she rented out the rest to area ranchers and to ranchers from as far away as San Antonio de Béxar. She was also a banker of sorts in that she loaned money to her neighbors. Believing strongly in the Catholic faith, she owned two carved crosses, five images (possibly of saints) on canvas, and one carved saint of La Divina Pastora, or the Divine Shepherdess, no doubt because she was a major breeder of sheep in this area of Mexico.[5]

After everything was assessed and losses taken from bad debts, the estate was worth 5,062 pesos, half of which belonged to Nicodemus and the other half to Gregorio. Gregorio also inherited the stone house in Mier. He was obliged to take care of the funeral arrangements and have fourteen masses said to the most holy Virgin of Agualeguas for his mother. From Gregorio's half, one-fifth was to be subtracted and given to the grandchildren of Doña Gertrudis, Don Pablo, Doña Nicolasa, Doña Gertrudis, Doña Casilda, and the granddaughter that she raised, Doña Juliana Vela. They each received 98 pesos and 5½ granos.[6] The asset list thus verifies the substantial position of Doña Gertrudis and the Vela family.

By the time Petra was born, her family had been ranching in what is now South Texas for over seventy years, establishing a legacy of raising cattle and sheep in what was then known as El Desierto de los Muertos, or the Desert of the Dead, the dry, thorny strip of land between the Nueces and Rio Grande that was home to feral animals.

Petra Vela de Kenedy

Petra was born on January 31, 1823, in the city of Mier, Tamaulipas, Mexico, to José Gregorio Vela and María Josefa Reséndez. I believe her deep Catholic faith was fostered by her proximity to the church, since she spent her early youth in the *sillar* house in Mier, which was very close to the Immaculate Conception Catholic church. Her mother, Doña Josefa Reséndez de Vela, died soon after Petra's thirteenth birthday in 1836. With Gregorio tending to his ranches and her mother dead, Petra was probably raised by her older sisters. She was becoming a young woman without the guidance of her parents when the young military officer Lieutenant Luis Vidal came into her life. No one knows when or where they met, but it might have been in one of the villas along the Rio Grande, where Luis had been sent in 1837 to join the Northern Battalion of the Mexican military, which was positioning its troops for a possible invasion to retake Texas.[7]

By 1842, Petra was living in Matamoros with Vidal. The census has them living at the military compound, with Luis's rank as captain and Petra listed as single and as a servant with two young girls, Luisa, two years old, and Rosa, eight months old. He was much older than she, forty-one years compared to her eighteen years. No record has been found of him of ever marrying Petra. Vidal would later go on to become a hero because of his role during the retaking of San Antonio de Béxar under General Adrián Woll in September 1842. During the battle, his horse was shot out from under him, and he was later commissioned as a brevet colonel. Vidal died in 1849 in Jalapa, Veracruz, of the *vómito*, which was induced from a bad case of cholera.[8]

In December 1842, Petra was living in Mier when the Texan forces tried to take the village but were soundly defeated by General Pedro de

Ampudia. Because she tended to the ill and wounded Texans, showing them love and care even though they tried to take over her hometown, Petra was remembered with a requiem mass in her honor at the cathedral in Brownsville on March 17, 1885.[9]

Vela Family Tree

Lázaro Vela + María Antonia García
1. José Nicodemus 2. María Gertrudis

1. José Nicodemus + María Gertrudis Ramírez
A. José Gregorio

A. José Gregorio + 1st wife Josefa Moreno
1. María Nicolasa 2. Pablo José 3. Juliana
4. Cecilia 5. Casilda 6. Gertrudis

A. José Gregorio + 2nd wife María Josefa Reséndez
7. José Antonio 8. José Lucas 9. María Petra
10. Pedro 11. Francisca 12. María Angela
13. Josefa Romualda 14. Antonia

Time in Brownsville

After the Texas Revolution in 1836, Texas laid claim to the land known to Texans as the Nueces Strip, a strip of land between the Nueces River and Rio Grande. Mexico also laid claim to it, as it was never part of Texas but part of the northern frontier of the Mexican state of Tamaulipas known as the Llanos Mesteños, or Mustang Plains. During the Spanish Colonial period it was the northern fringe of the colony of Nuevo Santander, also known as El Desierto de los Muertos. Although Texas claimed, colonizers were never sent to the area, as most of it was rangeland with ranches established by the early Spanish and Mexican settlers. This was the area where Petra's ancestors had made their living raising cattle and sheep for the past one hundred years. In 1845 the United States annexed Texas, which became the twenty-eighth state of the Union. General Zachary Taylor was sent to Corpus Christi in charge of the US Army, and by the following spring half of the army was in Texas.[10] In the spring of 1846 his troops marched south toward Matamoros, where they encountered the Mexican Army at Palo Alto and engaged in the battle that commenced the war with Mexico.

Shortly afterward, Mifflin Kenedy arrived in Texas. Kenedy, a Quaker from Pennsylvania, was a sailor and steamboat pilot. In 1846 he had been hired by Major John Saunders of the Quartermaster Department to pilot steamboats with supplies and troops for the army up the Rio Grande, where they would later disembark for their invasion into the interior of Mexico. The war lasted until September 14, 1847, when after much fighting US troops took the National Palace from General Santa Anna, who had agreed to a truce and withdrew to Guadalupe Hidalgo, north of Mexico City. The Treaty of Guadalupe Hidalgo was signed there on February 2, 1848, officially ending the war and setting the boundary between the United States and Mexico at the Rio Grande, from the Gulf of Mexico to the southern boundary of the then Mexican state of New Mexico, then west along the Gila River to the Gulf of California, and to the Pacific Ocean.[11]

After the war, Petra made her way to Brownsville, looking for a better life for her young children in the newly established town. The 1850 census of Cameron County shows the independent and financially able woman that Petra was, as she is listed as head of household with seven children—Luis, Vidal, Juana, Louisa, Rosa, Adrian, and Vicenta—all ten years old and younger. One more daughter, Concepción, was not counted in that census, making eight children that she had with Luis Vidal. Of those eight, only the last five would live to become young adults, marry, and have children. By contrast, her future husband, young steamboat captain and merchant Mifflin Kenedy, lived in a house with twenty-three other men. Sometime after the war with Mexico she met Mifflin Kenedy, who on March 1, 1850, had set up a steamboat business on the Rio Grande with partners Richard King, Charles Stillman, and James O'Donnell and named it M. Kenedy & Co. Even though Kenedy was a Quaker, he and Petra married at St. Mary's Catholic church in Brownsville on May 10, 1854, a church that she and Mifflin had helped establish financially as well as spiritually.[12] Together they had six children—Thomas, James, John Gregory, William, Sarah Josephine, and Phoebe Ann—all born in Brownsville.

The late 1850s saw turmoil and trouble in Brownsville with the Cortina Wars (1859–1860), when Juan Nepomuceno Cortina, a member of a landed Mexican-Tejano family, brought havoc to the Anglo citizens of Brownsville. He was trying to avenge the taking of lands by the newly established Anglos in South Texas from the long-established Mexican-Tejano families. In September 1859 he shot and wounded the sheriff of Cameron County, who had mistreated a former ranch worker of his family. This was the beginning of the Cortina Wars up and down the Rio Grande, which lasted until the following year, when Colonel Santos Benavides routed Cortina's army close to Carrizo.[13]

In 1861 the US Civil War commenced and brought more turmoil to Brownsville. Petra had already been through the battle of Mier in 1842, war with Mexico, and the Cortina Wars; now a new war in a new land was on her doorstep. But this war brought financial gain to Mifflin and his partners Richard King, Charles Stillman, and Francisco Yturria. They ferried bales of Confederate cotton on their steamboats down the Rio Grande to the open waters of the Gulf of Mexico under Mexican registry. Yturria was a banker and merchant and had registered the steamboats under his name to avoid bombardment by the Union forces that had blockaded the mouth of the Rio Grande. Mexico was neutral in the US Civil War, and aggression by the Union would have been unwelcome.[14] Mexico had its own problems, as it had been invaded by French forces who later installed Maximilian of Habsburg as emperor of Mexico and leader of its imperialist forces.

Petra and Mifflin experienced their own personal tragedy when Petra's son Adrian Vidal was executed on the morning of June 14, 1865. He had joined the Confederates at the beginning of the war, switched sides to the Union army, and then left to join the Mexican Juaristas, who were fighting the imperialist forces, when he was captured in the village of Camargo, Tamaulipas, a few miles from Rio Grande City, where he was executed. It was said that Mifflin tried to save him by sending money, but he was unsuccessful. After the war, life on the Rio Grande with the new Reconstruction government was not the same for King, Kenedy, and company, so the steamship firm was dissolved. The Confederacy was in shambles and many citizens wanted to leave the Union and start a new life south of the border. Emperor Maximilian gave a grant to organize the American and Mexican Emigrant Company, with General J. B. Magruder to head the office. Most of the principal participants were former Confederate generals or governors, with the only exception and only woman being Mrs. Mifflin Kenedy. Little is known about Petra's involvement in this group, but her connections to families in Mexico most likely played an important role.[15]

Life at Laureles

On May 31, 1868, Mifflin and Richard King amiably dissolved R. King & Company, which was vested in land and cattle. They gathered and sold all their cattle and other ranch holdings and then went their separate business ways. Three days later, Kenedy bought twenty-six leagues of land (116,480 acres), the Rancho Los Laureles, from Charles Stillman's brother, Cornelius. He later acquired adjoining land grants, which expanded the ranch to over 240,000 acres. Kenedy registered his Laureles ranch brand in Nueces County in 1868. Petra had already registered her own brand in the spring of 1856, when they had livestock on the Veleño ranch, her family's ranch on the Nueces River.[16]

Petra and Mifflin moved to Los Laureles in 1869. Petra's daughters with Colonel Vidal were now married and living in Brownsville except for Concepción, who had married Manuel Rodriguez of Nuevo Laredo. The boys were at Spring Hill College, a boarding school in Alabama, and Sarah was at the Ursuline Academy in New Orleans.[17] At Laureles they expanded their cattle herd into the thousands and employed several families who lived on the ranch as their herders, vaqueros, and laborers.

The 1870s brought new trouble to South Texas ranchers, as bandits stole livestock every day. Even so, Petra still traveled to Brownsville in her personal coach to visit family and friends. On one of those trips she and her entourage settled in for the night in the brush and were awakened by intruders. Mifflin's bodyguards for the trip kept them at bay until Petra jumped out from the coach and recognized one of the young men. She told him that if he did not behave properly she would tell his mother of his bad conduct. Shortly after that, the men disappeared into the chaparral, not to return.[18] The Mexican men were very obedient to their parents, especially their mothers, and they did not want to cause harm to a close family friend.

In 1882 Mifflin sold Los Laureles to a Scottish syndicate known as the Texas Land & Cattle Co. for $1,100,000. The sale consisted of 242,000 fenced acres, 50,000 head of cattle, and 5,000 head of horses, mares, and mules. He then purchased La Parra Ranch, which consisted of 23,000 acres, to adjoin his other Spanish/Mexican land grants in Cameron County. That move brought his total acreage to 400,000. Mifflin and Petra then moved to Corpus Christi in 1883, renting a house while he commenced building a grand house resembling an Italian villa, with all the modern conveniences, on the high bluff overlooking Corpus Christi Bay. It was close to St. Patrick's Catholic church, the church that he and Petra patronized and that was constructed with the help of their funding, much as they had done in Brownsville.[19]

Unfortunately, Petra did not get to live in the grand house for long. They finally moved in on February 26, 1885, but she died a few weeks later, on March 16. Mifflin brought the renowned Dr. Herff by special train to examine Petra, but uterine cancer had spread throughout her body; there was nothing he could do except make her comfortable during her last days.[20]

Legacy

During her lifetime Petra experienced the deaths of several of her children: Adrian Vidal by execution in Camargo; Phoebe Ann in infancy; William at sixteen years of age of consumption; and James of consumption just a few months before her own death. She was spared the traumatic death of her eldest son with Mifflin, Tom, when he was gunned down in Brownsville in 1887, two years after she died. But she did get to see her only surviving daughter with Mifflin, Sarah Josephine, marry the well-respected surgeon Dr. Arthur Spohn. Although she was too ill to attend the wedding, she was alive when her son John Gregory married the Louisiana-born Marie Stella Turcotte in New Orleans.

Petra made it through all the grief of losing close family members and her own approaching death because of her deep faith in God and her Catholic upbringing. She was an immensely caring person who saw to it that the very poor were always taken care of with food and clothing. Even after her death, as a letter that Mifflin wrote to John Gregory in August 1892 testifies, Mifflin fed fifty to one hundred people weekly for over six months through the convent in Corpus Christi.[21] It is fitting that the local Metro Ministries food kitchen for the homeless is now named the Petra Vela Kenedy Center.

To paraphrase the late Father Kelly Nemec, former director of the Oblates of Mary Immaculate's House of Prayer at the former headquarters of the Kenedy Ranch, "Petra's legacy of faith is rather like a spiritual DNA which courses through one's whole being and affects every facet of one's life. Moreover, something of this faith is passed on from generation to generation."[22] How very true his words are. Petra passed on that faith in God and the Catholic Church to her children, who in turn passed it on to their children. That legacy lives on, caring for people through her granddaughter Sarita Kenedy East's foundation, the John G. and Marie Stella Kenedy Memorial Foundation; and her grandson John G. Kenedy Jr.'s estate, the John G. Kenedy Jr. Charitable Trust, which benefits several Catholic institutions. Petra would find comfort in knowing that her work caring for others continued and will continue long after her passing.

Notes

1. Carl Duaine, *With All Arms: A Study of a Kindred Group* (Coahuila, Mexico: Nuevo Santander Press, 1987), 188.

2. *Estado general de las fundaciones hechas por D. José de Escandón en la colonia del Nuevo Santander, costa del seno Mexicano,* Publicaciones del Archivo General de la Nación (Mexico City: Talleres Gráficos de la Nación México, 1930), 14:409; Florence Johnson Scott, *Historical Heritage of the Lower Rio Grande* (Ciudad Camargo, Mexico: Texian Press, 1966), 83; Galen D. Greaser, *New Guide to Spanish and Mexican Land Grants in South Texas* (Austin: Texas General Land Office, 2009).

3. *Mier Census of 1782 & 1790*, compiled by Minerva Overstreet (Corpus Christi, TX: Spanish American Genealogical Association, 1990); *Estado general de las fundaciones hechas por D. José de Escandón*; Scott, *Historical Heritage*, 83; "Gregorio Vela—Rancher," *El Mesteño* 6, no. 1 (Winter–Spring 2003): 48.

4. Petition to Supreme Court of Tamaulipas, Mier Municipal Archives, copy in author's possession; *Book of Mier Deaths* (Corpus Christi, TX: Spanish American Genealogical Association, 1989); asset list compiled by Nicodemus Vela in 1822, Mier Municipal Archives, copy in author's possession.

5. Asset list compiled by Nicodemus Vela.

6. Asset list compiled by Nicodemus Vela.

7. *Immaculate Conception Church, Mier, Tamaulipas Book of Baptisms*, 1823, Immaculate Conception Church, Mier, Tamaulipas, copy in author's possession; *Book of Mier Deaths*; Jane Clements Monday and Francis Brannen Vick, *Petra's Legacy: The Ranching Empire of Mifflin Kenedy and Petra Vela* (College Station: Texas A&M University Press, 2007), 18.

8. Archivo Historico Municipal de Matamoros, census de 27 de Abril 1842, Exp. 1, Cja. 7, No. de Inventario 34, Fojas Utiles 7, Padrón de Vecinos del Ayuntamiento del 1 (Primer) Cuartel de la Sección del Oriente Plaza Hidalgo Poniente, Casa Mata Museum and Archives, Matamoros, Tamaulipas, Mexico; Monday and Vick, *Petra's Legacy*, 20, 22.

9. Monday and Vick, *Petra's Legacy*, 21; *El Mesteño* 6, no. 1 (2003): 51.

10. K. Jack Bauer, "Taylor, Zachary," *Handbook of Texas Online*, Texas State Historical Association, 2015, https://www.tshaonline.org/handbook/entries/taylor-zachary.

11. Mary Margaret McAllen Amberson, James A. McAllen, and Margaret H. McAllen, *I Would Rather Sleep in Texas: A History of the Lower Rio Grande Valley and the People of the Santa Anita Land Grant* (Austin: Texas State Historical Association, 2003), 98, 102–3.

12. 1850 US Census, Cameron County, Texas, LDS Genealogy, https://ldsgenealogy.com/TX/Cameron-County-Census-Records.htm; Monday and Vick, *Petra's Legacy*, 32, 34, 45.

13. Jerry Thompson and Lawrence T. Jones III, *Civil War and Revolution on the Rio Grande Frontier: A Narrative and Photographic History* (Austin: Texas State Historical Association, 2004), 34, 39.

14. Monday and Vick, *Petra's Legacy*, 91.

15. Monday and Vick, 105, 143, 171.

16. Monday and Vick, 162, 165; "Livestock Brands," *El Mesteño* 5, no. 2 (Summer–Fall 2002), 78.

17. Monday and Vick, *Petra's Legacy*, 179.

18. Monday and Vick, 174.

19. Monday and Vick, 280–81, 291.

20. Monday and Vick, 344, 347.

21. Monday and Vick, 272.

22. Father Kelly Nemec, "Petra Vela Kenedy and the Kenedy Family's Legacy of Faith in South Texas" (paper presented at the Texas State Historical Association conference, Corpus Christi, TX, March 7, 2008).

4

Sarita Kenedy East

DAVID SABRIO

Sarita Kenedy East was a towering figure in South Texas as a rancher and philanthropist. During her lifetime, ranching and philanthropy were decidedly dominated by men. Quietly and efficiently, without fanfare, and probably without consciously thinking about her actions, Sarita Kenedy East went about demonstrating that ranching and philanthropy were not gender-specific domains.

Background

To better understand Sarita Kenedy East, one must know something of the geographical and historical dimensions of the South Texas ranching culture of the latter half of the nineteenth century (1850–1900). Geographically, deep South Texas is an enormous triangle of land. From Corpus Christi south to Brownsville is about 160 miles; from Brownsville northwest up the Rio Grande to Laredo is about 200 miles; from Laredo east to Corpus Christi is about 141 miles. Now imagine a line beginning at Rockport, Texas (about thirty-three miles north of Corpus Christi), and going due west through Sinton, Sandia, Encinal, and on until the line intersects the Rio Grande, about forty miles northwest of Laredo. The area below this line covers approximately 16,550 square miles, or about 10.6 million acres. The states of Connecticut and New

Jersey could fit comfortably within this area, with over two thousand square miles to spare.

In the nineteenth century South Texas was inhospitable even to the strongest, best-prepared inhabitants. US general Philip Sheridan, whose first posting after graduating from West Point in 1853 was to Fort Duncan near Eagle Pass, Texas (on the Rio Grande about 218 miles west-northwest of Corpus Christi), famously said that if he owned Texas and hell, he would rent out Texas and live in hell. He could very well have been speaking about South Texas. People living in South Texas came into frequent contact with animals and plants that could bite, sting, scratch, stick, and hook. The heat was oppressive, and there was little drinking water. Official law enforcement was virtually nonexistent. Living in this kind of environment helped Sarita Kenedy learn something about independence and toughness.

Historical dimensions also influenced Sarita and the world she was born into. The first part of the nineteenth century set the tone of upheaval in South Texas. The Mexican Revolution (1810–1821) caused unrest and violence on both sides of the Rio Grande. Just fourteen years after Mexico gained its independence from Spain in 1821, the Texas Revolution began in 1835, bringing more violence to South Texas. After Texas declared its independence in 1836, the new republic had neither the funds nor the personnel to keep the peace south of San Antonio. Raids by bandits and rustlers and efforts by Native Americans to press their own claims to the land were frequent enough to prevent any kind of successful, large-scale ranching operations at this time in South Texas.[1]

The second half of the nineteenth century was a time of uncertainty and opportunity in South Texas: the independent Republic of Texas had just been annexed to the United States in late 1845. The Mexican War of 1847–48 "erupted over a border dispute following the annexation of Texas into the United States. The US claimed that the boundary was the Rio Grande. Mexico argued that the true boundary lay 130 miles to the north, along the Nueces River."[2] Legal deeds to vast tracts of land were often disputed, especially the hundreds of thousands of acres known as the Nueces Strip, the area from the Nueces River (which empties into Nueces Bay just north of Corpus Christi) south to the Rio Grande. Adding to the instability, Texas seceded from the Union to become part of the Confederate States of America from 1861 to 1865.

Two men who emerged from these trying times were Richard King and Mifflin Kenedy. These were men of vision, men who took risks, men of strong will and resourcefulness who worked tirelessly to achieve success. They could not accomplish their tasks alone, so they did what many effective leaders do: they adapted to existing conditions. One of those conditions was the *patrón* system. Daniel Arreola, author of *Tejano South Texas*, defines this system as "a semifeudal arrangement derived from Hispanic colonial roots. The *patrón* was a political overlord who controlled ranch *peones* (peons) through social and economic patronage."[3] Both the Kenedy Ranch and the King Ranch practiced the patrón system.

It would be too simplistic to suggest that all *patrones* were benevolent or that all participants felt equally comfortable in such a condition. As in many complex social systems, one's position and perspective invariably influence judgments about the benefits and fairness of the system. A complicating factor for contemporary readers is to put themselves in the position of those living in South Texas around the turn of the twentieth century, when Sarita Kenedy was an eleven-year-old girl. Robert Denhardt describes the patrón system on the neighboring King Ranch as follows; this description could apply equally to the Kenedy Ranch:

> A curious bond arose between the Kineño [employee of King Ranch] and the *patrón* in those dangerous early years, when they depended on each other for their lives. A feeling of mutual responsibility and trust arose that still clings. The Kineño rode not only for the *patrón* but with the *patrón*. There is a difference. The Kineños belonged to the Santa Gertrudis, and the Santa Gertrudis belonged to the *patrón*. When they fought off bandits and rustlers, they were fighting for their homes and jobs and for the homes and jobs of their fathers and their sons. The welfare of the ranch was the goal of both *patrón* and Kineño. Thus was born a loyalty too personal to buy.[4]

The two largest ranches in South Texas are the King Ranch (about 825,000 acres) and the Kenedy Ranch (about 400,000 acres). Establishing their South Texas ranches in the nineteenth century, Richard King, Mifflin Kenedy, and their family members quickly developed a sense that they had a unique relationship to their employees and the land, and responsibilities that extended beyond their immediate families. In this sense the sheer size of their ranchlands and the uniqueness of their situations had some influence on how they lived their lives.

The philosophy of Mifflin Kenedy toward cattle ranching influenced and made possible the philanthropic activities of Sarita Kenedy East many years later. In the introduction to *Voices from the Wild Horse Desert*, Ana Carolina Castillo Crimm states that Mifflin Kenedy and Richard King, during their years of piloting steamboats up and down the Rio Grande, became familiar with profitable livestock operations in Mexico. These Mexican haciendas (large ranching or farming estates) and latifundios (haciendas "of immense size") were "economically-oriented, profit-motivated capitalistic ventures involved in livestock raising."[5] Kenedy and King established their South Texas ranches on these Mexican models, with some modifications and adaptations. Authors Jane Clements Monday and Betty Bailey Colley elaborate:

> Richard King and his lifelong friend, Captain Mifflin Kenedy, . . . borrowed heavily from Mexican ranching tradition, . . . and spent their lives devising systematic ways to add monetary profit. . . . As a component for financial success, both were committed to keeping their huge land holdings intact. According to the September 26, 1984, *Corpus Christi Caller*, ". . . John [G.] Kenedy Sr. passed the philosophy of his father [Mifflin Kenedy] on to his children [John G. Kenedy Jr. and Sarita Kenedy]: Never, under any circumstances, split up the 400,000-acre ranch, the father preached to his children."[6]

Had Mifflin Kenedy's descendants chosen not to adhere to his philosophy of keeping the ranch intact, the likelihood of Sarita's far-reaching philanthropic activities and legacy would have been greatly reduced.

About sixty-five miles south of Corpus Christi on US Highway 77 is the small, unincorporated town of Sarita, the seat of Kenedy County. The estimated population of Kenedy County in 2012 was 431, making it one of the five least populated counties in the entire United States. The major buildings in Sarita are the public school (kindergarten through grade 6), the courthouse, the Catholic church, and the Kenedy Ranch Museum, housed in the building that was formerly the headquarters of the Kenedy Pasture Company. If one drives about four miles due east from Sarita on a narrow, two-lane blacktop road, one will arrive at the gates of the Kenedy Ranch. Mifflin Kenedy named his ranch La Parra,

Spanish for "grapevine," because of the abundant wild mustang grapevines growing among the underbrush and short oak and mesquite trees of South Texas.

Because the main house of the Kenedy Ranch is only about twenty-five miles due west of the Gulf of Mexico, the land surrounding the house contains gently sloping, low hills, which are actually sand dunes that have been formed over the centuries from the prevailing southeasterly winds and occasional hurricanes blowing in from the Gulf of Mexico. Over the years these dunes became covered with brush, vegetation, and low trees, mainly mesquite and live oak. In addition, many palm trees were planted near the ranch house, giving that area a somewhat tropical, forestlike atmosphere even though this part of South Texas is semiarid, receiving only sporadic rainfall. Mifflin Kenedy chose the tallest of these low dunes, about thirty-eight feet above sea level, to build his original ranch house in the 1880s soon after he bought four hundred thousand acres in 1882, forming the nucleus of La Parra Ranch. The architecture of this house was influenced by Kenedy's many years of familiarity with steamboats.

The "Big House," which has come to symbolize the Kenedy Ranch, was constructed by Sarita's father, John Gregory Kenedy, beginning in 1918, after the original ranch house had been carefully dragged by teams of mules and oxen about two hundred yards east of its original site. On the low dune where the original ranch house stood, John Gregory constructed an imposing Spanish Colonial Revival style ranch house, with the characteristic thick stucco exterior walls painted white, and a red tile roof. The three-story house looks even more massive than it already is, not only because it sits on a thirty-eight-foot hill, but also because it is topped by a watchtower rising another ten feet above the roof. Standing in the tower, then, is like standing eighty feet above the surrounding coastal plains. One has a commanding view in every direction for miles. This tower served a very practical purpose at the time: bandit attacks in South Texas were still common. The tower served as a lookout post, as an ideal defensive position for ranch sharpshooters, and as an emplacement for a Gatling gun if more firepower were ever needed.

By the time construction began on the Big House, Sarita was twenty-nine years old and had already been married to Arthur Lee East for about eight years. When the house was completed in 1923, Sarita and her husband moved into a wing of the new ranch house.

Not far from the Big House are the family chapel and an adjoining family cemetery where some members of the Kenedy family are buried. The chapel was dedicated to the Sacred Heart of Jesus on October 20, 1897. "This structure served as the family chapel for the Kenedys and the focal point of worship for the many employees of the ranch headquarters at La Parra."[7] The interior of the small, low-ceilinged chapel is simply decorated. Sarita was buried from this chapel after an all-night vigil. Immediately west of the chapel is a small, well-manicured family cemetery (its official name is the Kenedy-Turcotte Cemetery), where Sarita and other Kenedy family members and relatives are buried.

Sarita Kenedy East

With this background on geography, history, and the patrón system, we can better understand Sarita Kenedy. Children of wealth and privilege grow up with a sense that they are different from most others with whom they interact. For example, when Sarita was a teenager her father named the town of Sarita after her. This sense of difference is often heightened if these children are raised in an isolated, sparsely populated area, as Sarita Kenedy was. The offspring of wealth take many different paths. On one extreme are those who feel entitled, who feel that most rules do not apply to them, who take full personal advantage of the privilege they were born into. Other children of wealth feel a sense of responsibility to their family and the larger community, a sense that they are stewards of a legacy that they had little hand in building. This perspective is encapsulated in the following biblical passage: "From everyone who has been given much, much will be demanded; and from the one who has been entrusted with much, much more will be asked" (Luke 12:48, New International Version). From all the available evidence, Sarita Kenedy followed this latter path in life.

Born in Corpus Christi, Texas, on September 19, 1889, Sarita Kenedy was the daughter of John Gregory Kenedy (1856–1931) and Marie Stella Turcotte Kenedy (1862–1940), and the granddaughter of Mifflin Kenedy (1818–1895) and Petra Vela Kenedy (1825–1885). Her older brother, John Gregory Kenedy Jr., was born three years earlier, in 1886. Sarita ("little Sarah" in Spanish) was named after her aunt Sarah Josephine Kenedy.

When Sarita was a child, she and her family sometimes lived in the Kenedy home in Corpus Christi (located on the bluff overlooking Corpus Christi Bay and occupying the site where the Corpus Christi Cathedral now stands) and sometimes lived on the Kenedy Ranch, about seventy miles south of Corpus Christi. Although little is known about exactly how Sarita spent her childhood, we can assume that the love of the outdoors she exhibited as an adult began to develop in her childhood. Living so close to the water, she probably spent time at Corpus Christi Bay, which was very close to her family's Corpus Christi home, and at Baffin Bay, just a few miles from La Parra Ranch. She also enjoyed "roundups, hunting, fishing, and campfires."[8] She was educated at Incarnate Word Academy, a Catholic school in Corpus Christi. She continued her education in New Orleans at Sophie Newcomb College, a women's college loosely affiliated with Tulane University. Sarita did not complete a degree at Newcomb College; rather, she returned home and, on December 8, 1910, married Arthur Lee East, who, like her father, was a South Texas rancher.

Sarita Kenedy East Partial Family Tree

Mifflin Kenedy + Petra Vela
1. Thomas 2. James 3. John Gregory 4. Sarah
5. William 6. Phoebe

3. John Gregory Kenedy + Marie Stella Turcotte
A. John Gregory Kenedy, Jr. + Elena Seuss
B. Sarita Kenedy + Arthur Lee East

A trait that distinguished Sarita from most of her contemporaries was her family history of travel and exposure to non-US cultures. Her grandfather Mifflin Kenedy was born in Pennsylvania, attended boarding school, worked on a ship that traveled to India, worked on other ships and boats that plied many rivers in the southern United States, lived in Mexico, married a Mexican woman, and spoke Spanish. For this period, in a frontier area as isolated as South Texas, someone with these kinds of multicultural experiences was rare indeed. Sarita's father, John Gregory Kenedy, the son of Mifflin Kenedy, had to have been positively influenced by the variety and extent of his father's travels and exposure to other cultures. In fact, Sarita accompanied her parents on their travels around the United States when she was young. Moreover, Sarita's mother was from New Orleans and Sarita attended college there, which further exposed her to broadening experiences. Later in her life, Sarita traveled to Europe and South America.

Sarita's Love of Ranching and Love of People

Though there are few written records of how the young Sarita spent her years, we do know that after her father died in 1931, she assumed a more hands-on role in the management of the family ranch. Even before her father's death, she became increasingly involved in the daily operation of the ranch because her aging father was suffering from complications of diabetes. Her willingness to take on such a role and the way other family members accepted her leadership strongly suggest that she took an active interest in the family ranching operation from a young age. Working on the ranch would have meant that Sarita worked alongside the *Kenedeños*, the Mexican American and Mexican employees of the Kenedy Ranch. Sarita would have witnessed firsthand what her father and grandfather experienced: the Kenedeños taught them the most about how to run a successful ranching operation in South Texas. According to Colley and Monday, "Of necessity, the vaqueros [cowboys of Mexican descent] and the ranch owners had to rely on each other. On the King Ranch, and later on the Kenedy Ranch, a very special relationship between the vaquero families and the owners developed from mutual need. Each depended on and respected the other."[9]

Many people remember Sarita's love of ranching. For instance, Seferino Gutierrez (1906–1990), a lifelong Kenedeño and vaquero, remembered Sarita fondly in a December 1989 interview. Speaking of her taking part in working cattle, he said, "Sarita East went on the range to supervise. She was a very good rider and helped cut the cattle. She was good people." He also recalled, "Sarita took the men to the doctor when they got hurt on the ranch."[10] Also, in a June 2013 interview, Joyce Turcotte, the widow of

Louis Edgar Turcotte Jr., a cousin of Sarita, stated, "Sarita was definitely a horse lady, a ranch lady. Aunt Elena [sister-in-law of Sarita] would be doing needle work, and Sarita had her riding clothes on and her boots on ready to ride. She was out riding with the men. She was not one to sit at home." She continued: "She would leave the big house on Sunday and work cattle all week and come back on Sunday morning. She went way down south on the ranch. They would pile their supplies and bedding on the cattle truck and spend the whole week working cattle."[11] It was unusual for a woman to be so heavily engaged in the daily operation of a cattle ranch in South Texas at this time. Cattle ranching was a man's world. The work was dirty, dangerous, and physically demanding.

Many who knew Sarita over the years have commented on how respectfully she treated others, no matter what their station in life. As an adult, Sarita "took over the care and well-being of the Kenedeños. Like the King children, she grew up speaking Spanish among the vaqueros and their families. She knew them all intimately and cared deeply for them." Stella Cuellar Guevara, a fourth-generation Kenedeña, recalled Christmas celebrations on the Kenedy Ranch: "Sarita East was very nice. At Christmas, she sent gifts to the houses. Everybody in the family got a gift. The ladies got linens, towels, and the kids, toys; the men got a bonus. Nuts and candy were sent to the house. Sarita did this." Likewise, Enemorio Serna, a second-generation Kenedy vaquero, remembers Sarita's thoughtfulness: "On December 24th, we went to the Big House. We were given gifts of blankets, shirts, and coats. Then we had a dance."[12] In a recent interview, Jean Claire Turcotte, whose husband, Joe, was a cousin of Sarita, stated, "It's not only what she did for people; it's how she treated people. The lowliest person, no shoes, no shirt, she would go up and hug this person. She was a very caring, loving lady. She was very respected. She made sure that everybody had food in the commissary, had meat. She was a very caring person."[13] Former Kenedy County sheriff Rafael Cuellar, whose father and grandfather were Kenedeños, remembered Sarita as "a very beautiful lady with a very big heart. . . . You could see her everywhere, drinking coffee with the people, eating tortillas. She made sure nobody suffered needlessly." As the preceding testimonials demonstrate, Sarita's respect for and service to others went beyond lip service. One final example: "In her will, Sarita deeded ranch-owned houses to all the cowboys who had worked for her for at least 25 years."[14]

Philanthropic Activities during Sarita's Life

But Sarita Kenedy East's generosity extended far beyond the gates of the Kenedy Ranch and the small hamlet of Sarita. She is perhaps best known for her charitable and philanthropic activities during her lifetime and after she died. What caused her to give so much of her treasure to so many? Was it her devout Catholic faith? Her grandmother Petra Vela Kenedy (who died before Sarita was born) and mother, Marie Stella Turcotte Kenedy, were Catholics. Was it Sarita's sense of responsibility as a steward of great wealth to give back to local and larger communities in a way that would be ongoing and self-sustaining? Was it her sense of being part of a much wider world through her travels and knowledge of her family history? Was it her feeling of satisfaction and fulfillment experienced on a limited basis as *patrona*, which she wanted to expand beyond South Texas? Because she had no children and was the last surviving Kenedy, and because by all accounts she was such a "people" person and believed in family, perhaps her philanthropic work was her way of helping to create a worldwide family united by her generous bequests and legacies.

Sarita Kenedy East's giving nature was established while she was still living. Her generosity to the Kenedeños has been well documented, as in the specific instances recounted above. Less known are her charitable activities beyond the Kenedy Ranch. A partial list of recipients of Sarita's generosity during her lifetime includes the Norbertine Fathers; the Sisters of Purity (and of Mercy); Father Keller, founder of the Christophers movement; the Franciscans; the Jesuits; and representatives of a hundred other Catholic organizations, from the Negro Apostolate of the Divine Savior to the Marquette League for Catholic Indian Missions, including Father Flanagan's famous Boys Town, in Nebraska. Altogether, Mrs. East distributed from $40,000 to $100,000 a year to the Catholic Church and its causes.

Among other charities supported by Sarita were the March of Dimes, the National Braille Press, and the Red Cross. She also supported the Missionary Oblates of Mary Immaculate, an order of missionary priests who worked in South Texas; the Trappist monks; monasteries and missions in Argentina and Chile; a Catholic school in Laredo; the Catholic

Church in South Texas, especially the Diocese of Corpus Christi; and mission work in the Central American country of British Honduras, now called Belize.[15]

Although Sarita was not one to seek recognition for herself, recognition sought her out: "Because of her many contributions to charities and her many years of devoted service to the Catholic Church, Mrs. East received two special honors from the Pope—the medal Pro Ecclesia et Pontifice [Latin for "for the Church and the Pope"] and membership in the Equestrian Order of the Holy Sepulchre of Jerusalem."[16]

Philanthropic Foundations after Sarita's Death

If Sarita's charitable activities had ceased at her death, she would still be remembered as a remarkably generous, thoughtful woman. But these activities pale in comparison to the philanthropic work that she set in motion and that continues to function after her death. In the last year of her life, Sarita Kenedy East worked with spiritual and financial advisers to establish, in January 1960, a philanthropic entity named after her parents: the John G. and Marie Stella Kenedy Memorial Foundation. Sarita died on February 11, 1961, in St. Vincent's Hospital in New York City; her death was caused by an aggressive cancer. Almost immediately, legal jockeying began to take control of the newly established foundation. I will not attempt here to trace all the legal wrangling and lawsuits generated by the desire of various factions to influence the final disposition of the foundation's assets. Suffice it to say that when hundreds of millions of dollars are at stake—perhaps potentially as much as $1 billion or more over time—people take notice. The most detailed account of the intricacies of Sarita Kenedy East's wills, spiritual and financial advisers, lawsuits filed after her death, and related topics is the fascinating, extensively researched book *If You Love Me You Will Do My Will*, by Stephen G. Michaud and Hugh Aynesworth, published in 1990.

For the purposes of this chapter, I would like to focus on three charitable initiatives that emerged after Sarita's death: the Lebh Shomea House of Prayer; the Sarita Kenedy East Foundation; and the John G. and Marie Stella Kenedy Memorial Foundation.

The Lebh Shomea House of Prayer

The Lebh Shomea (Hebrew for "listening heart") House of Prayer grew out of the Kenedy family's relationship with the Missionary Oblates of Mary Immaculate, an order of Catholic priests who, beginning in the 1850s, fanned out from Brownsville over South Texas to minister to the widely dispersed inhabitants of the region between the Rio Grande and the Nueces River. One of the Oblate priests, Father Jean Breteau (known as Padre Juanito to the Kenedeños), ministered to the Kenedy Ranch inhabitants beginning in the late 1800s. As a native of France, Father Breteau developed a special connection with Sarita's mother, Marie Stella Turcotte Kenedy, herself of French heritage from New Orleans. The story continues: "Marie Stella spoke to her daughter [Sarita] about bequeathing their homestead and surrounding acreage to the missionary society to which Padre Juanito belonged. When Sarita Kenedy East died on the feast of Our Lady of Lourdes in 1961, she did in fact will to the Oblates her ranch headquarters with the specification that it be used for some 'religious purpose.'"[17] The Big House was first used as a novitiate for new seminarians studying to be Oblate priests. When vocations fell dramatically in the late 1960s and early 1970s, the Oblates turned the Big House into a center for those wanting a retreat in quiet, peaceful surroundings. To this day the Big House and the grounds surrounding it are used as a retreat center for spiritual renewal.

The Sarita Kenedy East Foundation

The Sarita Kenedy East Foundation, headquartered in the New York City area, grew out of Sarita's dealings with one of her financial advisers, J. Peter Grace, of New York City; he was a wealthy businessman who did charitable work for the Catholic Church. Grace originally had much more influence in the John G. and Marie Stella Kenedy Memorial Foundation. However, during the legal challenges relating to his degree of influence over Sarita in the last years of her life, the courts worked out a settlement among the parties. As a result, in 1964 the Sarita Kenedy East Foundation was "spun off" from the much larger Kenedy Memorial Foundation. The East Foundation began with approximately $14.4 million in assets.[18] Over the years this foundation has awarded grants generally ranging from $5,000 to $200,000 to various, mainly Catholic organizations, many of which are in the northeastern United States.

The John G. and Marie Stella Kenedy Memorial Foundation

The main charitable arm of Sarita's legacy is the John G. and Marie Stella Kenedy Memorial Foundation. Sarita and some of her financial advisers established the foundation on January 21–22, 1960, about thirteen months before she passed away in a New York hospital. The foundation's potential to generate income has greatly increased because in the 1950s Sarita began to allow oil and gas exploration and production on her ranchlands. By some estimates the oil and gas under the land controlled by the foundation are worth between $200 million and $500 million, probably more, given the ever-increasing cost of petroleum products. When details of the administration of the foundation became known, many of Sarita's closest family members and advisers from South Texas were alarmed that "outsiders" had too much control and undue influence over the establishment of the foundation. Those two outsiders were Brother Leo, a Trappist monk (Roderick Norton Gregory, before he took his monastic name), and J. Peter Grace, the New York businessman, both of whom had advised Sarita on spiritual and financial matters. Lawsuits flooded in, challenging the terms of the foundation. The main source of these lawsuits was South Texas: family members related to Sarita Kenedy East, local financial advisers, and church officials. The legal tangle was so thorny that it took the courts over twenty years to sort out the intricacies. Finally, by 1984, with most (but not all) litigation settled, the administrators of the foundation were ready to do what Sarita had wanted all along: help as many people as possible according to her wishes.[19]

The John G. and Marie Stella Kenedy Memorial Foundation is guided by the following mission and core values:

- Helping break the cycle of poverty;
- Assisting people to help themselves;
- Nurturing support and love for Catholic institutions;
- Developing the Catholic faith;
- Learning;

- Spirituality;
- Respect; and
- Cooperative/collaborative partnership.

The foundation encourages grants with large "ripple effects"—that is, those that generate benefits that spread beyond their primary grantee into the wider community, as well as "seed money" grants, whereby foundation support provides a needed catalyst or first step to very significant, and preferably ongoing, positive core value effects. Although its principal beneficiary is Catholic charities, the foundation supports nonsectarian charities in Texas to the extent of at least 10 percent of its annual distributions. Nonsectarian institutions are defined as nonreligious and not church related.[20]

In the early 1980s the foundation began disbursing grants. One of the first institutions to receive a sizable grant was St. Mary's University School of Law in San Antonio. The school's law library received $7.5 million and was renamed the Sarita Kenedy East Law Library. Another large grant went to "church and classroom construction and renovation in eight Texas dioceses." (In the Catholic Church, a diocese is a geographic area under the leadership and administration of a bishop.) In "Corpus Christi, where about $7.5 million was spent, the diocese built a state-of-the-art television and radio production facility." Among the nonsectarian organizations receiving early grants were the KEDT public television station in Corpus Christi, the Corpus Christi Public Library, the United Way, and the Food Bank of Corpus Christi.[21]

The foundation continues to fund various organizations within Texas:

> Nearly 90% of the total charitable contributions given are to Sectarian entities, primarily Catholic schools and churches . . . education has been strongly favored in recent grant-giving cycles, including Catholic schools, Catholic universities and public universities, all within the state of Texas. Health and human services are also favored, in keeping with the Foundation's core values.[22]

As an example of a typical funding cycle, during the 2007–2008 fiscal year, the foundation awarded more than five hundred grants totaling over $12.7 million. In accordance with the terms of the foundation, most of these grants went to sectarian causes. However, dozens of grants were awarded to secular organizations, especially in the areas of public health (American Cancer Society, American Heart Association, American Red Cross, American Diabetes Association); education (enrollment and tuition assistance for students at Texas A&M University–Kingsville, Texas A&M University–Corpus Christi, Del Mar College [located in Corpus Christi], University of Texas–Pan American, University of Texas at San Antonio); and human services (literacy programs, food banks, homeless shelters).[23] These examples are just a small, representative sample of the breadth of the foundation's grants.

Legacy

Few women have had a more positive impact on the people of South Texas than Sarita Kenedy East. Even fewer women have had a more positive impact on so many people outside South Texas. She was not the first woman rancher, or even the first woman rancher in Texas, but she was one of the most visible. As a result of her visibility, others could look to her and see what was possible, what it meant to defy a stereotype. Similarly, she was not the first woman philanthropist, or even the first woman philanthropist in Texas. But her level of commitment to her vision, combined with the financial resources designated to make that vision a reality, is rare. Ironically, Sarita Kenedy East would probably not have liked the attention and publicity focused on her by the *Mujeres a Través del Tiempo* mural and this accompanying chapter. Her interests would have been focused more on helping as many people as possible. Sarita Kenedy East invested in human capital. Over the years, she has caused the seeds of hope and opportunity to be sown among hundreds of thousands of people on two continents, North America and South America. And in a very real way this brief summary of her philanthropic activities is provisional and incomplete, because these activities will continue far into the future. The positive ripple effects of her efforts are incalculable. Undoubtedly the vast majority of those who have benefited from her legacy would not even recognize her name, and that is precisely the way that Sarita Kenedy East would have wanted it.

Notes

1. Jane Clements Monday and Betty Bailey Colley, *Voices from the Wild Horse Desert* (Austin: University of Texas Press, 1997), xxii–xxiii.

2. Gary Cartwright, "Sarita's Secret," *Texas Monthly*, accessed July 11, 2012, http://www.texasmonthly.com.

3. Daniel D. Arreola, *Tejano South Texas: A Mexican American Cultural Province* (Austin: University of Texas Press, 2002), 190.

4. Robert Moorman Denhardt, *The King Ranch Quarter Horses* (Norman: University of Oklahoma Press, 1970), 32–33.

5. Monday and Colley, *Voices*, xvi.

6. Monday and Colley, 48.

7. Historical plaque on the exterior wall of the Kenedy Family Chapel at La Parra Ranch.

8. Stephen G. Michaud and Hugh Aynesworth, *If You Love Me You Will Do My Will* (New York: Norton, 1990), 50.

9. Betty Bailey Colley and Jane Clements Monday, *Tales of the Wild Horse Desert* (Austin: University of Texas Press, 2001), 5.

10. Monday and Colley, *Voices*, 29, 154, 212.

11. Joyce Turcotte, interview with the author, June 7, 2013.

12. Monday and Colley, *Voices*, xxii, 141, 212, 216.

13. Jean Claire Turcotte, interview with the author, June 7, 2013; Cartwright, "Sarita's Secret."

14. Cartwright, "Sarita's Secret."

15. Michaud and Aynesworth, *If You Love Me*, 17, 65, 66, 73, 95, 118, 134.

16. The John G. and Marie Stella Kenedy Memorial Foundation, accessed July 18, 2012, http://www.kenedy.org.

17. "Lebh Shomea House of Prayer: The Legacy of Sarita Kenedy East," accessed July 11, 2012, http://www.lebhshomea.org/ske.htm.

18. Laurie E. Jasinski, "East, Sarita Kenedy (1889–1961)," *Handbook of Texas Online*, Texas State Historical Association, accessed July 2, 2012, https://www.tshaonline.org/handbook/entries/east-sarita-kenedy; Cartwright, "Sarita's Secret."

19. Michaud and Aynesworth, *If You Love Me*, 105, 295, 314, 342–43; Jasinski, "East, Sarita Kenedy."

20. John G. and Marie Stella Kenedy Memorial Foundation.

21. Michaud and Aynesworth, *If You Love Me*, 343.

22. John G. and Marie Stella Kenedy Memorial Foundation.

23. John G. and Marie Stella Kenedy Memorial Foundation.

5

Helen Kleberg

SANDRA REXROAT

We have an image of Helen Kleberg—a fictional image of Elizabeth Taylor's iconic screen role of Leslie in the 1956 movie *Giant*, adapted from Edna Ferber's novel of the same name. Elegant, headstrong, East Coast socialite embarks on a whirlwind romance with Texas rancher Bick Benedict. Elizabeth Taylor's portrayal of the East Coast socialite swept off her feet by the ruggedly handsome Texan who takes her to his family's sprawling ranch is arguably the image that is associated with the King Ranch, and with Bob and Helen Kleberg.

Ferber was a meticulous researcher, and she visited the King Ranch. There is no written account of the meeting of the Pulitzer Prize–winning author and the Klebergs, but presumably the idea for her novel was discussed, even if it might not have been welcomed by the ranch family. While Ferber's story is pure fiction, and one not authorized or most probably not approved by the Klebergs, the image of an elegant, intelligent, independent, horse-loving eastern socialite who falls in love with a Texas rancher and embraces life in the harsh environs of the ranch has a basis in fact, and that characterization could describe Helen Campbell Kleberg.

What we do know about the real Helen Kleberg comes to us from intimate family memoirs by her daughter, Helenita Groves, and by her nephew B. Johnson, who was raised by Helen and Bob after the deaths of his father, stepfather, and mother, Sara Kleberg, Bob's younger sister. Like her father before her, Helen Mary Campbell Kleberg kept a journal all her life. Her journals are not accessible, and our entry into Helen's personal accounting comes from the journal fragments revealed in Helenita Groves's homage to her parents *Bob and Helen Kleberg of King Ranch*, researched and written with Bill Benson.

Helen Campbell was born to Phillip Pitt Campbell, a Kansas lawyer, and Mary Helen Goff in 1902. The youngest of four children, Helen joined the family at 1903 North Elm Street in Pittsburg, Kansas. That same year, Phillip Campbell ran for Congress and was elected representative for the Third US Congressional District. He served in the US Congress for twenty years and then returned to the practice of law in Washington, DC, until his death in 1941. During his congressional tenure, he was a formidable presence as the chair of the powerful House Rules Committee. His legal practice included the Standard Oil Company of New Jersey. Because of her father's profession, Helen's upbringing was set in a political milieu that encompassed a large, influential, and international social circle.[1]

When Helen was thirteen, the Campbells moved to a fifty-acre estate overlooking the Potomac River in Arlington, Virginia, called Windsor. She loved the social scene and the mix of politics, wealth, and diplomacy that made up her parents' personal and professional circle of friends. Helen's upbringing was that of an East Coast socialite. But she also loved being outdoors—especially on a horse. And she loved to take pictures. Both passions prevailed throughout her life. Around the age of sixteen, she was sent to Villa Maria, a convent school in Montreal, in what seems to have been an attempt to curb her enthusiasm for life in general and boys in particular. She found that year difficult but ultimately rewarding and returned home to graduate two years later from the National Cathedral School and embarked on a European tour.[2]

Helen was twenty-four years old and visiting her sister and brother-in-law in San Antonio when she met Robert J. Kleberg Jr.—a "cowboy" from South Texas. They decided to get married five days after meeting. Family legend has it that Helen did not even know how to spell Bob's last name when she warily telephoned her father with the news of the upcoming nuptials. Another story told in the family is that Helen wore her sister's riding jacket for the wedding because hers was too dirty.[3]

The mythic sprawling ranch with the equally mythic ranch family in the movie *Giant* had some parallels with the Texas ranching family. The ranch was huge, extending to over nine hundred thousand acres. Robert J. Kleberg Jr., known as "Mr. Bob," was the grandson of the ranch founder, Richard M. King, and the son of King's attorney, who became his son-in-law with his marriage to Alice King. Kleberg was indispensable to the matriarch, Henrietta Chamberlain King, and worked with her after King's death to create the foundation for the modern King Ranch.[4]

His father sent Bob to the University of Wisconsin to study animal husbandry in order to build and strengthen the ranch livestock. Bob's interests lay elsewhere, in electrical engineering, so his father proposed a two-year trial in animal husbandry with electrical engineering in the future if Bob so desired. Bob never got the chance to consider the second option because Robert J. Kleberg Sr. suffered a stroke in 1916 and Bob came home to the King Ranch and took over as ranch manager. While at the university, Bob found his life's bliss in the study of genetics. His later development of a new cattle breed, quarter horses, and drought-tolerant grasses makes it doubtful that electrical engineering held any real interest for him by the time he came home to the ranch. His four siblings, Richard Mifflin, Sarah, Henrietta Rosa, and Alice Kleberg, were all on the ranch, as was his mother, Alice King Kleberg. His grandmother Henrietta Chamberlain King lived in Corpus Christi, about forty-five miles northeast of Kingsville, Texas. It was into this extended family and the vast acreage of the ranch that Helen was introduced for her wedding less than two weeks after the decision to marry. She arrived at her wedding wearing eastern-style riding breeches and boots.[5]

The King Ranch was one of the largest in the world, and "Mr. Bob" would become the "face" of the ranch and its driving force for the next fifty years. His brother, Richard (Dick), was elected to the House of Representatives in the mid-1930s and hired another young Texan, Lyndon Baines Johnson, as his personal secretary. His younger sister, Sarah, lost both her husbands and died tragically in an automobile accident, leaving two young sons, Belton Johnson (B.) and Bobby Shelton. Helen and Bob raised their orphaned nephews along with their daughter, Helenita, who was born in 1927, the oldest of the three. Their home was a seven-room cottage that had been the ranch foreman's quarters on the Santa Gertrudis division of the ranch. It gave the family more privacy than was afforded at the main house, which was close by. Helen and Bob lived in that cottage their entire lives, even though the children spent time off the ranch for their schooling. Helenita and B. spent extended periods with their great-grandmother in the house in Corpus Christi when Helen and Bob would go to Washington because of the failing health of Helen's father.[6]

The cosmopolitan eastern socialite and the Texas cowboy forged a solid partnership that extended to all facets of ranch life. They brought very different but complementary strengths to the management of the ranch. A great common bond was their love of horses. The King Ranch Stables were established in 1935 when Bob and Helen went to Kentucky to purchase thoroughbreds. It is safe to say that the King Ranch venture into thoroughbred racing had something of Helen's discerning eye and great store of knowledge behind it. Helen loved the thoroughbreds while Bob championed the quarter horse. Bob's fascination with genetics and breeding had led to the founding of the first American cattle breed, the Santa Gertrudis. It also led, with the inclusion of thoroughbred fillies, to the finest line of quarter horses sired by Old Sorrel. J. K. Northway, the ranch's longtime veterinarian, was also instrumental in the breeding of the quarter horses, as he had been in the development of the Santa Gertrudis cattle. Helen's role has not been told, but she did introduce Bob to the "sport of kings," and with her formidable store of knowledge and her connections in the racing world, he found a new outlet for his love of genetics. Pedigrees and track records meticulously studied and acted on for breeding, with both partners having an eye for a "good" horse, soon led to success at prestigious races. The pinnacle of success was achieved when Assault won the Triple Crown of racing—the Kentucky Derby, the Preakness, and the Belmont Stakes—in 1946. Middleground followed, with wins at two of the three, the Derby and the Preakness. Still other thoroughbreds added to the production of millions of dollars in both prize money and stud fees for the King Ranch Stables.[7] John Cypher, Mr. Bob's personal assistant, always said that Helen Kleberg was the most unrecognized influence on the ranch, particularly in thoroughbred racing. Helen and Bob instilled their passion for horses in daughter Helenita, and in her daughter Helen, who assumed the management of the horse operations when Bob was ill in 1963.[8]

Little written material on Helen Kleberg exists except the few paragraphs in which she is mentioned in works on the history of the King Ranch. In these brief glimpses, the term "elegant" invariably appears. Holland McCombs, the *Time-Life* editor who visited the ranch in 1947 to write a feature article on Bob Kleberg and the King Ranch for *Time* magazine, offered this observation: "To me she was a beautiful, composed, wise, witty, slender, auburn-haired Virginia Aristocrat—at times well-endowed with a patrician toughness and determination that could surmount and overcome a lot of obstacles."[9]

We do, however, have actual images of Helen Kleberg—photographs that capture Helen throughout her lifetime. Many of the photographs were taken by Toni Frissell, a prominent fashion photographer, war chronicler, and portraitist of the wealthy and the famous in postwar America. Later in her career, she became the first woman photographer for *Sports Illustrated* magazine, adding a new dimension to her already lengthy résumé, which included *Vogue, Harper's Bazaar, Fortune*, and *Time* magazines. Frissell met Helen and Bob Kleberg at the racetrack at Saratoga Springs, New York, in 1939 and struck up a friendship, particularly with Helen, who was herself an avid photographer.[10]

Helen's love of photography began early in her life. Her daughter, Helenita, recalls her mother's stories of "being bitten by the bug" as early as six years old when she began taking pictures with her Brownie camera. Helenita also recalled Brownie photos being snapped even in her own youth, prior to her mother moving on to a more professional Leica sometime in the late 1920s.[11] When Mr. Bob appeared on the cover of the December 15, 1947, issue of *Time* magazine, the article was accompanied by photographs taken by both Toni Frissell and Helen Kleberg. Frissell's photographs of the ranch include scores of images of Helen that capture her enthusiasm for and dedication to the ranch—the landscape, the people, the cattle, and of course the horses.

Both women loved the outdoors and this, too, is reflected in their photographs. There is a beautiful Frissell image, *Mr. and Mrs. Bob Kleberg at Work*, that appears in Frank Goodwyn's *Life on the King Ranch*. The Klebergs are on horseback, encircled by cattle. It is ironic, however, that in this book, the photograph shows only Mr. Bob surrounded by cattle, and immediately behind his silhouette is a horse's head with a slim hand on the reins. Helen Kleberg has disappeared into the binding of the book. Similarly, much of Helen Kleberg's story is hidden behind the silhouette of Bob Kleberg. Luckily, Toni Frissell's images of the King Ranch, and of Helen and Bob, can be accessed through her collection at the Smithsonian Museum. When Toni Frissell was first invited to visit the ranch, she asked whether she could bring her camera. She visited often and always brought her camera. The invitations were both personal and professional. Frissell became a good friend and mentor to Helen. Indeed, there are many instances of a shot being staged for both photographers, who then used different angles and light to create their images. Frissell's friendship with Helen and her access to the ranch enabled her to create the photographic essay on the King Ranch that introduced this nation to its preeminent ranch and rancher.

Other photographers worked on photographic assignments on the ranch. Eliot Elisofon's photographs accompany *Life* magazine's two-issue excerpts from Tom Lea's 1957 two-volume work, *The King Ranch*. Lea's work is the standard for the history of the ranch, but it is Frissell's photographs that became the iconic images of the "ranch" in twentieth-century America. Frissell's are the images that are associated with the ranch.

Bob sought to expand the ranch with overseas acquisitions, and Helen's influence on this venture is probably her most recognized contribution to the King Ranch. The Klebergs first went to Argentina on a honeymoon cruise to see, in Bob's words, "the best damn cattle country in the world." Bob had a vision that cattle ranching could support the stability of countries by providing protein for the world's population.[12] Helen's upbringing had prepared her well for socializing with an international clientele, a skill that proved to be of tremendous value for the ranch. Bob was outgoing and friendly, but Helen had the cosmopolitan experience.

The ranch expanded into Australia, Cuba, Argentina, and Venezuela with Helen advising Bob. Leroy Denman, Bob's attorney and business confidant, commented, "Through her relationship with Bob, she helped transform it [King Ranch] from a fairly provincial, local kind of operation into an international business of prominence." John Cypher, another of Bob's confidants, agrees with this assessment: "She broadened his horizon to encompass the world. She changed him, gave him an international outlook."[13]

Helen always traveled with Bob, if she was well enough. She was diagnosed with tuberculosis in the late 1920s and over the next twenty years fought recurring bouts of illness. Surgeries after 1946 forced her to spend extended periods away from the ranch but did not rid her of the condition. Both working the cattle with Bob and photographing the spectacle amid the swirling dust kicked up by the animals led to periods of quarantine in the house. She used the time inside to work with her prints.

Helen Mary Campbell Kleberg died of a brain tumor at the Columbia-Presbyterian Medical Center in New York City in June 1963. She was sixty-one. Unlike other women married to famous, powerful men, who at their husband's death took the reins of a family business or were appointed to their husband's seat in Congress and emerged from their husband's shadow to be recognized in their own right, Helen died leaving Bob to continue without her for another eleven years. She was a private person and did not seek the limelight. Mr. Bob's accomplishments have been chronicled, but Helen's influence on ranch management remains conjecture, except for those most closely associated with the Klebergs. In the foreword to Groves's book, Helen's great friend and neighbor Anne Armstrong wrote:

> We will never know how much influence she [Helen] had on all the wonderful things he [Bob] accomplished. She never bragged and continuously supported him. She was a lady through and through. To anyone who would meet Bob, Tom Armstrong, Johnny Kenedy, or the younger ones, they might say, "Ah, these wild and woolly Texans, they are a rough, tough lot." They were stopped in their tracks, however, when they met Helen. There was no one more elegant. She was never flamboyant and was a heck of a shot. . . . She learned everything Bob knew and was always at his side."[14]

Notes

1. Helen Kleberg Groves, *Bob and Helen Kleberg of King Ranch* (San Antonio: Trinity University Press, 2017), 44–45; for biographical information about Helen Kleberg, see "Helen Mary Campbell Kleberg," Find a Grave, accessed September 8, 2018, https://www.findagrave.com/memorial/125229184/helen-mary-kleberg; and Debbie Mauldin Cottrell, "Kleberg, Helen Campbell (1902–1963)," *Handbook of Texas Online*, Texas State Historical Association, accessed September 8, 2018, http://www.tshaonline.org/handbook/online/articles/fkl14.

2. "Helen Mary Campbell Kleberg"; "Kleberg, Helen Campbell." See also Groves, *Bob and Helen Kleberg*, 56–57.

3. Groves, *Bob and Helen Kleberg*, 64–67.

4. Alden Whitman, "Robert Kleberg Jr. Dies; Owned Huge King Ranch," *New York Times*, accessed September 8, 2018, https://www.nytimes.com/1974/10/15/archives/robert-kleberg-jr-dies-owned-huge-king-ranch-once-a-spanish-grant.html.

5. Groves, *Bob and Helen Kleberg*, 67.

6. Groves, 263–64.

7. For information about the King Ranch under Bob Kleberg, see "Robert Kleberg Jr. Dies; Owned Huge King Ranch," and Skip Hollandsworth, "When We Were Kings," *Texas Monthly*, August 1998, https://www.texasmonthly.com/articles/when-we-were-kings. See also Groves, *Bob and Helen Kleberg*, 86–87.

8. John Cypher, *Bob Kleberg and the King Ranch: A Worldwide Sea of Grass* (Austin: University of Texas Press, 1996), 53–54.

9. "King Ranch's Bob Kleberg," *Time*, December 15, 1947.

10. For biographical information on Frissell, see "Toni Frissell," Wikipedia, accessed September 8, 2018, https://en.wikipedia.org/wiki/Toni_Frissell.

11. Groves, *Bob and Helen Kleberg*, 98–101.

12. Cypher, *Bob Kleberg*, 141.

13. Groves, *Bob and Helen Kleberg*, 240–45; Cypher, *Bob Kleberg*, 54.

14. Anne Armstrong, foreword to Groves, *Bob and Helen Kleberg*, 7.

III

The Educators

6

Jovita González Mireles

MICHELLE JOHNSON VELA

Jovita González—Tejana, Chicana, Mexican American woman, and native Texan—was a pioneer in folklore studies and bilingual education in Texas. Born into a landowning South Texas Tejano family, over the course of her lifetime González would generously contribute to folklore studies, civic organizations, and the field of bilingual education. In many ways, González's literary and civic contributions were shaped by the borderlands themselves. She imbued her scholarship with a nostalgia that was ever mindful of the shifting linguistic, ethnic, physical, and cultural landscapes of South Texas in the early twentieth century. Uniquely qualified as a Tejana and a scholar to represent her ethnic and cultural heritage with personal dedication and loving tenacity, Jovita González has proven to be a landmark figure in the history of Texas.

Early Life and Education

Jovita González was born in Roma, Texas, on January 18, 1904. The year of her birth witnessed a dramatic shift in the borderlands of Texas. The rail line from Corpus Christi to Brownsville had been completed and began transporting farm products from the Rio Grande Valley, as well as hundreds of midwestern Anglos, into the region. As María Eugenia Cotera explains, "In the years immediately following the US-Mexico

War (1846–1848), relations between Anglos and Mexicans in the border region were marked by an ethos of relative tolerance for linguistic and cultural difference."[1] However, the influx of Anglos from the Midwest, as well as subsequent immigration from Mexico, stemming from the Mexican Revolution at the beginning of the twentieth century, dramatically altered the region over the next several decades. Ultimately, this transition became a central theme in González's works.

In her brief unpublished autobiography contained within the files and papers housed at the Mary and Jeff Bell Library at Texas A&M University–Corpus Christi, Jovita González describes her informal education at her family's ranch in South Texas, Las Víboras, as foundational for her subsequent academic formation. Jovita's father, Jacobo González, a believer in "pure" and formal Spanish, had come from a family of educators and artisans and was himself an educator who had directed the boys' school in Mier, Tamaulipas. In Mier, Jacobo met Severina Guerra Barrera, a descendant of a long line of colonizers from Mexico who, in 1749, had come with José de Escandón to settle the province of Nuevo Santander (named after his native province in Spain). Indeed, one of Jovita's ancestors, Don José Alejandro Guerra, had been surveyor to the Spanish crown. In Texas, Jacobo founded a school to bring Mexican education to the border boys, with Mexican books and curriculum. The girls were educated at home by the women of the family, specifically by Jovita's paternal grandmother, Mamá Tulitas, who narrated to them fantastic tales from medieval Spain as well as Mexican versions of fairy tales; and Tía Lola, Jovita's strong-willed widowed aunt, who taught Jovita and her sister Tula about their family history and cultural heritage. In addition, the ranch hands of Las Víboras contributed to the girls' knowledge of the folklore and culture of the region: Tío Patricio, the mystic; ugly Chon; Old Remigio, tortilla maker; Tía Chita; Pedro, the hunter and traveler; one-eyed Manuelito, the ballad singer; and Tío Camilo.[2] Though Jovita and her sisters could sew and crochet and were familiar with the Bible, Mexican history, and Sor Juana Inés de la Cruz, Jacobo realized that his daughters were not receiving the proper training and formal education they deserved. Although Jovita had been instructed in English for one year by Miss Elida García at the San Román Ranch, Jovita's father decided to move his family to San Antonio in 1910, so that his children would be educated formally in English. Jovita's elemental knowledge of English and fluency in Spanish allowed her to enter fourth grade at the age of ten and to be promoted at the end of the school year.

Jovita finished the equivalent of high school at the age of eighteen. After her graduation from high school, she enrolled in a "summer normal school" and acquired a teacher's certificate in two years. In Rio Grande City, with the assistance of her grandfather; her uncle Encarnación Salinas, county and district clerk; and Mr. Sam P. Vale, then county superintendent of schools, Jovita was granted a position at the city schools. Since she lived with her uncle and aunt, Jovita was able to save all her money, except for five dollars per month for incidentals, which contributed to her college fund.

In 1924, Jovita enrolled at the University of Texas but returned home to San Antonio after her first year, short of funds. For the next two years, she taught at Encinal as head teacher in a two-teacher school. Though she benefited from the experience, Jovita decided that she needed to pursue her college education and proceeded to enter summer school at Our Lady of the Lake University in San Antonio. The dean of Our Lady of the Lake, Mother Angelique, needing a teacher of Spanish in the high school department, offered Jovita a scholarship for the following year. As compensation for teaching two hours a day and a class of teachers on Saturday, Jovita received a private room, board, and tuition. Still, Jovita longed to return to the University of Texas, where she had studied advanced Spanish under Lilia Casis. In order to continue studying with Casis, Jovita began to tutor at Our Lady of the Lake.

The summer of 1925 proved to be life altering for Jovita, when she met J. Frank Dobie, renowned Texas folklorist and professor, with whom she formed a lasting professional and personal relationship. With his mentorship, Jovita fully realized the academic value of the legends and stories of the Texas borderlands. With his encouragement and support, she published several of her stories in *Folklore Publications* and *Southwest Review,* and from 1930 to 1932 she served as president of the Texas Folklore Society (the first female and Mexican American to hold the position), offering a distinctly Mexican perspective on the history of Texas.[3]

At the end of her sophomore year, Jovita was offered a position teaching Spanish half a day at St. Mary's Hall, an Episcopal school for girls in San Antonio. With this income, Jovita was able to assist her family and study in the afternoon. She continued to study at the University of Texas in the summers and enjoyed her friendship with the Dobies, Lilia Casis, and Dr. and Mrs. Carlos Castañeda. Jovita continued her studies at Our Lady of the Lake University during the long semesters and officially earned her BA there in 1927. She was then hired to teach full time at St. Mary's Hall in San Antonio. With the support of Ruth Coit, the headmistress of the school, and J. Frank Dobie, Jovita earned a Lapham Scholarship in 1929, which allowed her to continue her research in and on the borderlands and to advance toward earning her master's degree at the University of Texas. Jovita thrived during this time among the "border people" she loved and understood, feeding her hunger for knowledge of her homeland and sharing time with her friends and family in the counties of Webb, Zapata, and Starr in the Rio Grande Valley. To those in the valley who were not familiar with "the strange young lady, with long hair and a book full of notes," she was introduced as "maestro Jacobo's daughter, or . . . don Francisco Guerra's granddaughter from Las Víboras Ranch."[4] These introductions were all Jovita needed to be granted access to the border narratives that culminated in her master's thesis: *Social Life in Webb, Starr, and Zapata Counties.*

Collector and Interpreter of Folklore

Dr. Eugene Barker, the director of Jovita's MA thesis, was at first hesitant to approve it because of a perceived lack of historical references and "oddness." Jovita's friend, the scholar Dr. Carlos Castañeda, disagreed with Barker's assessment, commenting that "this thesis will be used in years to come as source material." González's thesis was indeed published posthumously as a "landmark Tejana thesis." In 1934, Jovita was nominated by the governing board of the Scientific Society of San Antonio for membership and was awarded a Rockefeller grant with the recommendation of J. Frank Dobie. Her research culminated in the production of two novels: *Dew on the Thorn* and *Caballero.* Jovita's future narratives, while conforming to Dobie's populist approach to South Texas folklore, eschewed the "imperialist nostalgia" of Dobie's narratives by embracing the "ideological contradictions of traditional culture . . . suggesting a complex social space inhabited by a host of frequently discordant voices and agendas." Furthermore, Jovita "allowed her subjects to speak, unlike the typical strategy of folklorists and anthropologists of the 1920s and 1930s, for themselves, without the overt mediating presence of the ethnographic narrator."[5] During her lifetime, some of her folkloric tales were published in literary collections and newspapers, but her historical novels and a comprehensive collection of her stories were not published until the late 1990s and early 2000s, more than a decade after her death.

The 1930s were a prolific and exciting time for Jovita. She published a series of stories titled *Catholic Heroines of Texas*, which was included in an exhibit at the Texas Centennial in Dallas; completed the novel *Dew on the Thorn*, which is believed to have been written primarily in the 1920s, even before Jovita's acquaintance with J. Frank Dobie; and co-wrote *Caballero* with her friend Margaret Eimer (whose pseudonym was Eve Raleigh). Though publishers resoundingly rejected the story line of *Caballero* (originally titled *All This Is Mine*) as being weak and uninteresting (even claiming that readers fell asleep while reading it), Jovita and Margaret developed a close friendship, later perpetuated through letters and postcards (Eimer relocated to Missouri) that revealed a lively humor and deep affection on the part of Margaret toward Jovita. The two commiserated about the obstacles to publishing their manuscript and other endeavors. The manuscript of *Caballero* was rediscovered and published in 1996, after both women were deceased. Now considered a significant contribution to Tejano literature, the novel depicts the ethnic, class, and sexual tensions that permeated nineteenth-century society and culture in South Texas, and that continue to do so today. With the posthumous publication of Jovita's significant works, it becomes increasingly clear that Jovita González was both among and away from her people, both an informant familiar with the realities of South Texas and a cultivated woman who set herself apart from the peon and the vaquero.[6]

Educational Reform

Jovita's personal relationship with Edmundo E. "E. E." Mireles, a fellow student at the University of Texas, continued throughout the early 1930s, though she struggled with the separation caused by their long-distance relationship. Leticia M. Garza-Falcón reports that "E.E. Mireles's mother was a sister of Venustiano Carranza, Mexican revolutionary leader and politician, while Jovita remained very loyal to the pre-Revolutionary dictator of Mexico, Porfirio Díaz." Indeed, ten-year-old E. E. had fought in the Mexican Revolution in 1915 with his father and later returned to Texas. While Jovita lived and worked in San Antonio and Austin, E. E. worked in the San Felipe Independent School District in Del Rio, Texas. Correspondence between the two reveals that E. E. worked arduously, teaching day and night school, while Jovita continued with her research and teaching, and both grew impatient for their marital union. Jovita and E. E. Mireles were married on July 31, 1935, in San Antonio at the mission of La Purísima Concepción by Bishop Mariano Garriga. After their nuptials, Jovita moved to Del Rio to reside with her husband. There, on the recommendation of Dr. Carlos Castañeda, she taught English, and E. E. Mireles was appointed principal of San Felipe High School. In Del Rio, the couple formed ties with "a group of Mexicanos responsible for the 1929 desegregation law suit (*Salvatierra v. Del Rio Independent School District*), the first suit to challenge the segregation of Mexicano school children in school facilities."[7]

Indeed, Jovita and her husband played "a significant role in shaping the public education of the community of San Felipe" until 1939, when they relocated to Corpus Christi, Texas.[8] In 1937, E. E. Mireles became a citizen of the United States, and in 1940 he was appointed the coordinator of the Spanish program in the elementary grades in the Corpus Christi Independent School District. His and Jovita's endeavors represent the first elementary school bilingual program in the United States. Operating against racial and social discrimination, the couple was instrumental in repealing legislation in Texas, dating back to World War I, which forbade the teaching of foreign languages in schools. At the time (1917), the law applied to German language instruction, not Spanish, but in the 1940s there was a relatively large Hispanic population in Texas, and E. E. Mireles and Jovita González believed in the necessity of teaching "proper" Spanish to students in the public schools. In 1941 the statute forbidding the teaching of a foreign language was repealed. Free textbooks were provided for Spanish language instruction at the primary school level. The couple collaborated on writing two sets of books on Spanish language instruction at the elementary level, which culminated in *Mi libro español*, a series of three books adopted by the state of Texas. The second series of six books, *El español elemental*, was used in Texas and throughout parts of the United States.

In 1943, E. E. Mireles initiated the formation of the Pan American Council, of which Jovita was a charter member, composed of Spanish- and English-speaking people addressing the needs of Hispanics in the city, particularly the economically underprivileged. Edmundo and Jovita were also pivotal in the formation of the Corpus Christi chapter of the League of United Latin American Citizens (LULAC). E. E. Mireles was well known by Texas politicians as a proponent of bilingual education and civil rights for Hispanics and African Americans, and Jovita supported him in his professional and political endeavors. Jovita began teaching Spanish and directing the Spanish program at Lamar Junior High School in Corpus Christi and then moved on to Corpus Christi High School in 1946, which was renamed Roy Miller in 1950. She was then appointed head of the language program at William Benson Ray High School in 1954. As an instructor, Jovita interwove Mexican and Spanish culture with grammar and vocabulary and by all accounts was a lively and engaging educator. A former student describes her as tough and demanding, with a good sense of humor, though she did not identify with Mexican American political causes. Jovita was deeply committed, however, to promoting and exposing Mexican American folklore to the Anglo-American public. One example of this exposure was through "*pastorelas*, pageants, and Christmastime *posadas* with local Mexican children as the pilgrims playing for the entertainment of a mostly Anglo audience."[9]

Though Jovita suffered from chronic depression, she was described by family, friends, and students as "charming," "gracious," "*justa*," "quick-witted," and "*cariñosa*." She maintained a busy domestic life, upholstering furniture, playing bridge and canasta, and sharing her knowledge of Mexican cuisine with her friends and family, often serving her favorite dish, arroz con pollo. She also enjoyed entertaining in her home and hosting bridal and baby showers.[10] Jovita frequently visited her sisters and brother in Querétaro, Mexico, at times spending the summer months there, while Edmundo followed his passion for chess, nurtured his friendships, and worked on professional and civic ventures. The couple remained childless and traveled frequently when not participating in their professional and civic activities. Jovita also continued to enhance her own education; in 1951, she enrolled in a six-week summer course on education and rural life at the Instituto Tecnológico y de Estudios Superiores de Monterrey, in Mexico. She continued teaching at Ray High School, sponsoring the "Conquistadores," the Ray High School language club for fourth-year Spanish students, and actively participating in the Pan American Student Forum, until her retirement in 1967. Jovita was involved in civic and social activities throughout the 1970s and was honored in 1981 in an exhibit at the Institute of Texan Cultures in San Antonio titled *Texas Women: A Celebration of History*. The exhibit featured 125 Texas women who had played pivotal roles in shaping Texas history.

Between 1978 and 1981, Jovita suffered the loss of several of her siblings, which by all accounts took a great toll on her both emotionally and physically. Already suffering from diabetes mellitus, chronic heart disease, and depression, Jovita was in declining health, and she died in 1983, officially of cardiac arrest. E. E. Mireles continued to live in the couple's house on Ohio Street with Isabel Cruz, the woman who had been their housekeeper and the manager of the Mireleses' personal affairs for decades, until his death in 1987. Isabel Cruz was instrumental in the preservation of the Mireleses' papers and their ultimate archiving in the special collections of Texas A&M University–Corpus Christi in 1992, as well as in archives and special collections at other major universities in Texas.

Literary Productions

The Mireles Papers remained relatively untouched until "Teresa Palomo Acosta and Cynthia Orozco resurrected her at the 1990 'Mexican Americans in Texas History' conference." In the years following the conference, scholars José Limón and María Eugenia Cotera recovered the manuscripts of *Dew on the Thorn* and *All That Is Mine*, gathered documents, and researched Jovita González's contributions to the folkloric literature of the borderlands. A critical analysis of the novel *Caballero* may be approached by considering three distinct historical perspectives: the period in which the action of the novel takes place (1846–1848); the era in which it was written by González and Raleigh (the 1930s); and the period in which the manuscript was rediscovered and published (1996). Some of the specific "changes González examines were caused by three related and powerful forces: the growing American influence in [the] area after the US-Mexican War, the 1904 arrival of the railroad, and the resulting shift in the region from ranching to farming."[11]

In *Dew on the Thorn*, written in the 1920s and '30s and published by Arte Público Press in 1997, González weaves her family's biography with folkloric representations of South Texas in the nineteenth century. Race, class, and female oppression are central to this narrative, though women's strength and sense of history give courage to confront the patriarchal figure. González relates stories of intermarriage in her narrative, hinting at the changing ethnic and cultural landscape of South Texas, which is more fully developed in *Caballero*. In this novel, as in her next, González criticizes the debt-peonage system while portraying South Texas as a sort of antebellum South.[12]

Though E. E. Mireles affirmed in an interview in the 1970s that the manuscript of *Caballero* had been destroyed, Jovita indicated otherwise to her interviewer, with the wag of a finger and a meaningful gaze. The manuscript was found among the Mireles-González papers and published in 1996 by Arte Público Press. The historical novel opens on the eve of 1846, more than a year after Texas's annexation to the United States and just before the onset of the US-Mexican War. The novel's action takes place primarily in Matamoros "in the border strip between the Río Grande and Nueces Rivers [in which] Mexicans remained the majority population until the twentieth century."[13] One year after the annexation of Texas to the United States, and decades after the Mexican government's recruitment of Anglos to populate Texas, cultural and political encounters between the Mexican (or Tejano) ranchero landowners and would-be US Anglo settlers became increasingly frequent. González and Raleigh accurately portray the historical and political transitions in South Texas in the mid-nineteenth century and the early twentieth century, as well as the ethnic and linguistic tensions that increased with Anglo immigration to Texas.

Ninety years mark the difference between the period in which González and Raleigh wrote *Caballero* and the time frame of the novel. Clearly, the perspective of the authors cannot be divorced from their literary creation. Historically, Texas had witnessed a Mexican uprising against Anglo domination, as well as the agricultural revolution. Racial and ethnic discrimination and notions of racial purity had increased dramatically, both locally and globally. Fixed notions of national and racial identities had led to the promulgation of fascist repression and enforced geopolitical borders. Mexicans in the United States were viewed as "degraded" products of racial mixture and therefore as racially unintelligible, a "bio-political" perception that was fueled by the National Origins Act of 1924. Ironically (or perhaps not), these images of Mexicans held by US Anglos are the very opinions expressed by *Caballero's* Mexican patriarch, Don Sebastián. Perhaps the novel's authors chose to represent in the character of Don Sebastián the very bigoted and racist attitudes exhibited in the United States at the time of the novel's production. As the characters defy and abandon Don Sebastián, through either death or voluntary departure, it becomes increasingly evident that González and Raleigh were socially conscious critics. In 2000, Arte Público Press published a collection of folk stories collected and written by Jovita González and edited by Sergio Reyna. Many of these stories had been published previously in *Southwest Review*. In his introduction, Reyna explains that Jovita, as a protégée of J. Frank Dobie, was a literary elaborator of folklore; that is, she enhanced and polished the South Texas stories she collected and remembered from childhood. Classified as a nativist, Jovita describes in her stories the storyteller within his or her natural setting as the central figure entertaining an audience, as a historian, and as a transmitter of cultural values.[14]

Legacy

Jovita González has proven to be a pivotal figure in the education of and about South Texans. In many ways, she embodies the contradictions and complexities inherent in the borderlands themselves. A descendant of Spanish aristocracy, of *gente decente*, landed, but facing economic, ethnic, and gender-based inequities under Anglo and Hispanic patriarchal domination, Jovita was both of her people and distanced from them. A Porfirista who believed in civil rights and racial equality as well as women's rights, Jovita also inhabited her prescribed role as housewife and subordinate to her husband, even though by many accounts she was perceived to be "a lot smarter than her husband." As well, Jovita faithfully upheld Catholic traditions and middle-class Mexican and Spanish cultural norms. Passionate, courageous, and confident in public, she was chronically depressed in private, expressing her desperation only to her family and close friends. Though she did not enjoy the magnitude of her scholarly success and acclaim in her lifetime, the decades following Jovita González's death have witnessed the fruition of her lifelong ambition and have shed light on the talent and vision she possessed. She was indeed a woman who defied prescribed gender and ethnic roles through her teachings and writings, who worked toward the preservation and transmission of her culture's mores and values even while questioning them, and who maneuvered within the principally Anglo-American academy. In effect, then, Jovita González was and is a political figure, though her "intellectual environment, her aspirations, and the climate of the times demanded that she leave her more blatant outcries against both the Anglo and the Mexican patriarchies and elitist/racist views . . . to future generations."[15] Thanks to the research and writings of scholars such as Cynthia Orozco, Teresa Palomo Acosta, José Limón, and María Eugenia Cotera, readers within Texas and beyond now may appreciate the literary, folkloric, and educational legacy left by Jovita González.

Notes

1. María Eugenia Cotera, *Native Speakers: Ella Deloria, Zora Neale Hurston, Jovita González and the Poetics of Culture* (Austin: University of Texas Press, 2008), 106–7.

2. E. E. Mireles-González Papers, Special Collections and Archives, Mary and Jeff Bell Library, Texas A&M University–Corpus Christi.

3. Cotera, *Native Speakers*, 119.

4. E. E. Mireles-González Papers.

5. E. E. Mireles-González Papers; Andrea R. Purdy, "Jovita González de Mireles (1904–1983)," in *American Women Writers, 1900–1945: A Bio-bibliographical Critical Sourcebook*, ed. Laurie Champion (Westport, CT: Greenwood Press, 2000), 142; Cotera, *Native Speakers*, 120, 124, 126.

6. Leticia M. Garza-Falcón, *Gente Decente: A Borderlands Response to the Rhetoric of Dominance* (Austin: University of Texas Press, 1998), 81.

7. Garza-Falcón, 77, 78.

8. Garza-Falcón, 78.

9. Garza-Falcón, 97, 98.

10. Garza-Falcón, 98.

11. Garza-Falcón, 74; Priscilla Solís Ybarra, "Borderlands as Bioregion: Jovita

González, Gloria Anzaldúa, and the Twentieth-Century Ecological Revolution in the Rio Grande Valley," *MELUS: Multi-Ethnic Literature of the United States* 34, no. 2 (Summer 2009): 177.

12. Garza-Falcón, *Gente Decente*, 106, 112.

13. Monika Kaup, "The Unsustainable Hacienda: The Rhetoric of Progress in Jovita Gonzalez and Eve Raleigh's *Caballero*," *MFS: Modern Fiction Studies* 51, no. 3 (Fall 2005): 564–65.

14. Pablo Ramírez, "Resignifying Preservation: A Borderlands Response to American Eugenics in Jovita Gonzalez and Eve Raleigh's *Caballero*," *Canadian Review of American Studies* 39, no. 1 (2009): 24–25, 26; Sergio Reyna, ed., *The Woman Who Lost Her Soul and Other Stories by Jovita González* (Houston: Arte Público Press, 2000), xv, xxii.

15. Garza-Falcón, *Gente Decente*, 89, 98, 132.

7

Mary Alice Berlanga Gonzáles

ADRIANA GARZA-FLORES

If education is the key to success, Mary Alice Berlanga Gonzáles has provided countless South Texas children with the essential building blocks of achievement for more than four decades. Even years after her retirement, Gonzáles warmly recalls the smiling faces of students in her first classroom at T. G. Allen Elementary School in Corpus Christi. Similarly, she remembers well her advocacy of teachers in the area school districts through support of local teacher unions. Her teaching assignments were often unenviable, teaching and leading in some of the area's most challenging schools in the heart of Corpus Christi barrios. Gonzáles met every challenge with a simple philosophy—all children deserved to attend good, quality schools, where facilities were safe and clean, teachers were thoughtful and encouraging, and principals' demands for order and discipline were matched only by their desire to change their students' lives.

Her proudest accomplishment remains the opportunity to serve as the founding principal of Corpus Christi's Rafael Galvan Elementary School in the 1990s. Her accomplishments in the classroom were not the only measure of Mary Alice Gonzáles's success. In addition to her career in education, she raised two children with her husband, Arnold Gonzáles Sr., a three-time state representative whom she supported throughout his career in politics and public service. Through her special combination of teaching effectiveness, care, nurturing, and encouragement of fellow teachers, Mary Alice Gonzáles exemplifies the generations of South Texas educators responsible for molding the future of the region.

Early Life

Mary Alice was born in Robstown, Texas, on September 14, 1940, to David Berlanga and Bertha Hinojosa Berlanga. Her family moved to Corpus Christi when she was three months old. David Berlanga was born in Robstown, Texas, while Bertha Hinojosa Berlanga was a native of Parás, Nuevo León, Mexico. Growing up, Gonzáles always felt connected to her parents' roots. As a child, Mary Alice Gonzáles acquired her mother's native Spanish tongue before learning English alongside her father. Her father was a hardworking provider from a migrant family that traveled to Michigan yearly to pick cherries. A steadfast proponent of education, David Berlanga Sr. became the first in his family to graduate from high school; he yearned to attend college at nearby Texas A&I University in Kingsville but lacked the one hundred dollars necessary for tuition, despite offers of campus jobs. He soon became a painter at the new Naval Air Station Corpus Christi. He raised his family on Coleman Street on the west side of Corpus Christi, a neighborhood in the traditionally Hispanic area of the city.

For David Berlanga Sr., the dreams of a college education that he was unable to fulfill would not be denied to his children. He always emphasized education as a top priority among his four children. He worked diligently to afford Catholic school education for his children while Bertha worked at raising the children and keeping the home. When it came time for Mary Alice to enter school, her father wanted his oldest child to have the best education possible. For the Berlanga family that meant Incarnate Word Academy, a premier Catholic school that first opened its doors in Corpus Christi in 1871.[1] It was there he believed his children would receive the best training to prepare them for a prosperous future.

When David Berlanga Sr. arrived to enroll his young daughter in kindergarten, he was initially turned away by the Sisters of the Incarnate

Word and Blessed Sacrament who operated the school; they told him there was no room in their school for Mary Alice. Determined that his daughter would have the best opportunity to learn, David Berlanga Sr. told the sisters he would "go to Sears and buy a desk" for his daughter if that meant she could attend. Gonzáles recalls the day vividly. "The sister, seeing his determination to have me attend IWA kindergarten, allowed me to come into the classroom and assigned me a seat at one of the tables," she said. Mary Alice was then asked several questions to test her readiness. "I knew all the answers, since my father had reviewed the very same questions with me many times," she recalled. By the middle of the year in kindergarten, Mary Alice was promoted to first grade. "I remember distinctly when my mother received the phone call from the sister telling her of my promotion. Excitement and pride reigned in our household."[2] Always a bright child, Mary Alice proved a fast, precocious learner. She practiced English with her father at home, and the extra work to sharpen her language skills paid off.

After three decades in education, Mary Alice Gonzáles credits the care, nurturing, and discipline she received from the nuns as inspiring her to become a teacher and shaping her educational philosophy. To Mary Alice Gonzáles, the sisters at IWA were models of both behavior and teaching. Structure, learning, and order were the cornerstones of her education at Incarnate Word Academy. The sisters expected all students to walk with pride, look others in the eye, be confident, and always display proper manners. From the Incarnate Word sisters she learned to be curious, studious, and dedicated, qualities she always hoped to inspire in her students.

At the urging of her parents and under the guidance of the Incarnate Word Academy faculty, Mary Alice continued to dedicate herself to her studies, becoming an all-A student. By the time she graduated as salutatorian of her senior class in 1958, she knew that teaching would be her calling. Her uncles on her mother's side of the family were teachers, and the profession was held in high esteem in both her family and the community. Mary Alice recalls her father encouraging her to pursue teaching since the profession attracted many women. "Being a teacher was a very important profession," Mary Alice Gonzáles said.[3]

Becoming a Teacher

After high school she earned an associate degree at Del Mar College in Corpus Christi in 1960 and then transferred to Texas A&I University in Kingsville. She borrowed the $300 needed to cover books and room and board and worked as a florist to be able to afford sheets for her twin-sized dorm room bed in Eckert Hall. Soon, the cost of living and attending Texas A&I forced Mary Alice to begin commuting to the campus, which was forty-five miles south of her home in Corpus Christi.

In 1961 she married Arnold Gonzáles Sr., an art and education major, also from Corpus Christi, whom she first met at a Favorites Dance at Incarnate Word Academy during her junior year of high school. She earned her bachelor's degree in elementary education in 1962, after doing her student teaching at Rose Shaw Elementary in the Corpus Christi Independent School District, where she would later spend most of her career in education. Her first school assignment as a classroom teacher came in 1962 when she joined the staff at Elizabeth Street Elementary School in Corpus Christi as a fifth grade teacher. There she worked with principal T. G. Allen, a strong leader for whom the school would ultimately be named. It was at T. G. Allen Elementary that Gonzáles crossed paths with the legendary E. E. Mireles, husband of Jovita González Mireles, who was in charge of the Head Start Program for the district. Head Start was a federal program launched after President Lyndon B. Johnson's State of the Union speech in 1964 and was first implemented in the summer of 1965. It provided preschool children of low-income families with a comprehensive program to meet their emotional, social, health, nutritional, and psychological needs. E. E. Mireles and his wife were among the founders of bilingual education in Texas. They wrote several books that were used throughout the nation.[4] E. E. Mireles observed and mentored Gonzáles during the summer of 1965 after she had just completed her first year of teaching fifth grade. He, too, had an impact on Gonzáles's development as an educator. She would later use the Mireleses' books in her classrooms and the schools she led.

During her first years she learned important lessons about classroom technique and management, helping her identify the type of educator she did and did not want to become. More than fifty years later, Mary Alice Gonzáles struggles with emotion when she recalls one student whose consistent misbehavior left her little choice other than sending him to the principal's office, where he received the punishment typical of the era, a paddling. For Mary Alice Gonzáles, it was one of the worst experiences of her early career. The image of the child marked by shame, pain, and disappointment was enough to prompt her to develop a style of classroom management that would lessen the probability of sending poorly behaved students to the principal's office, where they might meet a similar fate. From that point on, she employed empathy and compassion as important components of her teaching philosophy.

From 1962 to 1976, Mary Alice Gonzáles served as a classroom teacher in several Corpus Christi Independent School District (CCISD) schools including Woodlawn Elementary, Meadowbrook Elementary, Cullen Junior High School, and Oak Park Elementary. During this period Mary Alice and Arnold Gonzáles Sr. began a family: son Arnold Gonzáles Jr. and daughter Miriam Rose. During the 1970s, the family moved to Michigan while Arnold Gonzáles Sr. pursued graduate work. Mary Alice Gonzáles spent time working at Flint Community Schools, where she gained insight into the concept of community and education functioning symbiotically. "Schools don't belong to the teachers or the administrators, they belong to the communities," Mary Alice Gonzáles said.[5]

Flint Community Schools were open to parents who wanted to volunteer at the schools, and they were open to the community in the evenings for classes and tutoring. Mary Alice Gonzáles recognized the value in building a sense of community around a school. In Flint she also began to fully appreciate the integral role parents played in the success of their students and their schools. If parents were in the schools, as they were in Flint, students were more eager to come to school. She taught math in an open classroom setting, where students were free to learn and grow at their own pace.

These were lessons that helped shape her approach to school leadership when the Gonzáles family returned to Corpus Christi in the late 1970s and Arnold Sr. began his decades-long career in public service. Soon after returning from Michigan, Arnold Sr. successfully ran for the first of three bids for state representative, representing a portion of Corpus Christi. Mary Alice Gonzáles returned to her career in education. From 1976 to 1979 she served as facilitator and assistant principal at Fanning, T. G. Allen, and Menger Elementary Schools. Her approach to administrative leadership was rooted in her desire to help teachers and advocate for them rather than tell them how to do their jobs in the classroom. Teachers, she said, know what they are doing in their own classrooms. Soon, her advocacy for teachers led her to become involved in the Corpus Christi Classroom Teachers Association. Through her work with the union, she was able to help administration listen to the needs of teachers throughout the district.

Master Educator

While balancing marriage, motherhood, and career, she earned a master's degree in elementary curriculum and instruction from Corpus Christi State University in 1979. Five years later, Mary Alice tackled her most challenging role, as principal at David Crockett Elementary School. Located in the heart of some of Corpus Christi's most impoverished neighborhoods, Crockett Elementary was in disarray in 1984 when Mary Alice Gonzáles received the school key. It was designated a Title I school based on the Elementary and Secondary Education Act of 1965, which aimed to narrow the gap between schools in low-income areas and other schools. The first time she unlocked the doors to her new school, she saw kindergarten rooms that looked more like army barracks than classrooms, bathrooms stained by years of rust, single light bulbs hanging down from the ceiling, and cracks in the floors. She knew the challenge ahead and had heard the stories about the school. Teachers were not teaching. Students were running out of the school whenever they spotted an open door. "How can kids be excited about school when this is what they see?" she asked herself.[6]

Mary Alice Gonzáles immediately began upgrading the school, painting the kindergarten classrooms with bright colors, updating the bathrooms and light fixtures, and creating a Parents' Room for parents to visit and volunteer in the school. She also began a Partner in Education program with the city's Regional Transit Authority to provide transportation for parents to attend PTA meetings. Soon, an active PTA formed and began contributing to the school. Key to improving Crockett Elementary was motivating teachers to commit to developing challenging and appropriate instruction. Mary Alice Gonzáles sought to inspire her teachers and soon built a solid team of educators dedicated to effective teaching. Students had to come first. New reading programs ensured that every Crockett student owned books to create a library at home. She urged teachers to do their best, understanding that students would, in turn, do their best. Students began thriving in a positive environment that encouraged learning, creativity, and confidence. "We wanted kids to believe that they could be somebody," she said. "We had high expectations of them. We all would tell our students at Crockett to remember that they were somebody; that they were intelligent; that they were beautiful and that they could do work at our school."[7]

Soon, the school's performance on state and federal standardized tests improved. Mary Alice was successfully changing a culture that had nearly crippled Crockett Elementary, and she was replacing apathy with excitement and innovative learning. Crockett became a model school for the CCISD; when Texas first lady Linda White visited the district, administrators selected Crockett Elementary School for one of her stops. The professional highs in Mary Alice's career in the mid-1980s paralleled personal achievements, including her appointment to the Texas Governor's Commission for Women in 1985. In 1987, CCISD administrators selected her to attend the first Principal's Academy of the Texas Elementary Principals and Supervisors Association (TESPA). Three years later, she earned the Excellence in Education Award presented by Mexican American civil rights hero Dr. Hector P. García and the American GI Forum.

When the CCISD began searching for a principal for the district's newest school, Galvan Elementary, located on the city's expanding southwest side, her success at Crockett Elementary propelled her to the top of the list of candidates. In 1990, she was appointed principal of the new school. She visited with the architects who were building the school and assembled a dream team of teachers who were trailblazers in instruction. She implemented an interdisciplinary approach with a focus on social studies for teaching at Galvan. Mary Alice Gonzáles and her new staff attended training at Texas A&M University–Corpus Christi to learn about the interdisciplinary approach in order to make the new school a leader in innovative and effective teaching practices.

Each year, teachers and administrators developed a unit theme that would become the focus of learning in a variety of subjects. The units allowed students to discover the world beyond South Texas by hands-on learning. Students made presentations about the culture and history of countries around the world as part of the new learning style. Soon, her vision to make Galvan a pioneer in interdisciplinary learning garnered the attention of the community, and the school became recognized for the new teaching method. Mary Alice Gonzáles led the school with a constant focus on innovation and learning. In fact, Galvan became the first CCISD school to include special education students in regular classrooms and other school activities.

In 1993, Mary Alice Gonzáles received the Educator of the Year Award from the City Council of PTAs. By 1995, the school received a Recognized Award for excellence in academic performance from the Texas Education Agency. That same year, the school received an $87,000 Texas Education Agency grant that funded a Developmentally Appropriate Practices Program, which developed a new approach to teaching reading, writing, and spelling from prekindergarten through second grade. The approach was based on Montessori-style methods that encouraged the "natural development of children."[8] In 1996, Galvan again received Recognized status from the Texas Education Agency and was also given a "Three Star School" designation by *Texas Monthly* in a four-star rating system the magazine employed. That same year, Mary Alice was a nominee for the National Distinguished Principal Award. The next year she earned the Outstanding Achievement Award in Education by the Incarnate Word Academy Alumni.

Retirement

Mary Alice Gonzáles ended her career in education in 1998, when she retired as principal of her beloved Galvan Elementary School. After retirement, she continued her commitment to education as cofounder, owner, and chief executive officer of Promoters of Educational Concepts. The comprehensive language arts program Build-On Phonics helps children learn the foundations of literacy. Schools, both public and private, throughout Corpus Christi have implemented the model. Additionally, the program has been used by schools in Jackson and Mendenhall, Mississippi; Houston; Washington, DC; and Reynosa, Mexico. In an effort to continue inspiring and motivating the teachers of tomorrow, Mary Alice Gonzáles has served as field supervisor for the iteachTEXAS Alternative Certification Program since 2000. Through her role as field supervisor, she continues to mentor and observe first-year teaching in the classroom.

Molding the district's newest school into an example of excellence and teaching innovation along with transforming the struggling Crockett Elementary School were the crowning accomplishments of her more than thirty years in education. Her rise from classroom teacher to principal to curriculum developer serves as a testament to her love of teaching and commitment to improving the lives of students, while serving as a mentor and advocate for teachers. Balancing work with family was difficult, but she credits her son and daughter with being good children who were motivated to excel. Arnold Jr. graduated from Yale University and Michigan Law School, and Miriam graduated from Brown University and earned a doctorate degree in educational policy from Stanford University. Mary Alice Gonzáles served as a constant support for her husband, Arnold Sr., throughout his years of public service as a state representative, deputy land commissioner for the state of Texas, and Corpus Christi city council member.

Now a grandmother of four, Mary Alice Gonzáles takes pride in her career in education and continues to be active in the local community, serving as a member of the Board of Directors of the Corpus Christi chapter of the American Diabetes Association. More than fifteen years after she retired, students still stop Mary Alice Gonzáles at the grocery store and fondly share their favorite memories of their school years. The memories that touch her the most come from the students who thank her for making them feel special and for helping them believe in themselves. Those memories validate her career in education and her personal philosophies. She reflected, "I always asked myself and asked my teachers to ask themselves—am I providing the right environment for teaching? We always tried to make school inviting and interesting for the kids and the students still remember that."[9]

Notes

1. "History," Incarnate Word Academy, 2012. April 1, 2014, http://www.iwacc.org.

2. Mary Alice Gonzáles, interview with the author, December 13, 2013.

3. Gonzáles, interview.

4. "Head Start History," Office of Head Start, July 2015, accessed January 7, 2015, https://www.acf.hhs.gov/ohs/about/history-head-start; "Mireles, Edmundo Eduardo (1905–1987)," *Handbook of Texas Online*, Texas State Historical Association, June 15, 2010, accessed January 7, 2015, http://www.tshaonline.org/handbook/online/articles/fmi90.

5. Mary Alice Gonzáles, interview with the author, January 18, 2014.

6. "Parents / Prepare My Child for School: Improving Basic Programs Operated by Local Educational Agencies (Title I, Part A)," US Department of Education, September 2004, accessed June 5, 2014, https://www2.ed.gov/programs/titleiparta/index.html.

7. Mary Alice Gonzáles, interview with the author, March 27, 2014.

8. "Montessori," International Montessori Index, accessed June 18, 2014, https://www.montessori.edu/.

9. Mary Alice Gonzáles, personal interview, March 27, 2014.

8

Dr. Juliet V. García

MANUEL FLORES

When Juliet Villarreal was a fifth grade student in Brownsville, located in the Rio Grande Valley of Texas, she won a spelling bee at her elementary school. Neither she nor her teachers were surprised by her accomplishment. After all, she was a bright girl destined for better things, perhaps even college, something to which not many Mexican American girls could aspire in the 1960s. When she got home, she told her mother she had won the contest by spelling "Mediterranean" correctly. Her mother immediately saw it as more than just another award, one of many her bright young daughter would win during her lifetime. "You've been given a gift [from God]," she remembers her mother exclaiming excitedly. "You better figure out how you're going to use that gift to help others."[1]

Juliet would do that and more. Early on, she determined that her role in life would be to help others succeed by achieving a university education. With a steadfast commitment to education, Juliet became the nation's first Mexican American woman president of a college, earning countless honors along the way. She helped transform the lives of thousands of students in the Rio Grande Valley, historically one of the most disadvantaged areas of the nation.

After serving as president of Texas Southmost College and the University of Texas–Brownsville, she became the executive director of the new University of Texas Institute of the Americas. In March 2016, García was named senior adviser to the chancellor of the University of Texas System. Her career has been in higher education since 1972, but it all started after she won that spelling bee as a child.

Childhood

Juliet was born in Brownsville, Texas, on May 18, 1949, to Oscar García and Paulita Rico Villarreal. Her mother died of breast cancer in 1957 when she was nine. She knew from an early age the value of education and was taught that with drive and commitment, there were no limits to what she could accomplish. That attitude of strength, ambition, and courage was strongly rooted in family tradition.

In a documentary video about her titled *Against the Odds*, Juliet recalls how the concept of education was instilled by her *familia*. She recalls a tale of her grandfather fighting to ensure that his daughter Paulita, García's mother, and her brother would not go to an inferior school. "They had the Mexican school and the Anglo school," she says, recalling the family tale dating back to the 1930s. The story, she says, "gets better" with time. "He was determined that his children should go to the Anglo school 'cause they had better teachers, better equipment . . . you know. He left [home] with his shotgun and his babies and they were allowed into the school." Her mother went on to become salutatorian of her high school but should have been valedictorian, García said, referring to family lore again. "She graduated salutatorian from her high school graduating class. The number of Hispanic women graduating from Harlingen High School in those years [1940s] was I think two, my mother one of them. The story in the family is that she should have been valedictorian but there was no way a Mexicana was going to be valedictorian in Harlingen High School."[2]

The prejudice her mother and father experienced in their youth affected Juliet's view of her world, as well, she admits. "In Harlingen, the public pools were not open to the Mexicanos, except for one day a year," she recalled as she remembered more family anecdotes. "The next day they cleaned out the pool." From this environment and background she says she learned that one must fight for his or her rights. "But the lesson was not one of revenge," she says. "It was a lesson of *'mi hijita* [my darling daughter], you just have to be as smart or smarter than anybody else and eventually you'll get the jobs, you'll get what you need, but don't give in.'"[3]

From the lessons of her grandfather and her mother's experiences, she "learned you have to speak up; you have to be an advocate." When it came to standing up for his daughter, Juliet's father never hesitated. She recalls that when she was in the second grade at Los Ebanos Elementary School in Brownsville, "they had Mexican [American] children and Anglo children in another class. I was Mexican so I went in one class and Cynthia my friend went to the Anglo class, and I was okay with that."[4] One day, however, she came home crying. She had been told not to speak Spanish in class so she did not, but her friends in that class spoke mainly Spanish.

"I got called everything from '*Te crees muy gringa*' [You think you're very Anglo] to '*muy agrinda*' [very Anglicized]," she recalls. Juliet's parents had spent two years sending her to kindergarten and English-speaking classes for her to be ready for school. Her mother went to the school and insisted that Juliet be put with the other English-speaking students. The principal informed her that there was "no more room" in the English-speaking class. After Juliet's mother shared the story with her father, he dressed up and put on his Stetson hat to go visit Miss Sharp, the principal. He received the same answer. Oscar informed the principal he was going to place an "ad out in the [news]paper to inform the public" about his family's dilemma. As Oscar left the principal's office and was just about out the main door, the principal came out and told him to stop. "She said, 'Oh Mr. Villarreal, I think there's something we can do.' And I was put into the English-speaking second grade," Juliet recalled. From this, she said she learned that when your children's education is involved, you have to be an advocate for them.[5]

Higher Education

Her educational experience as a young girl in Brownsville helped shape her journey in higher education, which was marked with struggle but lots of determination, she says. After attending Texas Southmost College and Southwest Texas State University (now Texas State), Juliet married Oscar García in 1969. The couple moved to Houston to follow job opportunities. She received a bachelor of arts degree in English from the

University of Houston in 1970, and a master of arts degree in rhetoric and public address from the University of Houston (UH) in 1972.[6]

Juliet got her first taste of teaching at UH. She was appointed as a teaching assistant for speech while she worked on her master's. "I had a lot of students who did not want a 'García' teaching them how to speak," she recalls. "But it was okay once they met me, but it was obvious [at first] they were concerned." Her University of Houston experience convinced her she would be a college or university professor. While working on her undergraduate degree, she had done substitute-teaching duties in Houston between degrees, and it was not a pleasant experience. "*Me hicieron garras* [they tore me up]," she says almost painfully as she recalls the incident about her junior high substitute-teaching experience. "The kids locked me in a classroom one day. I mean I was yelling for the principal [to come save me]. I told my husband I have to go on to school [and get a higher degree] 'cause I cannot [teach] high school or junior high."[7]

With her master's degree in hand, she landed a job at Pan American University (PanAm) in Edinburg in 1972. She was the first Mexican American woman in the Speech Department at PanAm. More trouble in the classroom was looming. "In those days we had to give a speech test [to students]. PanAm had a requirement that if [a student] did not meet the speech test criteria you could not graduate. . . . In essence it was a Voice and Articulation class. It was speak like [*CBS News* anchor] Walter Cronkite. If you don't speak like Walter Cronkite, you're not going to graduate. Well, of course, it was aimed at the Mexicano." The test was based on the International Phonetic Alphabet. She would pass or fail students according to the results and never had problems. One day, an Anglo male student took the test, she recalls. The process worked until "I flunked a young Anglo boy, from probably Houston or somewhere [around there]. He flunked because he talked like this [using Texas twang]. And he flunked my little test and everything broke loose at PanAm." In a Speech Department meeting, Juliet had to explain her decision to flunk the student. In the end, the other professors and instructors agreed that the young man did not meet IPA standards and would have to take the special class to graduate, just like Mexicanos who had not met the standards of her test.[8]

From PanAm, Juliet moved to the Brownsville campus and taught for a year. Then she went to the University of Texas at Austin and earned a

PhD in communications and linguistics in 1976. Her experience at the University of Texas was life changing, she admits. "UT Austin for me was a tremendous experience," she said. "I came there to understand how powerful a university experience can be to a student and what [a] difference it could make in your life and in your family's life." Juliet loved studying and doing research in Austin. She found herself lost in a sea of libraries and ideas—a scholar's heaven. "I could study in libraries that were rich [in documents and sources]. There were 22 libraries [on campus] and my goal was to go to every one of the libraries while I was in Austin. I remember sitting in the library under the tower looking up at the ceiling, 'cause it was painted beautifully [with original artwork]. I remember thinking, 'Why can't we have this in Brownsville? What's so different about the people in Austin that they deserve this and we didn't?'"[9] The experience helped her create a vision of what higher education in the Rio Grande Valley should look like.

Return to Brownsville

In 1986, Juliet was named president of Texas Southmost College (TSC), the first Mexican American woman to become president of a college or university. In 1991 she and a group of community leaders spearheaded the establishment of a new university in Brownsville, the University of Texas at Brownsville (UTB). They then created a partnership between the new university and the existing community college, TSC.[10]

Juliet harked back to her years in Austin when she was tapped to lead UTB in 1992. She led the campus in creating a "university atmosphere" with stately buildings on the UTB campus, where she served as president until 2014. Along with the booming construction, the campus experienced a growth spurt in 2009. Not only was a new state-of-the-art recreational center—called "the REK" by students—built, but also a new library and classroom building. Students and visitors to the 43,000-square-foot library are greeted by a mosaic tile mural by renowned Mexican artist Sergio Higareda. Inside there is an atrium-style reference computer section complete with large arched windows, providing an ample view of the greenery surrounding the adjacent Lozano Banco Resaca. A picturesque art center and other structures were built and renovated. The concept behind the construction aimed to create an ambience of pride for the college and its students. The question Juliet pondered as a UT doctoral student—"Why can't we have this in Brownsville?"—was answered. They could, and it all happened under her visionary leadership. "Together we helped create a beautiful campus with a sense of place designed to honor the heritage of the people in our region," she said. "We built it, of course, to reflect our [Hispanic] roots."[11]

Juliet became not only a strong advocate for education but also an innovative leader in educational design. Her work is influenced by the cultural values of the Latina community and her own commitment to the South Texas community and the education of its youth. As the president of TSC and UTB, she aggressively advocated for access to higher education through innovation and experimentation. In her twenty-three-year tenure as president of UTB, the campus and surrounding TSC campus grew from 49 to 460 acres, more than 120 endowments for $21 million in scholarships over ten years were established, dozens of degrees and new classes were added, and enrollment grew from seven thousand to more than seventeen thousand. More importantly, the number of bachelor's degrees tripled, and the number of master's degrees quadrupled.[12] Under her leadership, research expenditures increased exponentially. The university was ranked in the top five public universities in Texas for research expenditures in aerospace technology and biomedical research. It became known for its Center for Gravitational Wave Astronomy, its chorale program, and its highly competitive chess team.

Student graduation rates increased dramatically because of Dr. García's efforts to establish a campus culture that initiates innovative ways to promote student success. Juliet takes the most pride in the degrees earned by the students. During her tenure at TSC and UTB, she has seen more than thirty-nine thousand degrees granted.[13] These accomplishments are a testament to her dedication, philosophy, and desire to bring quality higher education opportunities to the Rio Grande Valley.

Juliet's career is marked by her service and sense of community. She has served as chair of the Advisory Committee to Congress on Student Financial Assistance, chair of the American Council on Education, and member of the White House Initiative on Educational Excellence for Hispanic Americans. She was also a member of the San Antonio Board of the Federal Reserve and the Carnegie Foundation for the Advancement of Teaching and served on several boards including the Ford Foundation.

She was named one of the top ten university presidents in the nation by *Time* magazine, was recognized in the "World's 50 Greatest Leaders" list by CNN, and served on President Barack Obama's transition team. A champion of diversity and educational attainment, Juliet traveled to Rhodesia after apartheid and to the jungles of Chiapas in southern Mexico to spread her vision of education and to learn from others. Her work earned her a place in *Hispanic* magazine's list of the "100 Most Influential Hispanics."[14]

Along the way, her Rio Grande Valley institutes of higher education—Texas Southmost College and the University of Texas at Brownsville—as well as the University of Texas System chancellor would be sued by the Department of Homeland Security (DHS) in 2008 for refusing to allow surveyors access to the campus property during the construction of the 670-mile fence along the US-Mexico border. The fence would have cut through the campus of Texas Southmost College and the University of Texas at Brownsville. She opposed the wall because it would have (1) jeopardized campus security; (2) run counter to the mission of the colleges; and (3) impacted the historical value of the site.

"To support a plan that would build an 18-foot-high steel barrier between two friendly countries would be to directly contravene our mission and destroy the campus climate that has been so painstakingly and carefully created," she wrote in a memo to the University of Texas System regents in January 2008. The DHS and both universities were heading to federal court to resolve the matter. On August 1, 2008, the DHS and the two Rio Grande Valley colleges reached a compromise before the two parties entered federal court. García, her RGV colleges, and the UT System had won. The compromise stated that the DHS would not build additional fencing on the UTB campus. And, any fencing that had been started would not be eighteen feet high. She was, as they all said, the champion of higher education for the Rio GrandeValley.[15] But that victory represented more than simply keeping the campuses secure and protecting the beautiful landscape. It was a testament to Juliet's character and her ability to take on anyone, including the federal government, to ensure that the quality of higher education in the Rio Grande Valley was secure and of the highest caliber.

In September 2014, she was named the inaugural executive director of the University of Texas Institute of the Americas, which provides a nonpartisan venue for discussions of critical issues facing the Americas and the Global South. Operating throughout the University of Texas System, the institute convenes seminars, leadership programs, public events, and policy programs for consensus building and problem solving. As executive director of the institute, García reflects on her mother's charge of finding out what to do with her "gift" as something that inspired her to make a difference in the lives of others. She was awarded an honorary degree by Smith College, a private liberal arts college for women in Northampton, Massachusetts, and as a testament to her commitment to education, in May 2015 she delivered the keynote address at the college's commencement ceremony. The address was translated into Spanish and Mandarin Chinese during its presentation, a first for the college. She encouraged the graduates to use their opportunity: "We are the privileged few; we must not squander the opportunity that we have been given. We must use it to find our own strength and having found it, to become steadfast, powerful and incessant advocates for others."[16]

Her Legacy

She would accomplish all these things without ever losing focus on her primary passion, opening wide the doors to higher-education opportunities for students in the Rio Grande Valley, who are mainly Mexican American and Hispanic, and whom she insists are as smart as or smarter than any students in the nation or the world. "It was time for kids to get to run the race," she says about the emergence of universities in deep South Texas. "Our students can run the race with anybody else, but don't let them be barefoot while everyone else has Nikes. Give us the same pair of tennis shoes that everyone else has and we will do the same kind of running and even win the race." That is the type of attitude she had about the future of higher education in the Rio Grande Valley when Texas Southmost College and the University of Texas at Brownsville merged to form the new University of Texas–Rio Grande Valley, or UTRGV. The new university will borrow from the old and even have a medical school with campuses spread throughout the area. She feels the best is yet to come for higher education in the Rio Grande Valley. "You will see this campus grow faster than it ever has before," she says, "so hold on because the story is just beginning for us."[17]

Notes

1. Juliet V. García, "Smith College 2015 Commencement Speaker," YouTube, May 17, 2015, accessed June 16, 2015, https://www.youtube.com/watch?v=LBld pII0s1Y.

2. Manuel Medrano, "Los Del Valle—Dr. Juliet V. García, against the Odds," *Texas Humanities*, Texas Southmost College–University of Texas at Brownsville, 2013, accessed June 16, 2015, https://txarchives.org/utlac/finding_aids/00459. xml.

3. Medrano.

4. Medrano.

5. Medrano.

6. Medrano; "About Us/Quienes Somos," University of Texas, accessed June 18, 2015, http://utb.edu/vpaa/Pages/AboutUs.aspx (site discontinued).

7. Medrano.

8. Medrano.

9. Medrano.

10. "About Us/Quienes Somos."

11. "Campus Construction Taking Shape, Construction Update: REK Opens," *Orange & White*, Summer 2009, 1, 3; Medrano.

12. "About Us/Quienes Somos."

13. "About Us/Quienes Somos"; "2016 Hispanic Heritage Month: Honorees," Congressional Hispanic Caucus Institute, accessed December 2, 2021, https://web.archive.org/web/20160326091207/http://hhm.chci.org/awards-gala /honorees/.

14. "Dr. Juliet V. García," New American Alliance, accessed June 23, 2015, https://www.naaonline.org/dr_juliet_v_garcia; "Another First for a Latina," Being Latino, accessed June 20, 2015, http://www.beinglatino.us.

15. "Getting Sued over the DHS Border Fence," Security Infowatch.com, January 23, 2008, accessed December 3, 2021, https://www.securityinfowatch.com/government/news/10561877/getting-sued-over-the-dhs-border-fence.

16. "Commencement Address, 2015," Smith College, May 17, 2015, www .smith.edu/about-smith/smith-history/commencement-speakers/2015; Dave Eisenstadter, "Juliet Garcia, First Hispanic Woman to Lead U.S. College or University, Will Be Commencement Speaker at Smith," *Daily Hampshire Gazette*, last modified February 19, 2015, https://www.gazettenet.com/Archives/2015/02/SmithSpeaker-hg-021915.aspx.

17. Medrano; University of Texas at Brownsville, Wikipedia, accessed December 3, 2021, https://en.wikipedia.org/wiki/University_of_Texas_at_ Brownsville.

IV

The Politicians

9

Frances Tarlton "Sissy" Farenthold

SUSAN L. ROBERSON

Frances Tarlton "Sissy" Farenthold talks softly into her omnipresent cordless telephone, surveying a panoramic view stretching north from her artistically furnished downtown Houston apartment, answering repeated calls and plotting, as she has for most of her adult life, a campaign against a seemingly immovable monolith: the impervious Texas political machine. When she was interviewed for this chapter three years from her ninth decade, she had lost none of the energy she employed to become a liberal legend: South Texas legal aid lawyer and director, lone woman elected to the Texas legislature, first serious woman candidate for Texas governor, candidate for the Democratic vice presidential nomination who polled more votes than Jimmy Carter or Senator Edward "Ted" Kennedy, founding member and chair of the National Women's Political Caucus, president of Wells College, and an internationally recognized human rights campaigner who has been a rights observer from Iraq to the Soviet Union.[1]

But to describe her strictly according to her achievements would be unfair and inaccurate. So much written about her is two dimensional, ignoring a gentle, disarming toughness that is rarely, if ever, described. A seldom-used word best describes her personal approach to issues and opposition. She is gracious. In the best sense of the word, often misused as implied sexism, she seems to find the decency in the opposition amid her intolerance of the intolerant. She suffers fools neither lightly nor boorishly. She walks around nothing, yet she carries herself with dignity. She may deserve her reputation as a gadfly, someone who challenges the status quo, but if so, she is a gracious gadfly.

Background

To understand Farenthold's life and career, one must understand a political system that, by law, has no conscience. Texas state government grew out of a constitution designed to decentralize power and consign it to consensus. Written in 1876, it was a reaction to Reconstruction governance and an effort to return to the *patrón* system as adapted from Spanish, then Mexican, cultures by prewar Jacksonian whites. It is susceptible to favoring power over human rights and based almost exclusively on deals through a weakened executive branch, biennial sessions, gerrymandered districts, and abbreviated terms with salaries so low only the wealthy can afford to hold office. In sixty-three thousand words of amendments, its primary intent has changed little.[2] It is a system with power to do little other than protect itself. Term lengths, for example, were expanded once Texas politicians recognized the value of incumbency. Rather than personal wealth running the legislature (although it certainly has maintained a prominent place), campaign funding plays the dominant role in directing the triad of power:

> The comparatively powerless governor, who augments his position by heading the majority political party and through his many appointments to boards and commissions.
>
> The Lieutenant Governor, far more influential than the governor because the "Lite Gov" controls the Senate agenda.
>
> The Speaker of the House, elected by the lower house members, runs it with an iron clad authority of committee appointments, rules settings and agenda control.

Farenthold may have traded opportunities to be what most would consider successful for an uphill climb as an irritant and a conscience—a gadfly. She was born into a world where being a woman carried different expectations, but those expectations were commonplace compared to those of being a Tarlton. Her grandfather was Judge Benjamin D. Tarlton Sr., chief justice of the Texas Court of Civil Appeals, member of the

Texas legislature, and University of Texas at Austin (UT) School of Law professor. The UT Tarlton Law Library was named for him. Her father was among the most successful and prominent lawyers in South Texas. She could have moved quietly and easily with the flow of traditional Texas politics and culture. Instead, she railed against the monolith to become the voice of the powerless and the harpy of the powerful. And it was in Corpus Christi that her political twig was bent.

She began her education inauspiciously: "I was born in Corpus Christi, and went to parochial school, but couldn't get out of the first grade. I stayed in the first grade about three years. I remember the dunce's cap," she said, speculating that her inability to read and write for more than three years was a form of dyslexia, which she overcame with help from her mother and a small private school. Public school was a learning experience, she said, most of it negative. First there was the bus ride through the "poor white" neighborhoods north of Agnes Street, coupled with frequent visits to the family maid's home in the Sam Rankin area. She still recalls the impressions of poverty as she entered the pristine new Wynn Seale Middle School and learned her first lessons in politics. Second, she said, she was humiliated by a teacher. Onstage for a school office, she talked and joked with the group of boy candidates, only to be told she was not "acting like a lady. I was just crushed. I hadn't thought about that, but I remember that, oh, so well. A kid doesn't even know how to respond. I didn't have it in my own family. Later, I used to say when I was a teenager, that all girls had was, 'Thou shalt not!'" Finally, she ran for student office against the "football hero" with the idea that "if I could just get the girls together"; instead, she was "clobbered." She did not run for political office again until her campaign for the Texas legislature. She said that although her father was a great believer in public education, she simply was not learning much. She departed Corpus, first for the rigorous curriculum of Dallas's prestigious Hockaday private school for women, then to Vassar, graduating in three years and becoming one of three women admitted to the University of Texas School of Law, neutral ground for her, but trespass for her sex. She was one of three in a student body of eight hundred.[3] She saw all the male stereotypes of women, even though she was not directly affected by them.

Musing about those days, she explained, "It was a mixed deal. I was privileged and I recognized that. The privilege that I had was that my grandfather had taught there. Many of the senior professors had him as their law professor. My father was a contemporary of the senior professors. They had been to law school together. He was class of 1911. For one reason or another, I was not put in the embarrassing position that some women were. Now we didn't have our own restroom, so the staff let us use theirs. . . . I was outraged because [male students] were betting how long I would be there before I was engaged. The last thing I was interested in, having had my Eastern education, was getting married. That was not where I was, no more than belonging to a sorority. I said, 'No I don't want that.' I can't imagine going out and serenading. I had it much easier than a lot of women did," she said.[4]

Introduction to the Political Fray

Graduating in 1949, she returned to Corpus Christi and practiced law, first with her father, then with the Nueces County Legal Aid Program, becoming director in 1965. By then she had become interested in politics, first as a member of the Corpus Christi City Council's human relations commission, then during John F. Kennedy's presidential campaign. Three years later, she was elected from Nueces and Kleberg Counties to the Texas House of Representatives.[5]

She did not realize it was a declaration of war. "I used to say by the time I got to the legislature, my law school colleagues were in the greener pastures of lobbying. Twenty years before they were in the legislature, they were with the big companies. There was a lobbyist I had been in law school with. I knew him and that was it. He came to see me and was with Shell or Gulf or somebody. He and my son started talking, and he told my son, 'I don't enjoy doing this, but it's a job.' We don't know how our system works actually." She continued, "I don't know what I had in my head but by the time I got down to see the Texas Legislature I was appalled. I didn't have any background in seeing the way it operated. For example, 'This little old bill is not gonna do anything; just pass it for me.' It was that kind of thing. And God knows what was in it. It absolutely stunned me over and over again," she said.[6] Texas government has always been a complex mix of money, power, and alliances. The principals were either wealthy before ascending to their offices or had grown wealthy through them with a series of loans, "business opportunities" from favor seekers, or campaign contributors. Campaign laws today are powerlessly complex and were virtually nonexistent then. Texas is still run on power and favor, and then it was exclusively male.

"There's the thing of women being trivialized. This came from not my immediate family but relatives. One cousin said he'd support me if he thought I was really serious. Another cousin said my voice was too soft to get anywhere. One day I let into someone. I really lost my temper; it didn't happen often though," she said. "I was out campaigning in Corpus Christi, this was for the legislature, and I was on the west side, and flyers were there and I had been parked there about a half a block away from the park, and it was my runoff opponent that had his name on it, and it said 'send a man to do a man's job. Vote for Abel Chaplain.'" That kind of sexism would continue, as she reflected, "I say the same thing about the legislature, once it was known I was an elected official. Often they would say to me 'who do you work for? You can't be on the floor of the Senate.' And I would say, 'Yes I can.' That was a constant reminder. In the legislature, members could park around the Capitol. I would hear the whistle from the guard, saying, 'You can't park there, that's just for men.' That went on until the last day I was in office. . . . One thing that stands out was that our constitutional amendment committee was meeting, and the chairman from Central Texas decided to have it down at one of the private clubs at Stephen F. Austin. That's when there were only two hotels, the Driskill and Stephen F. I went to join them and they said, 'You can't come in, we don't have women at noon.' I told them I was expected here. I went in and talked to the chairman and they never made a move, so I left to the cafeteria and had a cup of cottage cheese, and I was furious. I was even angrier the next day because a year before I had got there, the same thing happened to Curtis Graves, who was an African American from Houston, a legislator. When it happened to him, his friends all stood up on personal privilege and criticized the policy. When this happened to me, not one person stood up for me. I should have gotten up, but I was waiting. The only acknowledgement I had of this outrage was the chairman, late that afternoon, brought me a box of candy the day it happened."[7]

"You put up with that kind of thing all the time," Farenthold said. "I could feel it because I knew it. Hispanics were a big part of my constituency, and I had been in legal aid in Nueces County so I would force myself to object to things, and I would say, 'You know you're representing people that can't get up here and can't take you to lunch' and when I would stand up, you could feel—it was just so prevalent—the hostility. It was so prevalent. I was out of place. For example, on Valentine's Day, they had the poet laureate of Texas and he read a poem to me. I wanted to be on the penitentiary committee, I didn't want a valentine. I'd hear stories about what happened to other women. There was one woman that was a widow. By and large they would come in to fill terms of the deceased husbands or deceased fathers. The names will remain out of it. I was told that the chair of the appropriations committee—he was powerful—sent her to his office for a crucial vote. I was told that. I developed a theory from my experience, and I think this is a Southern thing. There's a kind of surface politeness toward women on one level. If you accommodate, and smile, and agree, you could become what I call a pet. You stay in your place and things are very pleasant. This came to me with the valentine, and before the valentine. The speaker said to me, 'We had such difficulty in deciding what to get you for the speaker's breakfast.' Because all the males were given ties, and they got me a string tie. I mean, they spent time figuring that out, like the valentine."[8]

Texas Politics

To understand her foray into first Texas, then national prominence, it is necessary to understand the Sharpstown Stock-Fraud Scandal and its principals. Frank Sharp was a banker and insurance entrepreneur who literally built his own town, Sharpstown, now a suburb of Houston. Through his wealth he was a conspicuously influential figure in legislative regulatory politics. His weight was felt in both houses. Beginning in the early 1970s, Sharp came under scrutiny, first from the Federal Deposit Insurance Corporation (FDIC), then the Securities and Exchange Commission (SEC).[9]

He crafted a scheme, according to the SEC and both federal and state indictments, to lend about $600,000 from his Sharpstown State Bank to Governor Preston Smith, House Speaker Gus Mutscher, several Mutscher cronies, and other state officials, with which they would buy stock in Sharp's National Bankers Life Insurance Company. Sharp in effect "dried up" the stock by limiting the issuance, which artificially created huge profits from the sale, primarily to the Houston Diocese of the Catholic Church, to which Sharp had made regular and hefty contributions. In exchange, according to state and federal indictments, the officials shuffled through the legislature a bill that would have allowed private insurance companies to insure the deposits in state banks, which would have, Sharp thought, exempted him from FDIC regulations. Smith vetoed the bill, but not until after he and the other state officials had reaped profits from the sale. That action earned Smith the distinction of unindicted coconspirator. Mutscher was not so lucky. He and three others were convicted of accepting bribes, although his conviction was overturned on appeal and Mutscher was later elected county judge of his native Brenham. Much of the evidence was based on Sharp's testimony, for which he was granted immunity from prosecution by federal authorities. Lieutenant Governor Ben Barnes, personally anointed by President Lyndon B. Johnson as the next Texas governor and expected to springboard from there into even higher office, had been peripherally associated with Sharp but wasn't charged. All the officials in the case denied any wrongdoing.[10]

Simultaneously, the University of Texas at Austin periodically erupted in student protests of up to one hundred thousand or more participants, primarily over American involvement in the Vietnam War, but also significantly against the policies of UT Board of Regents chair Frank C. Erwin, a lawyer and Democratic Party apparatchik who was politically appointed by the Johnson-Barnes ruling faction. Erwin was accused of ruling with an iron fist, firing faculty based on their politics, hiring faculty and staff through cronyism, and letting contracts based on favors and favoritism.

Added to this mix were thirty liberal-to-moderate legislators, Farenthold chief among them, popularly known in the press as the "Dirty Thirty," who regularly used their positions to protest the legislative oligarchy. They found themselves regularly shut out of the investigations, frequently contrary to the leadership's own rules. Once the SEC investigation began, they became a perpetual voice to keep the issue alive in the legislature, demanding, unsuccessfully, that the leadership step down pending results of the investigation. Failing that, they asked, equally unsuccessfully, that the legislature initiate its own inquiry. The majority took its revenge, isolating the Thirty and in some cases, like

Farenthold's, gerrymandering their districts to eliminate them from the legislature.[11]

As Farenthold explained, "The first people that were onto it were the Republicans, and they dropped out. See, when I first was meeting over the issue, it was [James Bradshaw "Jim" Earthman III] leading the charge, and then after a couple a weeks, the young Republicans stayed in, but the older ones weren't into it any longer. I asked one of them . . . and he said our county chair said to drop it. Why they dropped it, I don't know. Then Gus got into trouble again after the speaker thing," she said. "I would always go to Gus Mutscher and tell him what I was doing. I guess it was when I took the resolution asking for an investigation, I wanted to know what had happened, actually. Anyway, I couldn't get it out of the Senate. I wanted a joint resolution that both houses said it was time to investigate this. I took it to [Senator Oscar] Mauzy, he just sat on it. Then I went to Mutscher, and Mutscher said, 'You can't get it out of the Senate. You can't even get Jordan because they all took their orders from Barnes.' Mutscher used the term with a sense of real antagonism; he referred to Barnes as Mr. Clean. I could never find any connection between Barnes and the Sharpstown bill."[12]

"I loved Smith's explanation of the borrowed money," she reflected. "He said 'Well, it all went for debts.' That's where it usually goes. You know, who knew about that? On the first bill, I voted for it. I didn't know what I was doing, I had no time. On the second bill, I had a little time, so I went over to Bill Patman and said tell me about this, and he said, 'It is a bad bill.' So that gave me my marching orders as far as I was concerned. It was so interesting because that's the summer I was working on the resolution against [Senator] Jerry Sadler [D–Hickory Grove, although he actually lived outside his district], and I always reported to Gus what I was doing, in my naïve way. And I asked, 'Where is the speaker,' and [his office staff] said, 'He's in Houston with the astronauts.'" Although he denied it, he was with Sharp, engaged in the stock transaction.[13]

Prompted by general electoral unrest over the scandal, she ran for governor twice, first in 1972, eliminating Barnes and Smith but falling well behind Uvalde banker Dolph Briscoe, who had been trounced by Smith in the 1968 Democratic primary. Briscoe was a quiet, unassuming man who had a virtually unlimited war chest, which he used to craft the appearance of a Texas political outsider. He was an acceptable compromise to both the old and new Texas power brokers. He again defeated Farenthold in the 1974 primary.[14]

Briscoe didn't play dirty, she said. He had that done for him. "I later learned that Briscoe, with the resources he had, kept his staff intact from 68–72," she said. "I didn't know where it came from, and years later I learned it came out of the headquarters of that campaign. The last day, they put a heartbeat on Spanish radio in San Antonio, and they said I'm a baby killer. I didn't know about it, and Dr. Hector García was just furious and he called and told me and he could never find out. And then I learned . . . it came out of [candidate Briscoe's] headquarters."[15]

Briscoe was often accused of being overinfluenced by his wife, Janey. Still, Farenthold said the races left her without animosity. "I used to say that there were two women wanting to be governor, but only one was running. I have no animosity towards Briscoe whatsoever, but I've heard that it was his wife that really wanted him to run. I think she was right there on the desk with him. . . . My target really wasn't Briscoe, but . . . I thought we had a chance at reform to make our state government more compatible with serving the people, and it's gone further away," she said. While she was not destined to be the first real woman governor (Miriam A. Ferguson served in the office as a surrogate for her impeached husband, James "Big Jim" Ferguson), "Sissy" opened the mansion door for Governor Ann Richards. "She wrote me that [I made it possible for her to be governor]."[16]

Leaving Politics

Leaving politics, but not political causes, Frances Farenthold worked with a variety of human rights groups. In 1976, she was named president of Wells College in Aurora, New York, a position that would add to a growing thesis that was to become what many consider her most significant writing, her speech titled "Women's Search for Peace," presented to the Federation of Houston Professional Women in 1988. In it she assailed "patriarchal structures," which, even when women receive equal pay and position, continue to maneuver them institutionally into a "male ethos" so endemic to our society's "language, logic, power, and relationships" that real change is bound to fail.[17] She explained, "What I did find—which really startled me—I was the first woman president of that college. A women's college that started in 1873. I was the first woman president. It was very difficult for some people to accept that, starting with the senior students. The younger ones didn't seem to have a problem. Some of them didn't know who the former president was, who was a male. They had trouble with my coming in. I also learned something that I think you can generalize . . . : There's an element of bureaucracy that's going to be there long after you go. There can be an attitude on some, 'Well we'll just slide through this; we don't have to make these changes.'"[18]

Reflecting on her experience at the college, Farenthold said, "One of the biggest problems I had was that I had young women that wanted to work on the grounds over the summer. I just had great difficulty in getting the person in charge of that department to accept that. That was one of the most difficult things I did. This was this example of the grounds. Then it dawned on me that these people can say, 'Yes, President Farenthold,' and go on their way and keep doing what they're doing, because they'll be there long after you go. If that goes on in a place as small as I was in, imagine what goes on in a massive [institution]." She continued, "What I found was, even though it was a women's college, there was a patriarchal deal. The college had a male president, but he would only come during graduation. The day-to-day work was handled by a woman superintendent. Then I found women not being paid the equivalent salary. What they had for a woman's center was just a little alcove by the restroom. Then of course there's a problem because the things that had been traditional there just didn't interest me. Like the president had always belonged to the Auburn Country Club. Well, I wasn't interested in the country club. The president always had a Buick. I had a Peugeot. Those little things were such a big change. I had a woman come to me . . . and she said, 'President Farenthold, it's so wonderful to see a woman's picture on the front page of the Aurora newspaper. That's never happened.'"[19]

Legacy

Now retired, or as retired as a person of conscience can be, she reflects on a world she tried to change, one that seems to be impervious to change. Or perhaps it is we, she said, so comfortable in our isolation, who fear to change. Still, she has maintained that aforementioned graciousness throughout most of her life. In answer to the traditional question "What would you do differently?" she concluded with a mild scolding. "I'm not going to second guess it. I'm not going to get into that can of worms. It is a silly question, but I don't want to dwell on it, because you do what you do at the time you do it. It would take a complete revision, and I might make a bigger mess of it than what I have. I don't really know. Maybe that's the unexamined life they're always scolding you about. This is another thing, and I just said it when I was at that college for four years. I told students 'quit planning in your life.' There's no planning in my life, but it was a different time. A very different time. I think now young women . . . know that they need to be responsible for themselves."[20]

Notes

Based on an interview conducted by Don Fisher in 2013.

1. Gina Bastone, "Frances Tarlton 'Sissy' Farenthold: A Noble Citizen," Bernard and Audre Rapoport Center for Human Rights and Justice, accessed October 6, 2013, http://www.utexas.edu/law/centers/humanrights/farenthold/aboutsissy.php.

2. Joe E. Ericson and Ernest Wallace, "Constitution of 1876," *Handbook of Texas Online*, Texas State Historical Association, accessed March 14, 2014, http://www.tshaonline.org/handbook/online/articles/mhc07.

3. Francis Tarleton "Sissy" Farenthold, interview by Don Fisher, July 19, 2013.

4. Farenthold, interview.

5. Frances Tarlton Farenthold Papers, 1913–2011, Dolph Briscoe Center for American History, University of Texas at Austin, accessed October 7, 2013, http://www.lib.utexas.edu/taro/utcah/00291/cah-00291.html.

6. Farenthold, interview.

7. Farenthold, interview.

8. Farenthold, interview.

9. Sam Kinch Jr., "Sharpstown Stock-Fraud Scandal," *Handbook of Texas Online*, Texas State Historical Association, accessed October 7, 2013, http://www.tshaonline.org/handbook/online/articles/mqs01.

10. Kinch.

11. John G. Johnson, "Dirty Thirty," *Handbook of Texas Online*, Texas State Historical Association, accessed October 7, 2013, http://www.tshaonline.org/handbook/online/articles/wmdsh.

12. Farenthold, interview.

13. Farenthold, interview.

14. Frances Tarlton Farenthold Papers.

15. Farenthold, interview.

16. Farenthold, interview.

17. Bastone, "Frances Tarlton 'Sissy' Farenthold."

18. Farenthold, interview.

19. Farenthold, interview.

20. Farenthold, interview.

10

Anne Legendre Armstrong

MARY LEE GRANT AND NIRMAL GOSWAMI

Introduction

Anne Legendre Armstrong was one of the most influential women in shaping the Republican Party in Texas. She was the first female ambassador to Great Britain and the first woman, of either party, to speak on the floor of a national party convention.[1] She wielded much of her influence not in the corridors of Washington, DC, or the Court of St. James's, but on her fifty-thousand-acre ranch in the brush country of South Texas. Here she entertained the prominent politicians of her day and Prince Charles of Britain, for whom she organized polo matches. The Armstrong Ranch was, for four decades, a gathering place where Republican leaders discussed election strategy over the kitchen table or while quail hunting.

The Early Years

Born in New Orleans to a French Creole family, Anne Legendre was the daughter of a wealthy coffee importer, Armant Legendre, and his wife, Olive. She attended the prestigious Foxcroft School in Middleburg, Virginia, where she was the valedictorian and president of the student body. She graduated Phi Beta Kappa from Vassar College in 1949 and first became politically active working for Harry S. Truman in his 1948 presidential campaign, describing herself as a liberal Democrat.[2] In 1950, after a brief stint as assistant editor at *Harper's Bazaar*, she married South Texas cattle rancher Tobin Armstrong. The 6'4" Armstrong, with his stable of polo ponies and custom-designed hunting cars, owned the South Texas ranch that his ancestor John Armstrong had obtained with bounty money from the capture of outlaw John Wesley Hardin. Tobin remembered his first encounter with his bride to be, when she came to visit her classmate Helen Kleberg on the 850,000-acre King Ranch, which adjoined Armstrong's property: "They were by the pool, and she looked so beautiful in her bathing suit. I was immediately smitten."[3] It would be the beginning of a fifty-five-year marriage of unusual love and devotion. Mary Lee Grant, who often interviewed the two as a reporter for the *Corpus Christi Caller-Times*, remembers being with them at a restaurant soon after Tobin was diagnosed with his final illness. He dropped his napkin, but Anne quickly—and so tenderly—reached to pick it up and hand it to him. For his part, he was not threatened by his wife's brilliance and success but instead admired her greatly.

The Armstrong Ranch

Though from a French Creole New Orleans family, Anne Armstrong took to her new South Texas ranch world with gusto, throwing hunting and fishing parties, riding horses, and establishing a reputation as one of the most accomplished hostesses in the state. Close ties between the Armstrong Ranch and the King Ranch were cemented when Tobin's older brother, John Armstrong, married the King Ranch's Henrietta Kleberg, and when his uncle Tom married her mother, Henrietta Kleberg Larkin, widow of John Larkin. So close were the ties that John Armstrong was the last King family member to serve as president of the King Ranch. Like the King Ranch, the Armstrong Ranch supported a colony of cowboys who lived in a community surrounding the Big House, working the 2,500 head of Santa Gertrudis cattle while riding thoroughbred horses, the Armstrong version of cow ponies. "I never rode a bought horse," Tobin Armstrong said. "I raised and trained my own thoroughbreds."[4] And like the King Ranch, the Armstrong spread had been forged out of the rough-and-tumble days of the nineteenth century but soon added the sophistication to be had from a first-class education. John Armstrong III, a Texas Ranger from Tennessee famous for the capture of outlaw gunslinger John Wesley Hardin, bought the ranch in 1852 and settled it in 1882. His sons combined the sophistication of an East Coast education with the independent spirit of a ranch upbringing. Charlie Armstrong, Tobin Armstrong's father, graduated from Yale University in 1908 and returned to South Texas to take over management of the ranch. Charlie's brother, Tom Armstrong, graduated from Princeton and Harvard Law School, then went to work as an executive for Standard Oil Company. Tobin Armstrong was tutored at home until he was nine, attending boarding school in San Antonio before attending the University of Texas and Texas A&M University.

Anne became an outstanding horsewoman, learning to ride western style. She truly became a Texas rancher and was as likely to talk about the weather or cattle as international politics. During one visit she told Grant: "Look how green the grass is. We haven't had it this way for years. It will be good for the cattle." She was also attuned to the political and social issues of South Texas. As Grant recalls, she interviewed Anne Armstrong and her husband many times while reporting for the *Corpus Christi Caller-Times*: "They would call me two or three times a week from their car, on the way to their office at the Kleberg Bank in Kingsville. Usually Tobin would make the call, complimenting an article I had written in that morning's paper, then taking apart points and criticizing and making suggestions. Sometimes he would hand the phone over to Anne and she would put in her two cents worth." Of the stories Grant wrote, they were particularly interested in the ones about immigration, an issue that was important to them as well as many other residents of South Texas.[5]

She also became a good shot, accompanying Tobin and guests on hunting expeditions. It was on the Armstrong Ranch that Vice President Dick Cheney accidentally shot Texas lawyer Harry Whittington in the face and upper body during a quail hunt in 2006. Whittington was not seriously injured. But the accident brought national attention to the important role the Armstrong Ranch played in political circles. "When you say, 'I've been hunting with the Armstrongs,' or 'I've been down on the Armstrong Ranch,' that implies a certain level of status and insiderness," Harvey Kronberg, editor of the *Quorum Report*, told the *New*

York Times. "The ranch itself is kind of a rite of passage for Texas Republicans. You go pay homage."[6] Guests have included the Rockefellers, Bushes, Cheneys, Karl Rove, James Baker III, Texas governor Rick Perry, and Senator Kay Bailey Hutchison. In an article about the importance of the Armstrong Ranch among Republican Party insiders, "Where the Politicians Roam," the *New York Times* said that the Armstrong Ranch rivaled "Hyannisport, Kennebunkport and the Hamptons as a setting where important relationships have been nurtured."[7]

Political Ideology and Activism

A supporter of the Equal Rights Amendment, Armstrong was the first woman to serve in a cabinet-level position, under both Richard Nixon and Gerald Ford. When the Watergate scandal broke, Armstrong stood firmly beside Nixon, leading one observer to say she sounded like "the cruise director on the Titanic." However, when the Watergate tapes were made public, directly implicating Nixon, she called for the president's resignation. She served as the first American woman ambassador to Great Britain under Gerald Ford and was the first woman to chair the President's Foreign Intelligence Advisory Board, under Ronald Reagan. She also acted as a mentor to longtime Texas Republican senator Kay Bailey Hutchison, who began her political career as Armstrong's press secretary.[8]

Soon after marrying Tobin, Anne Armstrong took on her husband's strongly conservative political affiliations, commenting that she was "ideologically not at home in the Democratic Party." She switched parties during the 1952 presidential campaign, volunteering as a precinct worker. While her five children were young, she worked in local politics and then became a member of the state Republican Executive Committee in 1961. In 1964, she supported the campaign of Senator Barry Goldwater and two years later became vice chair of the Texas Republican Party, serving from 1966 to 1968. In 1968, she became a Republican National Committee member from Texas. In 1971, President Richard Nixon suggested that she and Delaware committee member Thomas B. Evans join Senator Robert Dole of Kansas as cochairs of the Republican National Committee. She was the first woman to be cochair rather than assistant chair, a move meant to placate Texas Republicans who were disgruntled with Nixon's nomination of former Texas governor John B. Connally as secretary of the treasury. Connally was a Democrat at the time, even though he later ran for president as a Republican.[9]

Armstrong was one of three keynote speakers to deliver the address at the 1972 Republican National Convention, the first woman in either party to do so. In her speech, she attacked Democratic candidate Senator George McGovern, saying that "a small group of radicals and extremists has assumed control of the national Democratic Party." She also targeted the Democrats who were angry at the liberal antiwar policies of McGovern, saying they could find a place in the Republican Party. "The sudden storm of McGovern has devastated the house of Jackson, of Wilson, Roosevelt and Kennedy, and millions of Democrats stand homeless in its wake," she announced.[10]

As Nixon's second term began, Armstrong and members of Republican women's groups complained that the president had not honored promises to appoint more women. In 1972, she was named counselor to the president, the first woman to hold the post. "Republican men know there's been a change in Republican women," she told the *Los Angeles Times* in 1972. "Confidence breeds confidence."[11] Armstrong, who spoke Spanish to the ranch's cowboys and staff, became Nixon's link to Spanish-speaking Americans. The colonial city and art colony of San Miguel de Allende, Mexico, was like a second home to the Armstrongs, who also frequently hunted in Mexico. Her home at the ranch was also a bilingual one, as illustrated by a visit Mary Lee Grant made to the ranch while Anne was in Washington, DC. When the housekeeper brought Tobin and Grant a simple lunch of sandwiches, which they ate in the kitchen, "he switched between speaking Spanish to her, brusquely and formally, and in English to me."[12]

Watergate, Presidential Politics, Diplomacy

As the Watergate scandal developed in 1973, Armstrong disagreed with other White House aides by saying publicly that, like Senator Barry Goldwater, she felt that the scandal was hurting the GOP. But she maintained that President Nixon was taking steps "to see that we get to the bottom of this." When the tapes implicating Nixon in the scandal became public, however, she called for his resignation. After his resignation, she remained in Washington as a counselor to Gerald Ford, who placed her on the Council on Wage and Price Stability. This council was charged with investigating the causes of inflation. At her swearing-in, President Ford remarked that his wife was "always needling me" to appoint women to high-level posts. Armstrong responded: "I have the feeling Abigail Adams would have been just as excited as Betty Ford and I are" about her appointment.[13]

Then, as a result of Armstrong serving as one of the lead planners of the elaborate US bicentennial celebration in 1976, the *Washington Post* argued that she should be the GOP's presidential candidate in 1980. Journalist Clayton Fritchey said, "She is frequently spoken of as a possible vice president. But why not president?" He remarked that in addition to her broad experience in the political world, her winning personality would make her a good candidate: "To top it off, she has looks and charm, plus that great political asset, the gift of gab."[14] Though poised and dignified, Armstrong was able to talk to anyone, regardless of background or social station, and make them feel comfortable.

She was not chosen as Ford's running mate, but she continued to serve as a close counselor to the president. Then President Ford appointed her US ambassador to London in 1976. She served only a year, but during that time she made quite an impression on the British. She was the first woman to be assigned to a major American embassy since Clare Boothe Luce served the United States in Italy in the 1950s. The *New York Times* said that the British had "taken an instant liking to her because she is visible and direct and informal without turning informality into a cloying down-home soupiness." They were impressed with her expert horsemanship and shooting ability (she particularly loved hunting wild turkey) and called her "the most romantic diplomat that America has ever had" because of these attributes.[15]

As well, she had style, with her black hair, trim graceful figure, and magnificent wardrobe. Bringing her American style with her, she employed designers to help her present herself and her home to the British. She commissioned the noted American designer Halston (Roy Halston Frowick) to create dozens of outfits. When she was presented to Queen Elizabeth II, she wore a full-length white silk dress and white cloak by Halston that set off her dark hair and impressed the court. The hats she commissioned from Halston she dubbed the "ambassadorial version of the Texas broad-brimmed Stetson." To decorate the ambassador's home, Winfield House in Regent's Park, she brought designer Betty Sherrill with her. Walter Annenberg, a great art collector, had served in the ambassador's post previously, so Armstrong induced a contingent of wealthy Texas friends to establish a committee called "Art for Anne." They loaned her paintings so that her ambassador's residence would be up to snuff.[16]

She also demonstrated her daring when she made a trip to Northern Ireland during a heavy terrorist bombing siege after only a month into her tenure as ambassador. There she announced an Anglo-American initiative against gun running by the IRA. The first US ambassador to visit Northern Ireland, she was seen "jumping out of her bullet-proof Cadillac . . . to talk with citizens on embattled ground."[17]

She and Tobin became close friends with the Prince of Wales, who visited the Armstrong Ranch several times to play polo. Tobin Armstrong liked to show guests a photo he took at Charles and Diana's wedding, showing a distressed, devastated-looking Camilla Parker Bowles watching the ceremony, unseen. In 1977, Democrat Jimmy Carter became president and Armstrong was replaced as ambassador by Kingman Brewster, the president of Yale University. Anne Armstrong left Britain maintaining that her time there had been "the greatest year of my life."[18] Although she was offered the job of Republican Party chair, she opted to spend more time at the ranch with her family.

Later Years

Armstrong served as chair of Ronald Reagan's presidential campaign in 1980 and throughout the 1980s acted as head of the President's Foreign Intelligence Advisory Board. Later, she would serve as an intelligence adviser to George H. W. Bush. But in 1987, President Reagan awarded her the Presidential Medal of Freedom. "Her skill and unstinting effort in the service of her country have earned her the gratitude of our nation," Reagan said. "She set a high standard for all who recognized that government service is vitally important to our way of life."[19] As well as her political service, she also sat on the board of directors of many corporations, including Halliburton, General Motors, American Express, Union Carbide, Glaxo Wellcome, and First City Bank of Texas, cementing the Armstrongs' position among the corporate elite of the nation.

Anne Armstrong's many roles in the country's political realm, especially in the upper circles of the Republican Party, demonstrate that she was able to successfully navigate her way through political circumstances without getting mired in the typical liberal-conservative ideological confrontations of her time. While in some cases she did not serve in a high-profile position long enough to make a lasting impact, such as in her role as the US ambassador to Britain, she always seemed to have the political sense and dexterity that allowed her to work well with multiple constituencies with diverse political bases. Anne Armstrong was from South Texas, a region that is culturally, demographically, linguistically, and economically varied. It is also a region marked by a history of poverty and a legacy of discrimination toward Hispanics. Anne Armstrong was a witness to and influenced by these. That must have been why she was able to work with people from many backgrounds and with much empathy toward those who had less than she did.

Notes

1. Joe Holley, "Leading Texas Republican Anne Armstrong," *Washington Post*, July 31, 2008, https://www.washingtonpost.com/wp-dyn/content/article/2008/07/30/AR2008073002605.html.

2. William Grimes, "Anne Armstrong, Presidential Adviser and Pioneering Politician, Dies at 80," *New York Times*, July 31, 2008, https://www.nytimes.com/2008/07/31/washington/31armstrong.html.

3. Anne and Tobin Armstrong, interview by Mary Lee Grant, 1999.

4. Armstrong, interview.

5. Armstrong, interview.

6. Anne Kornblut, "Cheney Shoots Fellow Hunter in Mishap on Texas Ranch," *New York Times*, February 13, 2006, https://www.nytimes.com/2006/02/13/politics/cheney-shoots-fellow-hunter-in-mishap-on-a-texas-ranch.html.

7. Kornblut.

8. Kornblut.

9. Holley, "Leading Texas Republican"; Kornblut, "Cheney Shoots."

10. Grimes, "Anne Armstrong"; Holley, "Leading Texas Republican."

11. Grimes, "Anne Armstrong."

12. Armstrong, interview.

13. Holley, "Leading Texas Republican."

14. Holley.

15. "Anne Armstrong," *Telegraph*, July 31, 2008. http://www.telegraph.co.uk/news/obituaries/2481470/Anne-Armstrong.html.

16. "Anne Armstrong"; Holley, "Leading Texas Republican."

17. Holley, "Leading Texas Republican."

18. Armstrong, interview; "Anne Armstrong."

19. "Anne Armstrong."

11

Irma Lerma Rangel

MANUEL FLORES

There is a defining moment in the life and legacy of former Texas state representative Irma Lerma Rangel, and she was not even alive to enjoy it. On a sunlit but cold and blustery February 16 morning in 2007 on the back plaza of the Texas A&M University Health System College of Pharmacy named in her honor, a statue of her likeness was unveiled before a crowd of more than two hundred people. There, facing the Texas A&M University–Kingsville Student Recreation Center and in the shadows of fabled Javelina Stadium where the university's football team had won seven national championships, she came to rest.[1]

The location was appropriate, for she too was a champion for the people of Kingsville, Texas A&M University–Kingsville, South Texas, and the state. The moment was bittersweet, however. She would be honored with a statue in front of a building at her alma mater, but in a strange twist of fate and politics the building did not actually belong to Texas A&I University, now Texas A&M University–Kingsville. It was "the [Texas A&M University] System's" building. Rangel would not have liked that.[2]

That the pharmacy school and her statue had come to rest in Kingsville and on the campus of her university was not lost for those present on that February Friday. Rangel had passed away on March 18, 2003, after a valiant fight with cancer. Her once stoic and fiery stance on the floor of the Texas legislature for more than a quarter century while she fought and lobbied for an array of legislation that would impact the people of South Texas and state for years to come, however, was never lost. Now, her statue was there for all to see, a striking pose on top of a solid granite pedestal looking beyond the northern horizon—toward Austin—with her right hand outstretched, perched as if to start a lecture on the reasons she was backing yet another piece of social legislation.

After the customary dedication speeches and commemorative words, her sister, Minnie Rangel-Henderson, stepped up to the statue and slowly reached out her shaking white-gloved left hand, touching the left hand of her sister's statue, which was clutching the ledgers of law she seemed about to speak on that day. "It's a beautiful statue," she said in soft voice. "It looks like her, like she was."[3] But much taller. Rangel was 5'4" and the statue was more than 6' tall. Then, with a wry smile and a tear streaming down her left cheek, she turned to the reporter and said, "She is bigger in the statue than she was in real life."[4]

Early Life

"I am very proud of Irma," Minnie said that day. "I remember my parents when they told [us] 'go further in your education because it is the only thing you take with you when you die.'"[5] It is not surprising that the Rangel sisters grew up with a fervor for education. During the depression era of the 1930s, the family worked hard to survive not only economic pressure but also discrimination. The family survived in spite of many obstacles and, in the 1950s, made a move that would impact their lives. They moved from the Mexican side of Kingsville to a house just southwest of the Texas A&I college campus on Santa Gertrudis Avenue. It was on "the other side of the tracks," where the more affluent Anglo community lived. "As a family, we were faced with discrimination in a segregated community and we never accepted it. We were taught by our parents to fight injustices and stand up for the poor and oppressed. We never acted [as if] women were not equal to men and that Mexican-Americans could not be successful," Rangel-Henderson said.[6] In 1947 the Rangel parents had bought some land near the Texas College of Arts and Industry (later A&I and A&M–Kingsville). They later decided to build a home along the western part of Santa Gertrudis Avenue, close to the King Ranch gate.

But the land was in the "Anglo-White" area of Kingsville. One of the neighbors organized a petition to collect signatures against the Rangel family because he believed having a Mexican American family in the area would be bad for the neighborhood.[7] The family did not move. They resolved to stay and eventually built a two-story Spanish Colonial style stucco and brick house. With the college now across the block, the concept of education was reinforced for the three Rangel sisters. Minnie would go on to become a pharmacist, Olga would get her master's in education, and Irma would be a lawyer, a politician, a trendsetter, and a heroine for many.

Irma Rangel credits her parents for helping her and her sisters survive and persevere because of the lessons they taught their girls. "I never really had any problems [growing up] because we were raised with the idea that, you know, that I had to do more work than the other person because I was Mexican American, my parents would say."[8] Their father was Presiliano M. Rangel, known as "P. M." He was born in 1903 near La Rosita in Duval County. He was orphaned at the age of five and was raised by his sisters. He would go from family member to family member on "*un caballito* [a little horse]" and jump from job to job to survive. He would pick cotton in the Kingsville area and finally settle there. He had no education. Her mother, Herminia Lerma, was born in Los Arrieros, a ranch community in what is now Starr County. She, her father, and her brothers came to Los Hogos, a ranch community in Nueces County near Corpus Christi, in the 1920s. Known as "Minnie" and later "Big Minnie" because she would name one of her daughters after her, the Rangels' mother had a grade school education. An interview for *Tejano Voices* revealed the family's encounters with discrimination. The Lermas lived in a ranch house west of what is now Texas A&M University–Kingsville. They used the rental property to farm the area near the King Ranch. It would eventually become the site of their home. From that farmhouse, the nearest school was Flato Elementary, but Minnie could not attend that school. Instead, she had to go another mile to the school she was assigned to attend. "The Flato School was used for the Anglo students only and so [my mother] had to go like another mile or so to go to what was called the Mexican Ward at that time."[9]

That lease would become an important part of the Rangel family legacy. When P. M. and Herminia Rangel saw the old lease property the Lermas used to farm go up for sale, they bought the lot in the late 1940s.[10] "When she saw that this [lease] property was being sold, both she and my father went and bought it. And, as soon as they bought it, well, there were no Mexican Americans here in the neighborhood and so they wanted to buy it back from them and they offered five times more than they [her mother and father] had paid for it." The Rangels did not budge. The family moved into the new house in December 1951.[11]

P. M. Rangel was a respected member of the Kingsville and South Texas community. Rangel-Henderson remembers her father as a "hard-working" man who worked in farming, ranching, construction, and business. He became a merchant, owning an appliance store, a furniture store, a plumbing service, two barbershops, and a bar. He also helped his wife develop a successful dress shop just off the main street of Kingsville, not on the Mexican side of town.[12] P. M. Rangel was keenly aware of the obstacles Mexican Americans faced in order to vote. As detailed in Evan Anders's book *Boss Rule in South Texas*, those obstacles included a poll tax, permission from their boss, voting for whomever the boss or *patrón* asked for, facing armed gunmen at the polls, and just finding time to vote.[13] For these reasons he and the family became active in the 1940s in the Good Government League, which assisted politicians in staging political rallies and campaigning for office with support from progressive citizens who wanted everyone to have a fair chance to participate in the political process. The Rangel family was active in city, county, and school elections, but few Mexican Americans were elected to any of these posts until the 1980s. Later, "Little Minnie," Irma's sister, was elected to the Kingsville Independent School District board and served as president.[14] She was the first Mexican American woman to serve on the board and the first Mexican American to serve as its president.[15]

A Life in Politics

Armed and inspired with the lessons learned from her father and family, Irma Rangel set out on a trailblazing career. It started modestly: a college education at neighboring Texas A&I with a bachelor's degree in business administration in 1951, a job as a teacher in Venezuela and in South Texas at Robstown and Alice for fourteen years, a degree from St. Mary's University School of Law in San Antonio, a career as a prosecutor, and finally a life in politics.[16] Rangel's venture into law was the turning point in her life. After graduating from St. Mary's, she served as a clerk for federal judge Adrian Spears in San Antonio. She then moved to Corpus Christi, where she served as assistant district attorney for three years. She went into public practice in 1972 with Corpus Christi attorneys Tony Canales and Rudy Garza. In 1973, she finally returned to Kingsville to set up a law practice with Hector García. She took over the law practice in 1983 after García's death and kept it until 1993 (even as she served in the legislature), when she closed the office and decided to become "a full-time legislator."[17]

Her entry into politics came after she was invited to attend the Texas Women's Political Caucus convention in Austin. Lady Bird Johnson and Liz Carpenter spearheaded the TWPC gathering. There she noticed the lack of Mexican American women in politics. At the urging of other Mexican American women leaders, she was asked to consider running for the state legislature. "Because the incumbent house representative in Rangel's district, Greg Montoya, was under federal investigation he was considered vulnerable. The Latinas at the conference, who were also members of the Women's Texas Political Caucus, felt the time was right for someone to run against Montoya, and they specifically encouraged Rangel to run against Montoya.... Finally, after talking it over with her parents, she decided to 'take a crack at it'"[18]

With the support of her parents and the backing of Mexican American women leaders, she stepped into politics. It was not easy, as she recalls in her 1996 interview with *Tejano Voices.* All she had was her education, her family's good name and reputation, and a sincere passion to serve the people of South Texas. She was facing incumbent Greg Montoya and two other candidates in the Democratic primary. There were no Republican opponents, as Texas was essentially a one-party state at the time.[19] "Rangel had several things going against her when she ran for office the first time. First, she had been back in the Kingsville area for only a short period after being away seventeen years. Many people did not know her or remembered her only as a little girl."[20] But Rangel used her family roots to gain a foothold in the race. Her family was well known not only in Kingsville but also in South Texas. "[My parents] had always been loved and respected and so I remembered going to a Bingo and saying, you know, 'I am Irma Rangel, you know, P. M.'s daughter and *la hermana* [sister] of Minnie."[21] This tactic had worked a year earlier when professors Jim Hobbs, Cecilia Hunter, and Leslie Hunter at Texas A&I had encouraged her to run for Kleberg County Democratic chair. Now, however, she was running for the state legislature, and she admitted she "had never been to the Capital" in Austin. "Rangel frequently took her parents with her on the campaign trail, even having them sit with her when she attended a televised candidate forum for station KGBT in Harlingen. Her sister Minnie went door-to-door with her in Kingsville and rode with her in a car caravan through the entire district."[22]

There were other issues, too. Rangel's status as a single woman came into play, and there were even rumors she was a lesbian. In Elsa in the Rio Grande Valley, she had to visit with community leaders, including the mayor, to proclaim she was not a lesbian. "I am not going to go to bed [with you] to prove it to you," she told the men.[23] Her marital status was also a point of contention. Few knew that in 1954 she had had a relationship with a navy jet fighter pilot from San Jose, California, named Alfredo Carrillo. The two were engaged, but Carrillo was killed in a jet crash in California that year.[24] As Irma explained, "He [Carrillo] was killed and all that and then the older you become, the more particular you get, so you are trying to put all the good things you have met in other men, and I have never been able to find that guy, and then I was always very independent."[25]

Gaining financial support from power players and prominent lawyers was hard because she was not married. Instead, she ran a "very good grassroots campaign" with "great support" from women in her district, especially the farm workers' wives.[26] She had a small campaign chest, using her personal finances to fund a campaign that cost her almost $10,000. She had a hot dog sale to raise money and received a contribution from the TWPC of $1,850. With that, she bought some radio ads, yard signs, and candidate cards.[27] Mainly, however, Rangel's first campaign was personal. She recalls going door to door with her sister Minnie asking for votes and support. As she recalled, "And so I went to this house and I knocked on the house and I will never forget that. An elderly woman, *era una viejita* [she was an old lady], she came out *y le dije*, 'Mire Señora, soy Irma Rangel' [and I said, 'Look, lady, I am Irma Rangel']. And she said, 'Ah sí, yo la he oído en la radio y me gusta mucho la voz, esperese un momento' [Ah, yes, I have heard you on the radio and

I like your voice a lot, wait just a moment]. She came back with a dollar for my contribution. Oh, that was wonderful. I will never forget that."[28] Irma found that contributions from her supporters came from the heart. Rangel credits her victory in the primary to the knowledge she gained from working with rural citizens. "In a rural area, the people want to see you . . . you know, you go in and they offer you coffee, tamales, *pan dulce* [sweet bread], and all this. And you sit down and, you know, they just pass [their thoughts about your conversation] on to the others, you know."[29]

In the four-person race, Rangel managed to pull in enough votes to advance to a runoff with Jean Hines, a native of Riviera, just south of Kingsville. "Hines was from a well-known political family, her father having been Kleberg County commissioner for many years."[30] She would need help. State representative Gonzalo Barrientos came down from Austin to help with her campaign. She held her first political rally, standing on top of an old flatbed truck and urging people to vote. Hundreds of enthusiasts came to show support, and a friend gave her office space for the campaign headquarters. Neighbors, friends, and part of the Mexican American extended family cooked and donated money for food for volunteers. Word of mouth became her calling card as she and her campaign workers spread the word about the runoff election.[31]

Rangel's campaign gained momentum and she won by more than a 2-to-1 margin. With no Republican foe in the general election, she was heading for Austin. In 1977 she became the first Mexican American woman state legislator. She would be the only one until 1985, when Lena Guerrero from the Austin area was elected to serve in the legislature.[32] "I didn't know I was going to be the first one," she told reporters after she was elected. "I felt like I was really going to have to deliver. If I didn't succeed they were going to say 'All Mexican women were failures.'"[33] Rangel did not falter. She would serve for more than a quarter century and become the "Dean of Tejana Legislators."

Legislative Work

"People who knew Irma will remember her for her unmistakable voice," said Minnie Rangel. "She pronounced her words, syllable by syllable . . . she was very precise."[34] Detailing Irma's mannerism as a state representative, Jeremy Brown of the *Corpus Christi Caller-Times* said, "She spoke with the precision of an experienced orator. Her pitch rose and fell, rhythmically, as if she invests a steady but hefty dose of emotion in every sentence. Then there is that accent, which some have said sounds British, or at least European, but which Rangel said . . . might come from speaking Spanish and English syntax when she was a little girl, in a childish attempt to sound like she actually knew English."[35] When she arrived in Austin and walked into the Capitol and the House Chambers, she was determined to make a difference and to represent her people and the women of Texas with dignity and grace.

Her legislation was social, to say the least, and it started in her first year. During her first legislative session, she sponsored and passed House Bill 1755, which provided education and employment programs for mothers with dependent children.[36] As she recalls, it was late at night and some of the legislators were starting to pack up, including herself. But then the speaker (Bill Clayton, a Democrat like Rangel) called her bill up at the last minute, at about 9:30 or 10:00 p.m. She was surprised. Rangel picked up the memos on her bill, went up to the front marker where legislators stood, and said simply, "All right guys, you want us to have babies, then help us support them. . . . Let us help those who cannot help themselves and make them self-supporting." There was silence. "I think that is all I said and poof, the bill passed."[37] But she wasn't finished. The bill was good and it had passed, but her legislation needed money. When the appropriations bill came on the floor, Rangel, the first-term politician, was at it again. Appropriations are not easy to obtain in the Texas house. All the members are scrambling to get deals done to fund their legislation. She recalled, "There was a lot of smoke and a lot of noise. I wanted them all to hear me and I said, 'This is a good amendment, we need the moneys for that bill,'" hollering over the noise. But the noise continued. Then it happened; the attention getter she needed came as if a sign from above. To the day she did her interview for *Tejano Voices* in 1996, she believed she got help from above. "I am practically shouting on the mike and then all of a sudden, bang! What was that? A light bulb *de allí arriba* [from up there in the ceiling]. All the glass came on down and it hit . . . Smith Gilley [D–Greenville]. Smith Gilley was the one that got all the glass on his head and everybody was very quiet. Everybody got scared. You could've heard a pin drop." In the confusion and ensuing quiet, Rangel went up to the mike and said, "All right members, someone up there is trying to tell you something. I respectfully request a vote for my amendment [for funding]." It passed.[38]

Rangel was a hard worker and something of a perfectionist, the result of the expectations her parents had of the Rangel sisters and her own expectations of not failing her constituency, Mexican Americans, and women in general. When the Texas house was trying to pass a bill criminalizing abortion, Rangel again stood up for what she felt was right. "I am very strong pro-choice and I had been an assistant district attorney [in 1971] . . . I was the only woman prosecutor [in Nueces County]. And so all the rapes and the incest were coming to me."[39] Her experience of having to tell women that abortions were not legal in Texas solidified her prochoice belief, even if she was personally against abortion. Before a hushed house membership, Rangel spoke with vigor when the house and senate were trying to pass a law that would criminalize abortion. She recalled: "So, I went and I told them 'I do not condemn nor do I condone abortion.' I wanted [them] to know why this amendment has to go on. I told them that I had been a prosecutor. [I told them] it was not right that we, and you men here, be telling a woman whether or not she has the right to her privacy, to her own body. . . . Everybody was quiet where you could've hear[d] a pin drop."[40]

Advocate for Education

She returned to her next session having earned the respect of fellow house members but still learning. She would get key committee appointments that she felt enabled her to serve her constituency more effectively. During her more than quarter century of service to the Texas legislature, she served on more than fifty committees, chairing or vice chairing several. As chair of the Mexican American Legislative Caucus and as a member of the Higher Education Committee of the House, she had newfound power. Always a strong proponent of social legislation and always a strong voice on the house floor, she had extra ammunition now to push her agenda to help South Texas. Armed with new confidence, she set out to get a law school for South Texas, to be located at Texas A&I. She proposed the bill in 1991. Because of the respect she had in the house from her fellow legislators, the bill passed. It failed, however, in the Texas senate and died. "I will never forget Lt. Governor Bill Hobby saying that it was ludicrous to have a law school here in South Texas. But it wasn't ludicrous to have three law schools in Houston, you know. And so I sent the message to him and I told him, I said, 'How can you say that? You have got three law schools in Houston and that is not ludicrous, you know?' So, I couldn't get it passed.'"[41] The fact that they turned down a request for a law school at her alma mater in Kingsville offended but did not deter her. Cecilia Hunter and Leslie Hunter remembered the legislative battle:

> In 1991, Rangel and [state senator Carlos] Truan introduced legisla-
> tion to establish a law school at Texas A&I University. [Texas A&I]
> President [Manuel] Ibanez wrote a letter to *The South Texan* [the
> university's student newspaper] stating that a law school at Texas A&I
> "would be one of the finest things ever to happen to the entire state." It
> would have long-lasting benefits . . . and probably spawn other high-
> level programs [for South Texas].[42]

Even though the bill did not make it through both houses of the legislature, Rangel had sent a strong message. Higher education in South Texas, and the state for that matter, would be one of her priorities during her tenure as a state legislator.

From a meeting in San Antonio in 1999 of more than 150 Mexican American professionals, moderated by former secretary of housing and urban development and former San Antonio mayor Henry Cisneros, to develop higher education institutions in South Texas and along the border region with Mexico came a plan, a program. Rangel would be its leader. The plan included higher education initiatives for several universities: an allied health program for A&M–Corpus Christi; a medical school in the Rio Grande Valley at Texas–Pan American; a pharmacy school for A&M–Kingsville; and other professional schools for Texas–El Paso and Sul Ross in Alpine.[43]

Known as the South Texas Border Initiative, the plan had its roots in a lawsuit filed by the Mexican American Legal Defense and Educational Fund in 1987 and marked the momentum that had started to change the scope of border universities. With the passage of the South Texas Border Initiative secured, the border legislators from Brownsville to El Paso and all who represented South Texas now had more influence on future legislation. In 1993 Rangel secured $450 million for institutions of higher education in the border regions of the state.[44] Rangel had been appointed chair of the Texas Higher Education Committee in 1993 by newly elected speaker Pete Laney, in part thanks to some crafty political maneuverings when the Mexican American Legislative Caucus was split on whom it would support for the top position in the Texas house. Rangel had supported Laney and was not embarrassed to ask to chair the Higher Education Committee. "I am going to do a good job. I don't know what we are going to do, but I am going to do a good job. I won't embarrass you," she told Laney.[45]

From 1993 to 2003 Rangel served as chair of the powerful House Higher Education Committee. She would make a big impact and become the author of one of the most controversial pieces of legislation in the latter part of the twentieth century, the "Top Ten Percent Rule," guaranteeing admission to Texas public universities and colleges for all Texas high school students graduating in the top 10 percent of their class.[46] This legislation constituted a response to the US Circuit Court of Appeals decision in *Hopwood v. Texas* that essentially killed affirmative action measures in Texas. The case stemmed from controversy about admission to the University of Texas Law School. Affirmative action, to that point, had allowed universities to use some race-based criteria for admission. But with the decision, battle lines were drawn, and Rangel was charged by Laney with studying the impact of the *Hopwood* decision. Working with both Republicans and Democrats and meeting with members in both chambers, Rangel was able to gather a coalition that wanted an alternative. She even met with *Hopwood* lawyer Terrell Smith. She got Republican senator Ted Bivins, chair of the Senate Higher Education Committee, to eventually support the legislation. Laney was hesitant to allow House Bill 588 to make it to the floor and move up to the senate, where support seemed solid. He met privately with Rangel; many thought that was the end of the legislation. Always the political strategist, however, Rangel brought a cadre of nine Mexican American professional experts to support her case for the legislation. Still, when the bill came up for discussion on the house floor, Laney called for more "study." Rangel got up from her desk and shouted, "We've studied it."[47] Laney went quiet. HB 588 was approved in a nonrecorded voice vote, barely, and went to the senate, where it passed by a wide margin. It was now up to Governor Bush to make it law. Three days later he signed the bill.[48] In an article for the *Texas Observer* after Rangel's death in 2003, Myra Leo wrote: "The top 10 percent of students from the high school in Roma [in the Rio Grande Valley] were likely to be 100 percent Hispanic. The top 10 percent of students from Jack Yates High School in Houston were likely to be all black. And every one was automatically admitted to the state's best universities. That was Irma's legacy."[49]

Still, Irma's biggest battle was yet to come. The South Texas Border Initiative was always "the plan." Soon, the opportunity would arrive for her to make a difference in the higher education fortunes of her alma mater, Texas A&I, now Texas A&M University–Kingsville. In 2001 she introduced House Bill 1601, urging its passage to fund the first professional school in South Texas, a college of pharmacy on the Kingsville campus. She would get a professional school, but she would not live to see the building go up. Her battle with cancer claimed her in 2003 before the college was built and occupied by students. She had undergone successful treatment in 2002 for inflammatory breast cancer and ovarian cancer. As the signs of chemotherapy began to show, she seemed to generate greater support and respect from her fellow legislators. Soon, her hair short and not growing, she resorted to wearing brightly colored hats so that the impact of the cancer would not show as much. "One day, fellow female legislators walked into the House sporting hats in a show of support. With them were two male mascots—Rep. Tony Goolsby, R-Dallas, and Tom Uher, D-Bay City—also wearing woman's hats." They came in to roaring applause from the house membership.[50]

The applause would have been even louder if they had known the struggle it would take to make Rangel's last piece of legislation a reality. Construction and occupation of a pharmacy school at Texas A&M University–Kingsville almost did not happen. Finding funding became the chief battle until the Texas A&M University System announced on March 1, 2006, that it would transfer the management of the Rangel College of Pharmacy from Texas A&M University–Kingsville to the Texas A&M University System Health Science Center. Still, Texas A&M University–Kingsville president Rumaldo Juarez was desperate: "There is no change in the funding status of the college. We have done all the preparations we can do to open the program. However, without assured funding, we can't go any further. At this time we are exploring possible avenues of borrowing money. This is a most unfortunate situation that we must entertain." A bill creating the pharmacy college was passed in 2001 and lawmakers approved more than $300,000 in start-up money for construction of the college, much less than needed. A&M–Kingsville borrowed $3.1 million from the A&M System, but Juarez reported to the A&M System and the legislature that an additional $13 million would be needed to make the pharmacy college a reality. In May 2006, the legislature allocated $275,000 for 2006 and not a dime for 2007. Juarez lobbied the Legislative Budget Board, which recommended $10 million for the project. "Although $10 million was included at one point in the supplemental appropriations bill, at final passage the funding was denied."[51] Meanwhile, the building was going up and plans for preaccreditation were proceeding with Dr. Mauro Castro, Regents Professor of Chemistry at A&M–Kingsville, serving as interim dean. "We were going to make this happen. We couldn't wait," Castro said in a 2013 interview.[52] Nick Jimenez, editorial page editor of the *Corpus Christi Caller-Times*, wrote:

> There is a big empty building in Kingsville on the campus of Texas A&M University–Kingsville. That building was supposed to fulfill the dream of the late Irma Rangel, one of the great guiding forces of higher education in Texas. Her dream was that a professional school would be located in South Texas. . . . Yet, when the 79th Texas legislature was gaveled to a close this week, the $13 million to allow the Irma Rangel School of Pharmacy to open on schedule in 2006 wasn't there. . . . It is a chronicle . . . of political firefights and legislative hand-to-hand combat. But lost in all that are the students," Jimenez announced.[53]

Lost in the column as well was Rangel. Her death had robbed her of that moment. Rangel died on March 18, 2003, at age seventy-one of brain cancer after a lengthy battle with breast and ovarian cancer.[54] The day after her death, a glass vase with twenty-seven long-stemmed yellow roses, one for each year Rangel served, sat atop her desk at the Texas house as colleagues wept openly. "She lived and died full of passion, for higher education, for the poor," said Representative Pete Gallegos, D–Alpine. Rangel's seatmate in the house, Paul Moreno of El Paso, choked up as he recalled how they sat side by side for years. State senator Leticia Van de Putte, D–San Antonio, said: "I really cannot imagine a Texas Legislature without Irma." Texas governor Rick Perry ordered flags flown at half-staff at state buildings in Rangel's memory.[55]

Irma was gone, but the battle for funding for the pharmacy college continued for three more years. Finally, on March 22, 2006, funding was secured. It came from the Texas A&M University Health Science Center and ensured the opening of the Irma Rangel College of Pharmacy that fall. The first professional school in South Texas opened under the umbrella of the Health Science Center, not A&M–Kingsville as Irma had hoped.[56]

Now all that was left was to honor Rangel with a commemorative statue. On January 18, 2007, the statue went up. An article announcing its unveiling proclaimed, "Now students who enter the pharmacy school building that [has Rangel's] name at Texas A&M University–Kingsville will know her that way, too." Grateful for her leadership, vision, and dedication to her principles, those present honored Rangel. Kleberg County judge Juan M. Escobar, who represented Rangel's district and fought for the establishment of the school after her death, summarized her legacy: "It's a unique opportunity to show the people in South Texas how one person can make a difference. Irma got education and never forgot where she came from."[57] And so Irma Lerma Rangel was home. Facing north toward Austin, her feet are firmly on the ground of her alma mater—Texas A&M University–Kingsville.

Notes

1. Edwin Vasquez, "Irma L. Rangel Statue Dedicated," *South Texan* 81, no. 4 (January 27, 2007), 1.

2. Mauro Castro, interview with the author, November 12, 2014, Texas A&M University–Kingsville.

3. Edwin Vasquez, interview with the author, December 9, 2013, Texas A&M University–Kingsville.

4. Vasquez, "Irma L. Rangel Statue."

5. Vasquez.

6. "A Powerful Vision: The Legacy of Irma Lerma Rangel," *South Texan*, special edition, February 27, 2007, 3, 5.

7. "Oral History Interview with Irma Rangel, 1996," Tejano Voices, University of Texas at Arlington Center for Mexican American Studies, 61, accessed November 10, 2013, https://library.uta.edu/tejanovoices/.

8. "Oral History Interview," 1.

9. "Oral History Interview," 2.

10. "Oral History Interview," 2.

11. "Oral History Interview," 2, 3.

12. "Oral History Interview," 3.

13. Evan Anders, *Boss Rule in South Texas* (Austin: University of Texas Press, 1982).

14. "Oral History Interview," 5.

15. Anita Bradford, Nirmal Goswami, and Larry Knight, *Todo Por La Raza: Mexican-American Women's Political Activism in South Texas* (Texas A&M University–Kingsville, October 26, 2003).

16. "Powerful Vision," 5.

17. "Oral History Interview," 8.

18. Sonia García, Valerie Martinez-Ebers, Irasema Coronado, Sharon A. Navarro, and Patricia A. Jaramillo, *Políticas: Latina Public Officials in Texas* (Austin: University of Texas Press, 2009), 38.

19. "Oral History Interview," 9.

20. García et al., *Políticas*, 39.

21. "Oral History Interview," 10.

22. García et al., *Políticas*, 39.

23. "Oral History Interview," 40.

24. "Powerful Vision," 5.

25. "Oral History Interview," 21.

26. García et al., *Políticas*, 40.

27. "Oral History Interview," 10.

28. "Oral History Interview," 17.

29. "Oral History Interview," 18.

30. García et al., *Políticas*, 9.

31. "Oral History Interview," 16.

32. Teresa Palomo Acosta and Ruthe Winegarten, *Las Tejanas: 300 Years of History* (Austin: University of Texas Press, 2003), 266–67.

33. García et al., *Políticas*, 34.

34. "Powerful Vision," 5.

35. "Powerful Vision," 5.

36. Britney Jeffrey, "Rangel, Irma Lerma (1931–2003)," *Handbook of Texas Online*, Texas State Historical Association, accessed November 15, 2013, http://www.tshaonline.org/handbook/online/articles/fra85.

37. García et al., *Políticas*, 243.

38. "Oral History Interview," 33.

39. "Oral History Interview," 32.

40. "Oral History Interview," 31.

41. "Oral History Interview," 46.

42. Cecilia Aros Hunter and Leslie Hunter, *Texas A&M University–Kingsville* (Chicago: Arcadia), 184.

43. Hunter and Hunter, 184.

44. Jeffrey, "Rangel, Irma Lerma."

45. "Oral History Interview," 36.

46. García et al., *Políticas*, 44.

47. García et al., 44–47; 46

48. "Oral History Interview," 37.

49. Myra Leo, "In Memoriam: It Was Always about the Students," *Texas Observer*, April 2003.

50. "Irma Rangel, Legislator, 71," *Orlando Sun Sentinel*, March 20, 2003 (from *San Antonio Express-News*), accessed December 20, 2013, https://www.sun-sentinel.com/news/fl-xpm-2003-03-20-0303191294-story.html.

51. Adriana Garza, "Pharmacy School May Borrow to Get Under Way: A&M-K Consider Bypassing State for Needed $10M," Corpus Christi Caller-Times, January 22, 2006. "Regents Vote to Transfer Management of Rangel College of Pharmacy A&M-Kingsville to the Health Science Center," Texas A&M university System news release, March 1, 2006.

52. Castro, interview.

53. Nick Jimenez, "South Texas Gets a Big Empty Building," *Corpus Christi Caller-Times*, June 5, 2005.

54. Jeffrey, "Rangel, Irma Lerma."

55. Clay Robinson, "House Veteran Rangel Dies of Cancer at Age 71," *Houston Chronicle*, March 19, 2003, https://www.chron.com/news/houston-texas/article/House-veteran-Rangel-dies-of-cancer-at-age-71-2116106.php.

56. "Regents Vote to Transfer."

57. Adriana Garza, "Students Really Can Look Up to Rangel: A&M-K Pharmacy School Erects Statue of Late Legislator," *Corpus Christi Caller-Times*, January 19, 2007.

V

The Artists

12

Carmen Lomas Garza

MARY JANE GARZA AND
SANTA CONTRERAS BARRAZA

Out of the quiet stillness, the memories come—the handmade dresses, trips to the beach, eating *raspas con nieve* on hot dusty afternoons. They are as fresh and real as if they are happening the moment they are drawn on paper or painted on canvas. It is a long way from South Texas to the old naval shipyard at Hunters Point in San Francisco where artist Carmen Lomas Garza has rented a studio since the mid-1980s. With only the radio and some salsa tapes to keep her company, there are no interruptions here, no visitors, no mail, and for a long time she had no telephone because she used the pay phone down the hall.

Early Life in Art and Activism

Carmen Lomas Garza grew up in Kingsville, where she was born in 1948, surrounded by extended family. This small town of 25,315 inhabitants (in 2019) was founded in 1904 with the influence of cattle baron Richard King and the St. Louis, Brownsville, and Mexico Railway Corporation. Carmen's maternal family members were vaqueros at the King Ranch. The ancestors of Carmen's mother, María Lomas Garza, had been one of those original families who supposedly were enticed in 1854 by Richard King at Cruillas and Camargo, Tamaulipas, Mexico, to migrate to Texas and work at his ranch. Her family worked for the King Ranch for five generations, until they finally moved into the town. María's great-grandfather José Francisco Orta, one of the original immigrants, eventually became Henrietta King's personal bodyguard and cook. In 1923, Carmen's maternal grandmother, Elisa Medina, left the King Ranch at the age of fourteen to marry Antonio Lomas, who lived in town. The family eventually left the ranch and settled in Kingsville. Her mother was a homemaker who made all the clothes for the family, and her father was a sheet metal worker for the naval base, stationed in Kingsville.

Carmen was always fascinated by art in one form or another as a child: her grandmother's quilt patterns and crochet, the handiwork of her father in building their home, and the *lotería* boards her mother created for the fund-raising activities of the local chapter of the American GI Forum, a civil rights organization founded by Dr. Hector P. García. After observing her mother drawing and painting, she realized that she wanted to be an artist. The *monitos*, as her mother called them when she drew the lotería cards, made a lasting impression on Carmen. "I realized that she was an artist when I was about eight or nine years old. I was really impressed, I thought she was doing magic and I wanted to be able to do the same kind of thing," Carmen recalls.[1] To this day those lotería cards sit on a shelf in Carmen's home, a reminder of the source of her inspiration. She decided to teach herself how to draw because there were no art classes in elementary or junior high; she would draw anything or anyone in front of her. By the time she got to high school and was able to take an art class, she was ready. Her art teacher was so impressed with her talent that during Carmen's senior year she helped her get a scholarship to Texas A&I University to take art classes. Santa Barraza, retired professor of art at Texas A&M University–Kingsville, remembers: "Since I was also a student at H. M. King High School and graduated two years later, I recall Carmen as a unique student. She was highly revered as an upcoming young artist with a promising future. She, along with former classmate José Rivera whose family was also from the King Ranch, was the art star of the school. I would see their artwork all over the walls of the school." High school art teacher Noreen Newton groomed Carmen to excel in higher education. Most of the high school student art exhibitions featured Carmen Lomas Garza. She also was the art editor of the high school's literary journal, *Descant*.

Carmen loved Texas A&I University, excelled in her art, and received a bachelor of science in 1972. At that time the university did not offer a bachelor of fine arts in studio art, so she opted for a degree in art education. She was regarded with much esteem as the heart of the Art Department and a member of a new generation of devoted artists, to the point that years later she confided that while she was a student the department had provided her with a key to the print-making studio. Barraza recalls viewing and admiring many of her fine art prints on display in the department's hallways. Along with Amado Peña and José Rivera, Carmen was a star of the department. There was a lot of discussion among students, especially in the Art Department. William Renfrow, a professor in the department, would often host gatherings for students at his home on Friday nights. It was a unique situation that fostered an exchange of ideas, political thought, and discourse on current events. As a result of their demands to have more Chicano faculty and Chicano art, the Art Department hired Pedro Rodríguez, who set up a silk-screen print shop in the department.

During her college years at A&I, Carmen became active in the Chicano movement, which greatly influenced the direction her art and life would take. When she was just a sophomore at the university, Carmen was contacted by the Mexican American Youth Organization (MAYO) to organize the first Chicano art exhibit in Texas—her first curating job. It was held in Mission, Texas, in 1969 as part of a statewide MAYO conference. At that time, the country was in turmoil over the war in Vietnam. Martin Luther King Jr. had just been assassinated in 1968. Blacks were rioting in the streets; college students were requesting peace. Angela Davis and the Black Panthers were making history with their radical activism for social change. Young activists, both Black and Mexican American, were demanding civil and labor rights. Reies Lopez Tijerina in New Mexico reclaimed the Mexican and Native ancestral territory highlighted by the Tierra Amarilla armed standoff at the courthouse. The Mexican Americans were self-identifying themselves as Chicanos and aligning themselves with Cesar Chavez and the National Farm Workers Association of California.

The Mexican American students at Texas A&I, among them Carlos Guerra, began to organize themselves into political student organizations, such as MAYO. An underground newspaper was initiated through the assistance of the Art Department's William Renfrow. Even the writer Gloria Anzaldúa was commuting from her hometown to attend graduate education classes. Carmen, too, became involved in political student art exhibitions and activities. While at the university Carmen became interested in print making, pen and ink drawing, pencil, and charcoal. She was a good academic art student, but as a result of the Chicano movement she decided to look toward family and culture instead of class instruction to determine the direction of her work.

In 1971 Carmen did her student teaching for her degree at Robstown High School, thirty miles north of Kingsville. Most of the students were Mexican American or recent arrivals from Mexico who did not speak English. At that time teachers had to conduct their classes in English, but it was difficult for Carmen to ignore the new arrivals. While Carmen was at Robstown High the now famous school walkouts occurred. Even though she did not encourage any students to participate, her association with them caused conflict with the school superintendent, who subsequently requested her removal from the school. This incident had a profound effect on her emotionally, creatively, and politically. Later that year Carmen heard that the boys at Robstown who walked out and were eighteen years old were immediately drafted and sent to Vietnam. Upset by this knowledge, she said, "That's it. I'm going to dedicate my artwork to the Chicano movement and focus on being a Chicana artist and learning more about our own history, participating more politically, working on changing the curriculum in schools, changing attitudes about our language. If our boys can go and lose their innocence, their limbs, or, worse, their lives for our country, they have every damn right to enjoy their culture and their language and their history and fully participate in our society—in this society that we have contributed to. We have every right to be proud of who we are."[2]

Other Chicano artists were doing art influenced by the famous Mexican muralists with protest- or revolutionary-themed work. Others were using images of Emiliano Zapata or Pancho Villa or copying ancient pre-Columbian artwork. But there was very little that dealt with the ordinary lives of Mexican Americans. Carmen decided to depict those ordinary, everyday, and special moments she knew so well. She decided to print her own set of lotería cards and play boards, just as her mother had created many years before. She found a few of the older play boards with the monitos her mother had used as models, and in the process of creating her own she realized, "This is what art means. It's taking from the past, adjusting it, and creating new."[3] Carmen made the set of seventy-five cards for the lotería and printed a few play boards. She had been studying children's art in her education classes and understood how simple, direct, and upfront it was, an ideology she embraced. As she was doing the monitos on the lotería cards, she had an epiphany, noticing how wonderful it felt to draw them. It was a comforting moment, like coming home to familiar surroundings.

Because she also clearly understood the role print making served in the dissemination of an image, prints became very important for the movement. This understanding of print making and her decision to depict everyday life was a pivotal moment in Carmen's career as an artist. One such piece, a small etching, depicted a scene of her grandfather in his garden and herself sitting next to him on a box watching him water the garden. It was a memory that was special to her, done in a simple and direct style with disregard for perspective and convention, a style that she would stay with to create the visual narratives of her life. Those visual narratives allowed her to reaffirm and validate her experiences as a Mexican American growing up in South Texas.

In 1970 Carmen met Javier Gorena and Enrique Flores, artists and gallery owners from Mission, Texas, on one of their visits to Colegio Jacinto Treviño, where Carmen briefly studied. Enrique Flores owned the gallery property, which also included a Mexican movie theater and a frame shop. They became her friends and mentors and promoted her work. Javier and Enrique also taught her the business of art by giving her the only book on the subject at the time, titled *Marketing Art*. Carmen's first solo exhibit, called *Monitos*, showed in 1972 at Estudios Rio Gallery. While she was with Estudios Rio, Carmen started doing paper cutouts after looking through a book on Mexican folk art. Carmen grabbed some brown paper bags and scissors and started cutting, Javier joining her. Eventually they progressed to Exacto knives and finer papers and much more intricate designs. Javier went into more geometric and stylized patterns, while Carmen tried her hand at scenery. An important medium for her, the cutouts became bigger and more complex, using different media to represent the increasingly complicated scenery. These cutouts were used to decorate altars and public installations. The most famous of her cutouts are the large, commissioned pieces that adorn the San Francisco International Airport terminal and an apartment complex in Houston, Texas.

After teaching for one year in public schools in Austin, Texas, Carmen was ready to leave Texas. She was encouraged by Pedro Rodríguez, her instructor at A&I, to apply for funding and scholarships to go to graduate school at Washington State University in Pullman, where he was teaching. She received a scholarship to study color and lithography. Up to that point Carmen had worked mainly in black and white, avoiding painting or working in color. Not only were colors overwhelming for Carmen, but she also did not like wasting time or paint trying to figure out a certain shade she might need. Carmen decided to create her own color scales in several different media and all possible shades to understand how they worked. It was an exercise that proved valuable since she relies on her own hand-painted charts to quickly decide on a color. However, the facilities in the Art Department and the isolation of the school were difficult and disappointing for Carmen.

Recognition

In the summer of 1976 Carmen drove down to San Francisco to visit friends. After visiting Galería de la Raza and meeting director Rene Yanez, Carmen decided to drop out of Washington State and move to San Francisco. She volunteered and then worked at the Galería, a move that proved invaluable to her career. While working at the Galería de la Raza part time, she was able to get funding from the California Arts Council through artists-in-residence grants to enable her to continue doing her art at home.

In 1978 she organized a Day of the Dead exhibit dedicated specifically to Mexican artist Frida Kahlo for the gallery. She had been inspired the year before by Chicana artist Amalia Mesa-Bains's Day of the Dead *ofrenda* dedicated to five women, including Frida Kahlo. Carmen started inviting artists to the Galería to learn about Frida and the Day of the Dead by giving slide presentations of Frida's art. Her exhibit, as well as one by Hayden Herrera, triggered much interest in the art by Chicanos and women. Like other Chicana artists, Carmen benefited from the feminist art movement, which helped to break the European and American fine art barriers so many of them faced.

Many Chicano artists in those early years created work that was very political, which made it difficult to get it accepted into major museums. They were told that the quality was not there. In reaction to this attitude, the artists began putting political pressure on institutions that received taxpayers' money. If a museum received public money, the Chicano artists felt they had every right to be included in those exhibitions. Carmen was selected to sit on a panel for the California Arts Council to review proposals for institutional grants. The California Arts Council had been changing its policy and had no qualms about arguing that some institutions were not representing the Chicano community or the different communities where they were located. It was a struggle that took years of pressure, but eventually the museums gave in.

One of the first major Chicano/Latino art exhibitions was *Hispanic Art in the U.S.A.* in 1987. This controversial exhibit, which traveled around the United States, was able to secure funding from corporations and major institutions. The Corcoran Gallery in Washington, DC, for instance, cosponsored that exhibition along with the Contemporary Arts Museum Houston. Carmen was invited to be part of the exhibit, the only Chicana and one of three women in the show. The organizers asked her to show not only her paintings but also the Frida Kahlo ofrenda. She thought it would be awkward setting up this Day of the Dead ofrenda at the wrong time of year. But they wanted it because it would be educational; since nobody had seen anything like that, it would be a great opportunity. She had to go to every institution involved in the exhibit to do the installation, a tremendous learning experience for her. At the grand opening in Houston, there was a huge turnout from the local Latino community. It was an important achievement for the artists—the doors were finally opening.

Carmen had been directing her artwork to a Mexican American audience that would appreciate and best be served by the paintings and prints she was doing. It was also her way of fulfilling her own personal obligation and service to her community. In the process, she developed her collectors, the *padrinos* and *madrinas* that supported her in those lean early days, most acquiring their pieces on the "layaway plan." Carmen did not sell to non-Chicanos until she started to exhibit in museums with exhibitions like the *Hispanic Art in the U.S.A.* in 1987. That same year, she had her first major, important solo exhibition at the Mexican Museum in San Francisco, which published a catalog for the exhibit that was instrumental in disseminating information about her work. From that point on, she and her work were sought after. She had showings at a variety of venues, from Smith College to the Laguna Gloria Art Museum to the Whitney Museum of American Art. In addition to the many showings, Carmen's artwork was the subject of an interactive exhibition for children organized by the Austin Children's Museum in 2003 in Austin, Texas. The exhibition traveled for five years to children's museums in the United States before returning to Austin for a two-year display at the Thinkery, the new Austin Children's Museum. Just recently Texas A&M University–Kingsville purchased this three-dimensional installation for the permanent collection at the John E. Conner Museum. The exhibit is unique in that it took some of the more famous of Carmen's paintings such as *Tamalada* and made life-size dioramas that a person can actually walk into.

In 2003 Carmen returned to her alma mater, now Texas A&M University–Kingsville, and the chair of the Art Department, Santa Barraza, invited her as a visiting artist for a week to conduct several workshops for college and high school art students. A solo exhibition of her artwork was organized for the Ben Bailey Gallery at the same time. The city presented her with the key to the city and declared it Carmen Lomas Garza week. Barraza recalls Carmen's mother thanking her for paying the proper homage to her daughter, which she stated was long overdue.

Book Illustrations and the Meaning of Her Art

When Harriet Rohmer founded Children's Book Press in 1975 in San Francisco with a grant from the US Department of Education, she was the first publisher to focus exclusively on quality multicultural and bilingual literature for children. Children's Book Press forever changed the children's publishing landscape. Rohmer believed that "when a child opens a book and sees someone like herself or himself, it has the power to change that child's life and create an ongoing relationship to reading."[4] Carmen's artwork was the perfect vehicle for Rohmer's vision. In 1990 Children's Book Press published a bilingual book of Carmen's paintings and short stories titled *Family Pictures / Cuadros de familia*, which continues to sell. Celebrating birthdays, making tamales, picking nopales, and confiding to her sister her dreams of becoming an artist, these day-to-day experiences are told through fifteen paintings and their stories, each focusing on a different aspect of the culture. Writer Sandra Cisneros provided the introduction and poet Pat Mora the afterword for this touchstone of Latino children's literature. Three more award-winning picture books of Carmen's artwork were published in 1996 and 1999: *In My Family / En mi familia*; *Magic Windows / Ventanas mágicas*; and *Making Magic Windows: Creating Papel Picado / Cut-Paper Art with Carmen Lomas Garza*. Over seven hundred thousand copies of the books have sold since 1990. The books have received several awards including Notable Book, American Library Association; Pura Belpré Honor Award, American Library Association; Best Books of the Year Selection, School Library Journal; and Best Books of the Year Selection, Library of Congress. In addition, "In My Family" was a chapter in the third grade reader for public schools published by Scholastic Books.

Carmen's art has garnered reactions from a wide range of Mexican Americans, from a child saying, "Oh yeah, we did that last week," to an adult saying, "Well, I remember when my grandmother used to tell me stories of doing that."[5] The artwork stimulates discussion among family members about history, culture, and traditions. In the process of passing on the history to the younger generation, in the building of character, the base is built for survival, for without culture there is nothing. Carmen has always felt that from the very beginning Chicano artists were doing multiculturalism before it was popular to call it multiculturalism. Even though doing so meant much work and sacrifice and putting up with negativity, it has been worth the struggle. What kept her going through many dark moments was the support of not only her family but also the collectors and admirers who so loved her work. Now that the climate is better, Carmen notices the changes coming from the globalization of the internet and the effects on traditions. "I'm really curious to see how some traditional things are retained and how some traditional things are lost within this computer age," she says. "And how some traditional things are revived, for example, the tamalada. Families telling me, 'Well,

I remember my mother doing that, but I didn't do that, but now we're starting to get everybody together to learn how to make tamales.'"[6]

One of the first published illustrations by a mainstream publisher of Carmen's artwork, *Raspas con nieve*, a pen and ink drawing, appeared in the book *Chicano Voices*, edited by Carlota Cárdenas de Dwyer and Tino Villanueva. The publication incorporated the writings of thirty-three Chicano writers and illustrations by five artists, of whom Carmen Lomas Garza and Santa Barraza were the only females. Four of the artists had lived and/or been educated in Kingsville, Texas. At first glance, Carmen's *Raspas con nieves* appears to be a rather naive black ink rendering of a relaxed Sunday event with family at home or at the park, reminiscent of Diego Rivera's fresco *Sunday Afternoon at Alameda Park*. However, on closer inspection, the neighborhood becomes recognizable and tangible. The celebratory event is being held in front of the local *Tiendita*, where most community members purchased the renowned *raspas*. At the entrance to the store stands the owner wearing an apron and gently scooting a child inside. To the right of the entrance his wife, also wearing an apron, rests on a metal rocking chair. On the porch in front of these three people sits a father with his two children, who are enjoying and sharing snow cones with ice cream topping. The six figures are drawn in a linear, simplistic fashion. This stylistic approach is identified by Carmen as her monitos style. Her monitos are influenced by the hieroglyphics of ancient Mexico, which used bold, linear drawings with heads, arms, and legs depicted from a side view and including intricate clothing, headdresses, hair texture, and body accessories. In contemporary Mexico, this style of drawing continues to be used in the popular art of the iconographic retablo and the acrylic or tempera painting on a *mate*.

The *Lotería* series, intaglio prints on metal produced in Kingsville in 1970, is directly influenced by the artwork of her mother, María Lomas Garza. Her mother had produced play boards for Mexican bingo, lotería, for the local Catholic church to be used in fund raisers. Carmen was inspired by the cartographic images of the cards, which were framed under glass. They reimagine Mexican Colonial etchings such as the 1784 *Descripción de las Endechas Mudas de la Santísima Madre Santa Maria de Guadalupe; Dispuestas por Manuel Quiroz (Description of the Dirge of Mourning of the Holy Mother Saint Mary of Guadalupe; Produced by Manuel Quiroz)*, sold as *estampas* (prayer cards) to the general Mexican public.[7] In this etching, forty boxes bordered by a braided design contain linear illustrations depicting different prayers dedicated to the Virgin of Guadalupe. The entire page is visually akin to a lotería panel.

Importance of Her Work

Borrowing from the past, as with the *Lotería* and *Monitos* series, Lomas Garza's artwork illustrates the concept of countermemory, where attention is focused on something that has been forgotten and concealed from the public. "Chicana artists [like Lomas Garza] focused on their cultural identity using the female lenses of narrative, domestic space, social critique, and ceremony, which filtered these nutrient experiences, contradictory roles, and community structures."[8] Amalia Mesa-Bains states that Carmen Lomas Garza uses the techniques of cultural and collective memory as well as regional histories to subvert the dominant status quo and eliminate erasure of her culture. Her artwork reveals a highly articulated and meaningful visual interpretation of a revisionist and cultural refiguring, calling up memory, the personal, cultural, and countercultural. By narrating her own memory, she empowers the art while transforming it into a new meaning. Lomas Garza creates a web of worldly interconnectedness with her monitos that originally acted as a resistance to erasure but now has been refigured into an embodiment of a place without borders, imbued with empowerment and happiness. The ideal visual narrator for the Chicano experience, Carmen Lomas Garza paints stories that transcend borders and successfully reiterate her own poetry of truth to everyone.

"The first time that I realized that there was some success was when I sold my first etching to another undergraduate student at A&I during I think it was my first year, for five dollars. I didn't know what value to put on it. All I wanted was to get enough money to get some more paper," said Carmen Lomas Garza.[9]

Notes

1. Carmen Lomas Garza, interview by Mary Jane Garza, Austin, TX, 2004.
2. Garza, interview.
3. Garza, interview.
4. "Children's Book Press History," Children's Book Press,

https://www.leeandlow.com/imprints/children-s-book-press/articles/chil
dren-s-book-press-history.

5. Garza, interview.

6. Garza, interview.

7. Centro Cultural Arte Contemporaneo, *Maravilla Americana: Variantes de la Iconografía guadalupana, siglos XVII hasta XIX, Festival Guadalajara* (Mexico City: Patrimonio Cultural del Occidente, 1989), 82.

8. Amalia Mesa-Bains, *El Mundo Femenino: Chicana Artists of the Movement*, CARA catalog (University of California, Los Angeles, Wright Art Gallery, 1991), 131.

9. Garza, interview.

13

Selena Quintanilla Pérez

OCTAVIO QUINTANILLA

I never got the chance to see Selena in concert, but I know people who did. "She was amazing," they say. In the early 1990s, I played in a rock band and worked as an office manager for a plumbing company. When the plumbers and laborers arrived at the office from the different worksites throughout the Rio Grande Valley, they would often walk in humming one of Selena's melodies. It was the workers who one day brought the news of her death. She was twenty-three years old when she died on March 31, 1995. A few years later, I was teaching English at Harlingen High School and one fall morning, Rebecca Lee Meza, the girl who portrayed young Selena in the 1997 movie starring Jennifer Lopez, walked into my classroom. I didn't know who she was until a student revealed her to me: "That's her, sir. Selena."

Selena was part of our everyday lives in the late 1980s and early '90s. I heard her music on Tejano radio stations. I saw her perform on TV. In South Texas, everyone knew her name. Who didn't? It was hard to ignore her popularity in the Mexican American community. Although I didn't identify myself as a fan then, I often attended important events in people's lives where her music played in the background—quinceañeras (the coming-out parties for fifteen-year-old Latinas), weddings, and even funerals. Even now, thirteen years after Becky Lee Meza walked into my classroom, and eighteen years after Selena's death, Selena has once again entered my life. This time, I wanted to get to know her and contextualize her importance in our contemporary consciousness. After her death, Selena became the subject of numerous television and musical tributes; the subject of scholarship; the subject of film; and now, the subject of a mural, which is one more way to remember her and to confirm her importance in the lives of many South Texans as well as in the lives of thousands of fans around the world.

Rediscovering Selena

On a warm summer morning in 2013, I made my way from Harlingen to Corpus Christi, Texas, Selena's hometown and home of the Selena Museum. Built in 1998 by the Quintanilla family, the museum serves as a memorial to the achievements and life of Selena. The museum displays her red Porsche, awards, photographs, stage outfits, and other memorabilia. It is a popular destination for fans. I had arranged an interview with Abraham Quintanilla Jr., Selena's father and manager. When I first called asking to interview Selena's mother, Marcela Quintanilla, a clerk on the other end of the line, said, "That's not gonna happen." From what he told me, after Selena's death Mrs. Quintanilla stopped giving interviews. Seconds later, Abraham Quintanilla was on the phone: "I can make time for you next week. Be here at eleven."

I drove for more than two hours to get to Corpus Christi, making my way across the large expanse of South Texas ranchland, through the Border Patrol checkpoint at Sarita, through Kingsville and other small towns that dot Highway 77. I wasn't sure how the meeting with Abraham Quintanilla would go, the two of us with the same surname, though to my knowledge, unrelated. All I knew was that I wanted to talk to him, that I wanted to hear anecdotes about the Queen of Tejano from someone who had been close to her.

I arrived at the museum fifteen minutes before my meeting with Abraham, and as I waited in the lobby, people poured in nonstop. I tried to talk to the clerk, but it was almost impossible. "It's always like this," he said. "People come from all over." Oklahoma. Washington. The Netherlands. Fans in non–Latin American countries know Selena because of the movie. They identify with her story. They relate with the universality of having a dream and the dedication and guts to realize it. Fan letters pour in from all over the country and all over the world. At one point in our conversation, Abraham said, "Here, read this." It was a handwritten letter from a woman from the Philippines, expressing her condolences to the Quintanilla family for their loss. She explained that although she could not speak or understand Spanish, every morning she would listen to Selena's music on YouTube. Dance to it. The letter was one more reminder of the power of Selena's soulful voice, her power to move us.

If Abraham Quintanilla encountered visitors in the lobby or gallery, he would want to know where they came from. "Where are you all from?" he would ask. McAllen. Laredo. San Antonio. People who recognized Abraham Quintanilla often pointed at him in awe as he walked by and whispered, "That's the dad." They knew that he, too, had been part of Selena's journey. Abraham led me to a small office in the back of the museum and we talked. We talked about Selena's childhood, her character, her music. Born about fifty miles south of Houston on April 16, 1971, in Lake Jackson, Texas, Selena Quintanilla Pérez dreamed big.

Beginnings

The story is well known by now to Selena fans. In the early 1980s, Abraham Quintanilla Jr. opened a Mexican restaurant in Lake Jackson where Selena, then eight years old, would sing accompanied by her brother Abraham III on bass and her sister Suzette on drums. At first, Selena was shy. Supposedly, she was "gawky and unsure of herself," often bursting into tears when her father called her to the microphone. "She would sing, and as soon as she finished the last word of the song she would say, 'Thank you!' and leave," her sister Suzette said."[1]

The business, however, did not last long. The economic downturn of the eighties hit the Quintanillas hard; they lost their source of income and their home. Ceasing to be entertainment for the restaurant's patrons, Selena y Los Dinos, as the band was billed, became a means to survive.[2] Of this time, Selena once said, "We were literally doing it to put food on the table."[3] Touring in a van, Selena y Los Dinos played birthday parties and weddings, eventually graduating to honky-tonks and dances across South Texas.

In 1987, after years of playing these venues, fifteen-year-old Selena won the Tejano Music Award for Female Entertainer of the Year. Things were about to change for the band, and for Selena. The win brought a major label contract with Capitol Records, which led to six increasingly successful albums.[4] Selena was not only accomplished in singing polkas and *cumbias* (lilting, reggae-tempo sounds originally hailing from Colombia) but was also comfortable reworking songs by bands such as the Pretenders, whose eighties rock classic "Back on the Chain Gang" Selena transformed into a *cumbia* titled "Fotos y Recuerdos."[5] As we talked in his relatively small office, Abraham remembered Selena's taste in music: "She liked all kinds of music and she was influenced as much as she has influenced many performers." From Donna Summer to Madonna, Selena's taste in music could often be heard in the choices she made as a singer, and as a performer whose primary job was to entertain a crowd.

Abraham Quintanilla told me that Selena y Los Dinos played all kinds of musical styles as kids, from country to conjunto (traditional, accordion-driven Mexican music). Though Tejano music has evolved on its own since the 1930s, its musical and historical roots are traced to conjunto music from the Rio Grande Valley and to the sophisticated pan-Latino, big-band *orquesta tejana*. The orquesta tejana merged "the popular Cuban dance styles like the *bolero* and *danzón* (via Mexico), with Mexican *rancheras* and *canciones románticas*, with US swing and big band."[6] In the 1940s and 1950s, orquesta tejana groups filled clubs and concert halls throughout Texas and in communities across the United States where Texas Mexicans migrated. Selena's music is situated within these genres.

Of course, female conjunto singers paved the way long before Selena became the Queen of Tex-Mex, and long before contemporary Tejana performers carved careers in the Tejano music industry. Among them were Lydia Mendoza from Houston, Rosita Fernández from San Antonio, and Chelo Silva, who was one of the "biggest names in Tejano Conjunto music" in the 1950s, and who hailed from Corpus Christi.[7] Tejana performers such as Laura Canales, Patsy Torres, Shelly Lares, and Selena Quintanilla followed the lead of the first conjunto women. Despite the challenges all these women faced, such as low pay, little or no respect, discrimination, and the stigma they suffered in a male-dominated genre, they found spaces to succeed, often surpassing the male performers in popularity.

Possibly one of the biggest challenges that Selena faced, and overcame, was the male-dominated Tejano music scene. In an interview she said, "There's a lot of men in this business. If you can't speak for yourself they are going to run you down every which way."[8] Selena represented the "contemporary boom" in Tejano music, "a genre in which women have had to be resilient in their desire to stay and succeed within the industry."[9] And resilient she was. She broke gender barriers and her "musical accomplishments propelled her to become the foremost representative of Tejano music of the twentieth century."[10] Her rise within the ranks "disrupted the gendered institution of Texas-Mexican music, which had historically been represented by male figures."[11] Abraham Quintanilla was aware of Selena's influence: "She became very popular," he said. "I think she, along with Emilio Navaira, opened doors to a lot of Tejano performers."[12] Selena blossomed as an artist and, ironically, opened the doors of success and popularity throughout the United States and Latin America to a wave of male-led Tejano bands.

Scholars have pointed out that "Selena's music was embraced by a unique 'Tejano generation,'" a generation located somewhere between the post-Chicano civil rights era and the emerging pan-Hispanic identity formation of the mid-1980s.[13] This new generation of Tejanos needed someone to highlight their roots and their culture, and Selena helped express their unique American identity through her music. After all, Tejano music has its developmental origins *en este lado*, within the borders of the United States."[14] It bridged Mexican and American culture.

But Tejanos did not embrace just Selena's music; they embraced her persona, which resonated with many of them "in terms of gender, color, language, social class, and a regional history and culture."[15] For a new generation of Tejanos, it was easy to identify with Selena's working-class roots; they admired her decision to make her home on the same street where her parents lived even though she had enough money to live in a posh neighborhood. She made her home in Corpus Christi, where her father first started booking gigs for the band. "Selena was from the barrio," a disc jockey told mourners at a memorial service the day after her death. "She still ate tortillas and frijoles."[16] Young girls saw themselves in her. They moved like her, they dressed like her, tried to sing like her. But South Texas women were not the only ones who identified with Selena. Selena represented women from all Latino backgrounds. One of her fans put it best: "Selena is an icon to us because she is both culturally and physically like we are, someone born here in the United States and definitely an American, but also a Latina, proud of who she is and able to say she didn't have to lose her culture to be successful. She not only embodied ideals of Latina beauty but the struggle we live with every day, between two cultures, two languages and two sets of values."[17] Selena symbolized success, empowerment. She was the mirror Latinas wanted to see themselves in.

Selena's Influence Expands

Despite popular belief, Selena had a tough time breaking into some Latin American markets such as Mexico, where class is often associated with race or skin color. Her mestizo features contrasted with the "typically fair-skinned and light-haired soap-opera stars," and she was referred to as *naco*, an ethnic and class slur meaning coarse or vulgar.[18] Her music was associated with the lower working class in the upper-class neighborhoods of Mexico City. This perception of her, however, soon changed, as evidenced by her appearance in a few episodes of a popular telenovela of the time, *Dos mujeres, un camino* (*Two Women, One Destiny*), starring former *CHiPs* star Erik Estrada.

Because she grew up speaking English, Selena had to learn Spanish once her popularity spread to Latin American countries. At first she had to learn the song lyrics phonetically, but with determination, she learned to carry on a conversation in Spanish, illustrating the importance of the language as "a strategy for upward social mobility."[19] Traditionally, we tend to think that English is the language that brings economic advancement, but Selena proved that knowing Spanish can be an asset to an emerging star. One element that needs to be stressed, however, is that her struggle with Spanish had more complex implications: it symbolized "the legacy of violent language oppression over promoting Spanish-language use in Texas."[20] Some Tejanos still remember the verbal and corporal punishment inflicted on them for speaking Spanish in school. Abraham Quintanilla was familiar with this period of our history. He knew about the suppression of the Spanish language in schools. Selena reminded many of us of this legacy, and yet her struggle with learning Spanish demonstrated that the language of her forefathers, the language of many Tejanos, is vital in our modern world.

Furthermore, for Selena, a native Texan, learning Spanish became a means to reach her Latin American public and a testament to its importance in reaching new markets. New markets in Latin America meant more money, and in the music industry, money is the definitive measure of success. Tejanos embraced Selena because of her struggle with Spanish in public interviews and in Spanish-language television programs. Her broken Spanish resonated with her Tejano public because many of them also spoke "some version of Tex-Mex Spanglish."[21] A shared language connected them. Tejano audiences saw in Selena a representation of who *they* were. Her struggle disproved the notion that having Mexican ancestry means fluency in Spanish.

Success Comes to Selena

Though Selena reached superstardom in the Tejano music scene, she never boasted about her success. Sometimes she would worry about filling venues, but her father reassured her that the lines of people forming outside the places where she performed were for her. "I believe that Selena was not even aware of how successful she was, how popular she was," her father remembers.[22] Revered and respected by Mexican Americans, Selena reached out to her community, especially the youth, and recorded educational videos, including one just before her death in which she differentiates between different Mexican musical genres popular in the United States. Those who knew her personally or came into contact through her music and performances respected her status as an international entertainer and admired her values, her humility, and the good example she tried to be to others. Though she was known as the Madonna of Tejano music, she was guided by tradition and family. One of her publicists said, "She was sexy like Madonna, but never vulgar. Her sweetness came through."[23]

At the height of her popularity, she was making enough money to buy herself almost anything she wanted, but she kept herself in check. Once, while shopping at Caesar's Palace in Las Vegas, Selena found a piece of jewelry she liked. When she looked at the price, her mother commented, "Es mucho dinero" (It's too much money).[24] Although Selena bought it anyway, like her mother, she was startled by the price. Maybe the fact that her family had struggled with finances made her more cautious with how she spent her money. Or maybe she did not see herself as a "big star," and splurging was something that "big stars" tended to do. To her fans, Selena was not *creida*, or conceited. In the spotlight, Selena was a star, a performer at the height of her power, but the fact that she considered herself *del pueblo*, of the people, forged a powerful, personal bond between her and her audience.[25]

When it came to her fans, Selena could not refuse them. They wanted to get close to her, touch her hair, get her autograph. Often, her father would have to restrain them: "The fans don't understand. Sometimes they get so excited that they can hurt you. They don't mean to hurt you, but it happens," Abraham said.[26] When fans became too enthusiastic and Selena felt overwhelmed, she would give her father a "certain look" and he would jump into action and take her to safety.

But generally, Selena has been characterized by fans and family as a caring and compassionate individual, one who gave people second chances to prove their worth, so much so that when her father made her aware of Yolanda Saldivar's embezzlement and fraud, she responded: "Dad, maybe her family needs the money."[27] Quintanilla told her to be careful with Saldivar because she was dangerous. Selena did not see the danger. She had so much faith in the goodness of people that she could not detect the murderous intentions of her once number-one fan, Saldivar.

Had she lived, Selena would have been the first Tejana recording artist to break through the language barrier and achieve international stardom.[28] Of course, for a few naysayers, this is mere speculation. But to a great extent, she accomplished this feat after her death. Her talent ranged from her entrepreneurship as a businesswoman to stints in the world of acting. Selena knew how to brand and market herself and did so by opening two clothing boutiques—one in Corpus Christi and one in San Antonio. She designed her own clothes and worked with other designers to bring her vision to fashion. Furthermore, because of her popularity in the Tejano music scene, not only was Selena invited to participate in episodes of a popular Mexican soap opera, but Hollywood also came knocking at her door. In the movie *Don Juan DeMarco*, starring Johnny Depp and Marlon Brando, Selena played a mariachi singer, a small part, but significant for a young Mexican American from the barrios of South Texas. What young Mexican American woman growing up in the dusty *colonias* of any Rio Grande Valley town would not be inspired by her? Overall, her business ventures were successful. With record sales, fees from endorsements, and sales from her boutiques, in 1994, *Hispanic Business Magazine* ranked Selena eighteenth on a list of the twenty wealthiest Hispanic entertainers.[29]

Hailed as the Queen of Tejano music, Selena had achieved legitimate gold record status even *before* she started to work on English-language recordings.[30] Selena won a Grammy in 1994 for Best Mexican American Album with her 1993 release *Selena Live!* The record that followed, *Amor Prohibido*, sold more than five hundred thousand copies. The hit single "Amor Prohibido" went to number one on the Latin International Chart, unseating Gloria Estefan, who for some time had enjoyed crossover success. Tejano music and the Tejano scene were on the rise. Selena had brought it international attention.

But Selena's accomplishments thus far were not enough. As an artist and entrepreneur, Selena had ambition. She wanted not only to conquer the Tejano market in the United States and reach Latin American countries, but to cross over into the English-language market. By the time of her death, Selena had recorded songs such as "Dreaming of You" for her first English-language album, which she hoped would bring her the kind of crossover popularity enjoyed by artists like Gloria Estefan and Jon Secada. Though she did not get to fully experience her inevitable crossover into the US mainstream music scene, she did reach US Latinos in the Puerto Rican and Cuban communities, who did not usually listen to Tejano music. Selena kept reaching the goals she had set herself as an artist and opening the way for other female artists. Her accomplishments demonstrated to young South Texas girls that *sí se puede*! Yes, you can!

Selena's Influence

Today we see the impact Selena had on women who have "made it" as international stars. Think Jennifer Peña, who took over the airwaves once Selena was gone; and Jennifer Lopez, whose international career was launched by portraying Selena in the Warner Bros. biopic; and more recently, Selena Gomez, who was named after Selena and is known for singing Selena's songs onstage. Megastars such as Beyoncé, Shakira, and Mariah Carey speak of her as someone to be admired and as an influence. Eva Longoria sums up their thoughts: "She would've been bigger than all of us."[31] What is significant about Selena's success is that she attained it not in the "Anglo 'Hollywood dream machine' market of Los Angeles nor the US 'Latin' media capital of Miami, but South Texas, the 'home of Tex-Mex music.'"[32] In doing so, she opened doors to young Latina music artists of all races and acquainted mainstream America with the borderlands.

Artists continue to remember Selena by singing her songs. In 1996, the album *Recordando a Selena* featured international artists such as Yolanda Duke, Los Jovenes del Barrio, Tito Nieves, and Manny Manuel, who sang Selena's songs. In 2012, the album *Enamorada de ti* became the latest tribute to her memory, in which Selena duets posthumously with national and international artists such as Don Omar, Selena Gomez, and Cristian Castro. The latest recordings, which are often at the top of the Billboard Top Latin charts, are evidence of Selena's popularity even now, and of her lasting contributions, even after death, to the music world.

Selena's death was a cultural moment for the Mexican American and the general Latino community. Because of Selena, American corporations realized that there was an untapped market in the Latino community. For example, *People* magazine at first ran a story about her life but soon after dedicated a complete issue to her. The first and second runs of the issue sold out completely. *People en Español* came directly out of the success of Selena's tribute issue.[33] Her fans collected the commemorative issues. They shared them with their children. Some of her fans were not even born when Selena was alive, yet they know her. Fans keep the memory of Selena intact by sharing her music and her life. They do not want to forget her determination to reach the American Dream nor the values she upheld.

What director Gregory Nava has said about his movie *Selena* is also fitting to describe Selena the artist, the entertainer, the legend: "In a certain way, *Selena* is the story of a brilliant young woman, it's the story of family, it's a story of a community struggle to break through and cross over, and it's also the story about the American Dream."[34] Once, Selena was asked how she would like to be remembered.[35] To paraphrase, she wanted to be remembered not only as an entertainer but also as someone who cared and gave the best she could, and as someone who tried to be a good role model and the best person possible.

After three hours of talking to Abraham Quintanilla about his daughter, I realized that no one in the Tejano music scene in recent years has reached Selena's success and stardom. Fans all over the world seem to agree on one thing: there will never be another Selena. Not with that voice, that laughter, and that charisma that brought millions joy and empowered countless young women all over the world to dare, to dream. As I drove back to the Rio Grande Valley, the sun began to ease itself behind the South Texas horizon. This time I did not turn on the radio. No music. Just the road ahead of me and the dying sun. *She matters*, I thought. *She'll be here for a long time.* I knew that every mile I traveled, Selena had traveled before me.

Notes

1. *People Weekly Tribute*, commemorative issue (Spring 1995), 29.
2. *People Weekly Tribute*, 30.
3. *People Weekly Tribute*, 30.
4. *People Weekly Tribute*, 30.
5. *People Weekly Tribute*, 30.
6. Cathy Ragland, "La Voz del Pueblo Tejano: Conjunto Music and the Construction of Tejano Identity in Texas," in *Puro Conjunto: An Album in Words and Pictures*, ed. Juan Tejeda and Avelardo Valdez (San Antonio: CMAS Books, 2001), 221.
7. Ramiro Burr, "Women in Conjunto Music," in *Puro Conjunto: An Album in Words and Pictures*, 88.
8. "Selena en Cristina," YouTube, accessed June 20, 2013, http://www.you tube.com/watch?v=GPu1H5KI8PA.
9. Deborah R. Vargas, "*Cruzando Frontejas*: Remapping Selena's Tejano Music 'Crossover,'" in *The Chicana/o Cultural Studies Reader*, ed. Angie Chabram-Dernersesian (New York: Routledge, 2006), 315.
10. Vargas, 320.
11. Vargas, 320.
12. Abraham Quintanilla Jr., interview with the author, Corpus Christi, TX, June 17, 2013.
13. Vargas, "*Cruzando Frontejas*," 316.
14. Vargas, 316.

15. Vargas, 316.

16. *People Weekly Tribute*, 7.

17. Christy Haubegger, quoted in Larry Rohter, "A Legend Grows, and So Does an Industry," *New York Times*, January 1997, http://www.nytimes.com/1997/01/12/arts/a-legend-grows-and-so-does-an-industry.html.

18. Rohter.

19. Vargas, "*Cruzando Frontejas*," 318.

20. Vargas, 318.

21. Vargas, 318.

22. Quintanilla, interview.

23. *People Weekly Tribute*, 23.

24. Quintanilla, interview.

25. *People Weekly Tribute*, 7.

26. Quintanilla, interview.

27. Quintanilla, interview.

28. Rick Koster, *Texas Music* (New York: St. Martin's Press, 1998), 213.

29. *Corpus Christi Caller-Times*, April 9, 1995.

30. Koster, *Texas Music*, 213.

31. "Mariah, Beyonce, Katy, Jlo, Gaga Remember Selena Quintanilla," YouTube, accessed June 7, 2013, http://www.youtube.com/watch?v=3wq3YJmFyjc.

32. Vargas, "*Cruzando Frontejas*," 320.

33. Q-Productions, accessed June 10, 2013, Q-Productions.com.

34. "Biography Selena," YouTube, accessed June 5, 2013, http://www.youtube.com/watch?v=ArQEsu9xkvo (no longer available).

35. "Mariah, Beyonce, Katy."

VI

Women of Service

14

Dr. Clotilde P. García

PAMELA WRIGHT

Mention Dr. Clotilde P. García, or "Dr. Cleo" as she was affectionately known, and many begin to tell stories similar to Francisco Guerra's. He recalls that when Dr. Cleo delivered his uncle, his *abuelo* (grandfather) had just been buried, leaving his *abuela* (grandmother) with a family of eight and little money or hope. Shortly after his grandmother's return home from the hospital with the new baby, a nurse delivered a package filled with clothes and diapers, courtesy of Dr. Cleo García. Dr. Cleo's generous show of compassion did not stop there, however; as Francisco remembers, she never charged his mother for his pediatric visits and inoculations. He says that he is "the product of one woman who had the tenacity to teach me that I was a human being, despite the poverty that is my family's legacy." Guerra concludes that she honored an entire people with her "Herculean efforts to restore the dignity of being a Mexican in America."[1]

Aida Hinojosa, following Dr. Cleo on rounds for a week, recounts the story of a young Chicana who had been stabbed to death by her boyfriend. Dr. Cleo had treated the victim since the age of six. She had even delivered the young woman's babies. Hinojosa recalls how the doctor involved herself in the family's grief and treatment: "I saw the funeral, the victim's children, her mother's grief. Cleo helped to draw me into the experience, and I felt, however faintly, the pulse of Corpus Christi."[2]

With such heart-wrenching stories, it is not hard to understand why Dr. Clotilde P. García is so revered in South Texas.

Clotilde García (1917–2003) was one of ten children born to José G. García (1887–1957) and Faustina Perez García (1887–1941) in Ciudad Victoria, Tamaulipas, Mexico. Though born in Mexico, she grew up in Mercedes, Texas, once her parents returned to the United States after her father completed college in Mexico. Her grandparents Antonio García Valverde (1859–1917) and Antonia García Pena (1860–1942) had emigrated from Camargo, Mexico, to Mercedes, Texas, in 1905 to join other relatives who were grantees of the Llano Grande land grant. Dr. Cleo's "father was a direct descendent of the Spanish pioneers and colonists who settled along the Rio Grande in 1750 under the leadership of Count Jose De Escandon, colonizer of South Texas."[3] Dr. Cleo came from such deep family roots in this area, it is little wonder that she had such a heart to serve the people of this region.

A Dream Deferred

Dr. Cleo came from an extraordinary family by any standard. Her parents were educators, and though her father's teaching credentials from Mexico were not honored in the United States, her parents instilled a deep love and appreciation for education and service into their children. Six of the ten children became physicians; one was the famous doctor, civil rights activist, and American GI Forum founder, Dr. Hector P. García. The two siblings, Hector and Cleo, were so devoted to their education that they would hitchhike from their home to Edinburg, Texas, where they attended Pan American University. Dr. Xico García, a younger sibling, recalls that the pair "would get up at 6 a.m. and eat day-old or three-day-old bread and then go out and hitchhike 30 miles to Edinburg to go to school." With that same determination, Cleo went on to complete a BA in chemistry at the University of Texas, graduating in 1938. Her intention was to move directly on to medical school; in fact, she was accepted to the University of Texas Medical Branch. Unfortunately, the Great Depression, the failure of her father's business (J. A. García and Bros. Store, a dry goods store), and the fact that her two brothers Hector and J. A. were already attending medical school conspired to keep her from those plans for the immediate future.[4]

Cleo knew that she was needed by the family, so while completing her premed courses at the University of Texas she also secured her teaching certificate. After graduation, her mother told her she should find work as a teacher to help the family. "I didn't need to be told," she recalled. "I knew my family was making extreme sacrifices to keep the two oldest in medical school. So I understood perfectly and was ready to go to work. But it broke my parents' hearts just the same."[5]

When Clotilde began searching for a teaching job, she endured the humiliation that comes with discrimination, the discrimination that she and her brother Hector would eventually fight. She was surprised that she did not receive job offers after she registered her credentials with a teachers' placement bureau in Austin. When she questioned the placement officer about the situation, he explained that "nowhere in the state of Texas would they hire 'Spanish-speaking' teachers. He didn't say 'Mexican' because that had a bad connotation. When they wanted to be nice to you, they would call you 'Spanish-speaking,'" Cleo recalled. She did, however, eventually receive a job offer for a teacher-principal combination "in the middle of rattlesnake country." She accepted it, "bought a five-dollar 'teaching dress' on credit and went to work as a teacher for the next ten years."[6]

During this time, World War II erupted, and she married a young Chicano soldier, Hipolito Canales. They had a son, J. A. "Tony" Canales, who would grow up to be an attorney in Corpus Christi. When the war ended, so did her marriage to the man who wanted her to be "strictly a housewife." Cleo now continued to teach in order to "support her son Tony, her widowed father and her younger siblings." She had "all but abandoned plans to study medicine" in order to keep her marriage. She recalls that the divorce nearly ruined her life. She explains, "Among our people divorce was a terrible stigma, and I felt like a fallen woman, a total failure. I developed a low image of myself."[7]

A Dream Finally Realized

It was her brother Hector who encouraged Cleo to apply once again to medical school and to follow her dream of becoming a doctor. She did so and was accepted into medical school at the University of Texas Medical Branch–Galveston in September 1948. Clotilde P. García became the first

Mexican American woman to attend medical school in the United States, and upon graduation she became the first Hispanic female physician and surgeon in the country. In itself, becoming a physician is quite a feat. When one compounds the rigors of medical school with the discrimination she faced while completing her degree, her accomplishment becomes even more amazing.[8]

As a rule, the University of Texas Medical School did not accept women at the time. Cleo was one of only five women admitted that year. Professors would argue that women took up valuable space and taxpayers' money because women would inevitably get married and become pregnant, whereas men would go on to make a living in the medical profession. When professors and other male students realized she already had a child at home, she was told her place was at home with that child.[9] She would often tell the story of a boy she met on the elevator her first day at school. He asked her, "Cleo, why are you here taking up a man's place? You should be home raising a family." She told him, "Why, thank you. I accept your marriage proposal." The boy never talked to her again, but she would blow kisses at him whenever she saw him.[10]

As a poor sexist joke, the five freshmen women were led to believe they would be subjected to pelvic exams by the sophomore male students. Cleo was understandably horrified and angered by this. Even though the five women might be united in their fight against this supposed threat and against discrimination and sexism in general, they were somewhat isolated. They all lived in separate rooming houses because the university had no housing facilities for women at the time. This lack of housing left little opportunity for them to study together as the male students did. The next academic year, the five "girls," as they were called by condescending male students and professors, rented a house together. They had demonstrated their resolve to complete their studies, and Clotilde eventually graduated in 1954, at thirty-seven years of age, in the top 10 percent of her class.[11]

Though she was successful, she never forgot the discrimination she endured during her first year of medical school. Years later, she maintained, "We could have used a little affirmative action in those days." She supported "a slot system in medical school regardless of the argument for standards." She believed that standards did not "have to be sacrificed to give people a chance because there are many well-qualified people who would customarily be turned away because someone 'better qualified' is selected." She argued, "That someone invariably turns out to be Anglo male."[12]

La Doctora

In July 1953, Dr. Cleo began her internship at Memorial Hospital in Corpus Christi. Again, she was extraordinary, as she was the only woman in the group of interns. At the end of her internship, she joined her brothers Dr. J. A. García and Dr. Hector P. García and began practicing medicine in Corpus Christi. At first she was one of only two women physicians in Corpus. South of San Antonio, there were only five Hispanic doctors who were educated in the United States; three of them were Garcías.[13]

Dr. García enjoyed delivering babies, delivering over ten thousand during her career at Memorial Hospital. During the early years, it was not easy. The old Memorial Hospital was not air-conditioned, and the maternity ward was a building at the back of the hospital. Expectant mothers labored and delivered their babies with only the physicians and nurses present. Despite the lack of support for obstetrics, her dedication to her profession is legendary.

Santos Gomez, LVN, began working with Dr. Cleo in 1975 and remembers her dedication to patients: "Dr. Cleo came for every delivery, any time night or day. I remember times when she would stay all night, waiting at the nurse's station, occasionally nodding off to sleep in the chair. She never left the hospital when her patients were in labor." Gomez continues, "When the time came to deliver the baby, Dr. Cleo jumped up, wide awake, ready to go. Dr. Cleo would gather all the nurses and the residents in the room and give everyone a job. She was a great teacher and would tell everyone, 'If you're not doing anything, then you're not learning.'" Nabil Elmilady, MD, worked with Dr. Cleo for more than fifteen years and has similar memories of her dedication. He remembers her saying, "Have no fear—Dr. Cleo is here." He continues, "Dr. Cleo's patients loved her, and everyone had access to her office. She filled the vacuum for those who could not pay for medical care. She was a hard-working and dedicated physician." Dr. Cleo did in fact find that discrimination in medicine was not only racial but also economic. Tony Canales, Dr. Cleo's son, also remembers his mother's dedication to her work. He explains, "Although my mother was best known for her babies—more than 10,000 that she delivered at Memorial Hospital—she was also a great surgeon and assisted her brother J. A. with many of his surgeries. In the 1950s doctors did everything. There were very few specialists. Doctors worked in the office, in the hospital and made house calls."[14] Serving so many patients, she was upset by "elitist" doctors who refused to make themselves available to everyone, especially the poor.[15]

Prejuicio

Even though Dr. Cleo had the respect of colleagues and patients for her capabilities as a physician and surgeon, she still had to endure prejudice. At one time, there were two dining rooms at Memorial Hospital—one for doctors and one for staff and guests. One day, as Dr. Cleo and her son, Tony, were going into the physicians' dining room, they were stopped by a cafeteria worker. When Cleo explained she was a physician, the worker persisted, blocking the door. Exasperated, Dr. Cleo told the worker that if she was not a doctor, then he could have their trays. She dumped the food on the floor and left, heading for the administrator's office.[16]

Dr. Cleo was infuriated by this type of injustice anywhere it occurred, and she worked shoulder to shoulder with her brother Dr. Hector P. García in fighting against prejudice toward the Mexican American community. After World War II, Hector García founded the American GI Forum in order to organize Chicano veterans. Many saw this as a radical move, but the major push was for equal rights in education, employment, and health care. Like her brother, Dr. Cleo saw the medical community as a place to "revolutionize" her "patients' attitudes toward their own survival—economic and political as well as medical."[17]

Though she never aspired to hold political office, believing her role as physician, educator, and advocate more powerful, she and her brothers J. A., Hector, and Xico were proud to help the Mexican American community find a voice. Thanks to their efforts, South Texas Mexican Americans were becoming more knowledgeable about issues like school desegregation and fair and equal employment opportunities. Look through South Texas newspapers like the *Corpus Christi Caller-Times* and the *San Antonio Express-News* from the 1950s through the 1980s, and you will be hard pressed to find an edition that does not mention the Garcías, the America GI Forum, or a cause that they championed in the Mexican American community.

La Educadora

Not just a healer and medical practitioner, Dr. Cleo believed, like her parents and siblings, in education. Because of her humble upbringing, she knew the power of education and recognized it as a key to rising above poverty. Her own life exemplified this ideal; she had gone from hitchhiking thirty miles to junior college to graduating from medical school. She completely understood that knowledge was vital to bringing honor and dignity to the Mexican American community. Perhaps two of her most important contributions to formal and equitable scholarship came in the form of her twenty-one-year tenure on the Del Mar College Board of Regents from 1960 to 1981 and her service on the Texas Constitutional Revision Commission in 1973, where she sat on the education committee.

Dr. Cleo's time on the Del Mar College Board of Regents coincided with two turbulent decades in American history. The 1960s and 1970s saw the birth of the Black civil rights movement, the women's rights movement, and desegregation in public schools. The political scene was no different in South Texas, but it included the push for rights for Mexican American citizens. Dr. Cleo used her considerable influence, backed by her brother Dr. Hector P. García, to fight for the rights of poor children during the desegregation movement in Corpus Christi, which was no small task. In 1972, out of the one hundred largest metropolitan areas in the United States, Corpus was ranked third in the nation for the number of poor and impoverished.

On August 14, 1972, Dr. Cleo made a statement to the Corpus Christi Independent School District (CCISD) board, taking it to task for being negligent in not offering free transportation to Mexican American children under a "majority to minority" transfer policy and the school system's "free transportation" policy. These policies were part of a desegregation plan that would move students, at no cost to them, from a school where they were in the ethnic "majority" to a school where they were in the "minority" if it was more than two miles away from the student's home school. In fact, a conviction of constitutional violations regarding school segregation against the CCISD had held up in the US Court of Appeals just twelve days earlier. In her statement, using the board's own policies and citing the court's findings, Dr. Cleo demanded free and equitable transportation for Mexican American students in Corpus Christi.[18]

In another show of her indomitable spirit, mere days before she made her statement before the school board, Dr. Cleo joined the voices that were calling for the resignation of CCISD superintendent Dana Williams because of what many perceived as a lack of leadership and lack of commitment to desegregation. This attempt to oust Williams, however, would be less successful than her call for equitable transportation, as he continued to hold the position until his retirement in 1981.[19]

In 1973, as part of the Texas Constitutional Revision Commission, Dr. Cleo sat on the education committee, where she and her cohorts called for any new Texas constitution to require just and equal educational funding and opportunities. Though a new Texas constitution was not approved, Cleo's participation on the committee demonstrates her fervent dedication to impartiality and her understanding of the importance of education to impoverished Mexican American students.[20]

La Feminista

Just as Dr. Cleo supported equal rights and treatment for all, she also championed the rights of women. Treating women as a physician and educating them about how to take care of their bodies and their babies contributed to the self-esteem of many women who came from great poverty and little formal education. She recalled elderly women who had never had a pelvic examination: "It took years for me to train them that the womb was a part of the body just like the eyes and ears. But the younger women caught on surprisingly fast." Dr. Cleo also saw babies that were dehydrated and malnourished. She had to battle against traditional remedies and beliefs. She instructed mothers about modern medicine and taught them how to combine their traditional teas with more nutritious formulas and medical treatments. She once stated that it took her two generations to reeducate her patients about the health and welfare of infants and the female body.[21]

Dr. Cleo was so well known for her work with impoverished women that in 1967 Sargent Shriver—American statesman and political activist, considered the architect of President Lyndon B. Johnson's "war on poverty," and founder of the Peace Corps, Jobs Corps, and Head Start educational program—personally invited her to participate in the "Conference on Women in the War on Poverty." During this conference, she and other speakers offered their advice on how women could expand their roles in the war on poverty through public and private programs. Her work did not stop there. As the 1970s brought the ERA (Equal Rights Amendment) movement to public attention, Cleo found herself in the middle of the debates as part of the Texas Women's Political Caucus. In 1974, the caucus sponsored a Chicana Educational Conference at St. Edward's University in Austin, which combined Dr. Cleo's love for education with her desire to improve the plight of Mexican American women.[22] Amid all her serious activist work, though, Dr. Cleo still maintained her signature sense of humor. While she was on the Board of Regents for Del Mar College, she participated in Corpus Christi's First Annual Women's Lib Breakfast in February 1973, where she caused a great commotion when she publicly burned her bra.[23]

In the 1980s her efforts on behalf of women earned Dr. Cleo a nomination to serve on the Corpus Christi Area Steering Committee for the Governor's Commission for Women, and in 1983 she spoke about women in education administration as part of the "Professional Women Speak" lecture series at Texas Southmost College. In this talk her feminist beliefs were evident as she encouraged the young female audience members to believe that they were just as capable as men of achieving their dreams. She told them, "You have to discipline yourselves. Forget riding around the block in cars, looking at boys. You can do that, too. You don't have to be a nun, but you do have to be dedicated." She explained to her audience that her profession meant being disciplined, being available when called on, being responsible. She continued, saying that the independence that comes with responsibility meant she could be "free to be my own person. It means I can live in a $250,000 home and drive a Cadillac because *I deserve it.*" This is truly the epitome of what Dr. Cleo hoped all Mexican American women could achieve: independence, education, good health, and prosperity.[24]

SAGA

In addition to education and health, Dr. Cleo believed it important, even necessary, to uncover the Hispanic history of the South Texas area in order to restore dignity to Mexican Americans. She maintained, "Our past should be preserved so we know who we are. We Mexican-Americans have overcome so many obstacles. For generations we were kept back and worst of all, we were conditioned to think of ourselves as inferior."[25] She argued that to know a people's history enriches the culture and provides a very definite identity; for the Hispanic community this identity was little known or not recorded in history books. She would often speak about this lack of knowledge and the need to teach Mexican history in universities and high schools: "I think it is time for us to learn of our own heritage, our history," she would say.[26] Therefore, to aid South Texans in learning who they are and to help them reclaim an important history, she wrote ten books on South Texas history, and in 1987 she founded SAGA, the Spanish American Genealogical Association.

In 1971, Dr. Cleo's historical work led her to discover a burial ground on the banks of the San Juan River near Carmago, Mexico, used by the US Army during the Mexican War in 1846. She donated her findings, including a skull with blond hair attached, to the Corpus Christi Museum.[27] In addition to this discovery of such a precious piece of Mexican history, Dr. Cleo is also responsible for several historical markers being placed throughout South Texas. She collaborated with Herminia Balli Chavala on a paper about a secular priest, Padre José Nicolas Balli, for whom Padre Island is named. This paper was written as an application for the historical markers that are now placed in Padre Balli Park on North Padre Island and near the South Padre Island "Welcome" sign. In 1986, Dr. Cleo's research was again useful in dedicating a historical marker, this time near Corpus Christi City Hall, for Captain Enrique Villarreal, a soldier, colonist, Indian fighter, and explorer who held the original title to most of what is now Nueces County.[28]

In addition to the highly visible historical markers in the area, Dr. Cleo made another, arguably more important, contribution to this region when she donated all her research and books to Texas A&M University–Corpus Christi. The collection is regarded as an educational and research resource that fills many gaps in the little-recorded history of South Texas.

When Dr. García donated her research collection, she did so to "help South Texas students identify with their Mexican-American heritage."[29] Thomas Kreneck, TAMU–CC Bell Library's associate director of Special Collections and Archives, believes Dr. Cleo's collection is one of the most significant the library has acquired, as it will aid in the university's "goal of creating a local collection of national significance." Part of the collection holds birth and death records that Dr. Cleo gathered from Mexican churches. These are extremely important documents because the records might otherwise have been lost, since churches are no longer responsible for record keeping. Dr. Cleo valued these documents because of their importance to Mexican immigrants who settled this region.[30]

Premios y reconocimientos

Dr. Clotilde P. García received many accolades for her civic work. In 1969, she was honored with a Community Leader of America Award by the Education Board Commission of Latin America for her work supporting equal education for Hispanic students. In 1972 the American GI Forum presented her with the Outstanding Citizen's Award. In 1984, Dr. Cleo was named to the first Texas Women's Hall of Fame as the first Mexican American female physician in Texas, and for her work with "civic and charitable organizations involved in education, historic preservation and emergency food, health and jobs programs." Finally, in 1989, for her genealogy work, and for her books on South Texas history, the Spanish government bestowed upon her the Medal of Honor of the Order of Isabella the Catholic from the King of Spain.[31]

Albert Einstein said, "Only a life lived for others is a life worthwhile."[32] Dr. Cleo García's life was certainly meaningful and lived for a purpose. She shepherded ten thousand souls into this world, taught thousands of women how to take care of their bodies, worked for equal rights and education for all, and diligently recorded the history of the region, benefiting generations to come. Dr. Cleo's magnetic personality can still be felt throughout South Texas. To the many anecdotes that many readily recall, I would like to add my own. As I got to know her through my research, I felt compelled to visit her grave in order to show my respect for this incredible woman. Her humble grave marker belies the giant contributions she made to this region and to the plight of the impoverished. Then again, maybe its humbleness is befitting someone who lived her life for others.

Notes

1. Francisco G. Guerra, "'Dr. Cleo' Was a Liberating Presence in the Mexican American Community," *Corpus Christi Caller-Times*, June 4, 2003.

2. Aida Hinojosa, "Clotilde P. García: Doctor of the Barrio," unpublished typescript, 3, Dr. Clotilde P. García Papers, Special Collections and Archives, Mary and Jeff Bell Library, Texas A&M University–Corpus Christi.

3. Carlos Guerra, "Dr. Cleo's Legacy of Healing and Humor," *San Antonio Express-News*, May 29, 2003; Leanne Libby, "Family and Friends Send Love to Dr. Cleo," *Corpus Christi Caller-Times*, November 12, 2000; "The Doctor Hector P. García Family," unpublished typescript, 1, Dr. Clotilde P. García Papers.

4. "Justice for My People: The Hector P. García Story," KEDT, Latino Public Broadcasting, September 17, 2007, https://lpbp.org/programs/justice-for-my-people-the-hector-p-garcia-story/; Linda Roehl, "Remembering La Doctora," *Christus Spohn* (newsletter), 2003, 4, Dr. Hector P. García Papers, Special Collections and Archives, Mary and Jeff Bell Library, Texas A&M University–Corpus Christi; Libby, "Family and Friends"; Mari Saugier, "Family Donates Dr. Cleo García's Papers," *Corpus Christi Caller-Times*, September 6, 2005; Hinojosa, "Clotilde P. García," 3.

5. Hinojosa, "Clotilde P. García," 4.

6. Hinojosa, 5.

7. Roehl, "Remembering La Doctora," 4; Carlos Guerra, "Dr. Cleo's Legacy"; Hinojosa, "Clotilde P. García," 6.

8. Bailey Calvin to Clotilde P. García, Galveston, July 1, 1948, Dr. Clotilde P. García Papers; Deborah Mann, "Marshals Named for Diez y Seis Parade," *Corpus Christi Caller-Times*, September 12, 1986.

9. Hinojosa, "Clotilde P. García," 6.

10. Carlos Guerra, "Dr. Cleo's Legacy."

11. Hinojosa, "Clotilde P. García," 7; Sara Lee Fernandez, "Dr. Clotilde P. García, Who Birthed 10,000 Babies, Dies at 86," *Corpus Christi Caller-Times*, May 28, 2003.

12. Hinojosa, "Clotilde P. García," 7–8.

13. Roehl, "Remembering La Doctora," 4.

14. Roehl, 5–6.

15. Hinojosa, "Clotilde P. García," 12.

16. Roehl, "Remembering La Doctora," 5.

17. Hinojosa, "Clotilde P. García," 10.

18. Clotilde García, "Statement on Behalf of Free Transportation under the Majority to Minority School Board Policy" (statement, CCISD Board Meeting, Corpus Christi, TX, August 14, 1972).

19. Anne Dodson, "William Bonilla Quits Post on School Desegregation Panel," *Corpus Christi Caller-Times*, August 7, 1974.

20. "Unit Urges School Equality Requirements in Constitution," *Corpus Christi Caller-Times*, July 12, 1973.

21. Hinojosa, "Clotilde P. García," 10.

22. David S. North (from the White House) to Hector P. García, Washington, DC, April 21, 1967, Dr. Hector P. García Papers; "Caucus Takes Aims on Goals," *Corpus Christi Caller-Times*, August 17, 1975; Cathy Soete, "Caucus Warned of Dangers," *Corpus Christi Caller-Times*, August 17, 1975; Chicana Educational Conference agenda, sponsored by Texas Women's Political Caucus, Chicana Caucus, St. Edward's University, Austin, TX, February 23, 1974, Dr. Hector P. García Papers.

23. Margaret Ramage, "Few Targets 'Ms.'d," *Corpus Christi Caller-Times*, February 19, 1974.

24. Governor's Commission for Women Corpus Christi Area Steering Committee to Clotilde P. García, Austin, TX, April 27, 1984, Dr. Clotilde P. García Papers; Sallyanne Holtz, "'Women's Barriers Down,' Says Dr. Clotilde García," *Brownsville Herald*, April 8, 1983.

25. Hinojosa, "Clotilde P. García," 13; Mike Bratten, "Genealogical Group Leads *Familias* to Their Roots," *Corpus Christi Caller-Times*, n.d., Dr. Clotilde P. García Papers.

26. Ben Goodwin, "LULAC Speaker Touts Mexican History," *Corpus Christi Caller-Times*, May 6, 1987.

27. "Local Doctor Locates Bones Believed Mexican War Dead," *Corpus Christi Caller-Times*, March 14, 1971.

28. "Dr. García, Herminia Balli Chavala Collaborate on Padre Balli Paper," Dr. Clotilde P. García Papers; "Historical Markers to be Dedicated," *Corpus Christi Caller-Times*, April 18, 1986.

29. "Personal Collection of Papers and Books Donated to Library by Dr. Clotilde García," *Texas A&M University–Corpus Christi Island Waves*, August 3, 1994, 1.

30. Saugier, "Family Donates."

31. "Clotilde P. García," Texas Women's Hall of Fame, Texas Woman's University, accessed June 15, 2013, https://twu.edu/twhf/honorees/clotilde-p-garcia/; Fernandez, "Dr. Clotilde P. García."

32. "Albert Einstein Quotes," Quotespedia, accessed June 29, 2013, https://www.quotespedia.org/authors/a/albert-einstein/only-a-life-lived-for-others-is-a-life-worthwhile-albert-einstein/.

15

Merideth L. Howard

JENNI VINSON AND
RICHARD P. SPAINHOUR

If you mention Merideth L. Howard to many people, you may get a blank stare or quizzical expression. But to military historians, to grateful beneficiaries of her service, and most importantly to those who knew her, Merideth L. Howard was a consequential figure. A quick look for her name on the internet will reveal a multitude of articles and sites dedicated to her memory. Most of these articles focus on her last few years of life, during her military service. Although her military service is a defining part of her life, her impact on her community reaches far beyond her profession as a soldier.

Corpus Christi Beginnings

Merideth was born in Corpus Christi, Texas, on July 2, 1954. She was the only child of Frank Howard and Mildred Elisabeth Hill. Her father worked in the Corpus Christi area as a local dentist. Merideth had strong ties to her family. She and her father were always close; many people would say they were best friends. Not only were they close, but her parents instilled in her a strong desire to be the best, which she carried throughout her life.

In 1968, at age fourteen, Merideth started attending Haas Middle School in Corpus Christi. There she met Melissa Addison, who became a great friend. The girls ensured that they had most of their classes together so that they could spend more time with each other throughout the day and work together on homework.[1] During middle school Merideth became heavily involved with sports, particularly tennis. She constantly drove herself, never settling for anything less than her best effort. The school did not have a coed tennis team, having a boys-only and a girls-only league. She often questioned why she could not compete against the boy's league since she believed in free competition.

During her high school years, she attended the same school as her cousin, Debbie Stevenson. Although they seldom had classes together, Debbie would sometimes spend the night at the Howards' home. During these visits, she noticed that Merideth was close to her family and influenced by their values. Her relationship with her father was genuine, and she inherited many of his traits and work ethic as well as his humor. Family was her cornerstone and gave her the courage and individuality to "not sweat the girly stuff." While many of her peers were consistently worried about teenage crushes and boyfriends, she exclaimed, "That is just plain silly."[2]

During her high school years, Merideth also enjoyed water sports and fishing. Growing up in Corpus Christi, constantly surrounded by the waters of the Gulf of Mexico, made it natural for her to take an interest in aquatic adventures. She spent countless hours fishing near her home, and according to many of the Laguna Madre locals, she became a great fisher and crabber. Merideth graduated from King High School in 1973. With her natural affinity for the water, she decided to pursue an education that would enable her to remain close to it. She earned both a bachelor's and a master's degree in marine resource management at Texas A&M University at College Station, where she also helped establish and participated in the first women's tennis team at the university.

Merideth's first major life challenge came as a result of her passion for marine study. Although she loved the water and spent most of her life near it, she was unable to fully immerse herself in marine management. After graduating, she became increasingly seasick each time she conducted a research mission aboard a boat. Sadly, this growing sickness inhibited her ability to conduct the type of research she hoped to accomplish. So, instead of staying with her degree and doing research only at a reduced capacity, she decided to find another career she could be as passionate about. Luckily, she found that passion in firefighting.

Wanting to remain close to the water, she tried to get a position with a fire station in her hometown of Corpus Christi. She attended fire school training at College Station, one of the nation's best schools for firefighters. The facility, Brayton Fire School, has the largest live-fueled firefighter training facility in the world. She became the second female ever to graduate from the school. While there, she stood out from the crowd, always going above and beyond. "She was one dynamic woman," said David White, her fire school instructor and now publisher of *Industrial Fire World* magazine in College Station. "She was a good, dedicated, hard worker. She always did more than what was expected. . . . What she didn't have in strength, she made up for with determination."[3]

At the time, none of the Corpus Christi stations would hire a female firefighter. The only way for her to become a firefighter was to take a position in Bryan, Texas, near her university. In 1978 she joined the Bryan City Fire Department and became the first female to be hired. She worked as an engine driver at Station #1 for about three and a half years. "While there, she gained the respect of her colleagues, no easy task, being the lone woman in an all male department, but she was more than up to the challenge. Innovative, she developed a way to recharge the department's respiration tanks on site. Compassionate, Howard helped start a car wash to benefit the Muscular Dystrophy Association and 'Jerry's kids.'"[4]

She continued to excel at her job until one day, after a colleague died while fighting an apartment fire, Howard decided her job was too dangerous. Following her passion for firefighting, she began a career as a fire risk management specialist. Now instead of responding to fires, she had the chance to prevent them from occurring. In 1985, her work took her to Alameda, California, where she was employed by Industrial Risk Insurers in fire safety and investigations.

On to California and Wisconsin

Although she worked hard, the insurance company did not offer many benefits. She always feared that she would one day wake up and realize that she was an old lady who had nothing to show for her life and end up living on the streets. So, in 1988, she joined the US Army Reserve. Enlisting ensured that she had access to multiple medical and retirement benefits while giving her the opportunity to serve her country. She felt it was her duty to serve the people around her, and military service would enable her to meet her calling. When she arrived at basic training, only a few of her instructors and none of her fellow trainees had ever seen such an old woman show up at boot camp (she was thirty-two at the time). Her age never bothered Merideth; she used the fact that she was the oldest one in class as a motivation. After graduating from basic training, Merideth was assigned to Fort Sam Houston to complete Advanced Individual Training (AIT), where she would become an army medical equipment repairer. Immediately after completing this training, she advanced to the rank of specialist. Her first Army Reserve duty assignment was with Headquarters, 6253rd US Army Hospital, Hamilton Army Airfield, Novato, California. Balancing the reserve with her full-time job was often a challenge. After logging forty-plus hours a week at her normal job, she spent half her weekends conducting drill at the airfield.

In 1991, Merideth met Hugh Hvolboll through a mutual friend. At the time, Hugh worked for Lockheed Martin Corporation as an engineer and lived in nearby Concord, California. Hugh was fascinated by fireworks and on holidays would work as a pyrotechnician at a fireworks company in the area. Although the commute between Merideth and Hugh was only thirty minutes, their jobs kept them quite busy. Often the only chance they had to see one another was on the weekends when she was not consumed by her duties with the Army Reserve. That meant she was normally available on holiday weekends. Since Hugh was normally busy on those weekends, she would help him with his work. Merideth and Hugh would often have humorous conversations about the disparity between their chosen professions. She once stated, "You set them off, and I'll decide how much damage they cause."[5]

In 1992, after serving in her position in the reserve for many years, Merideth was promoted to sergeant as a medical noncommissioned officer. This promotion caused her to change her military occupational specialty to medical health care specialist. Now a leader in the armed forces, she dedicated even more of her time to her military profession. She did not stay in this position long, however; in 1994 she was approaching the end of her enlistment contract. Since her unit of assignment was in the initial stages of being disbanded (the unit was completely disbanded by 1996), she decided to transfer into the Individual Ready Reserve (IRR). This decision enabled her to spend more time with her boyfriend, and although she would no longer be paid by the federal government, it allowed her to maintain many of her military benefits while continuing to accrue time in service to count toward retirement.

By 2000 Merideth had accumulated enough experience and assets in fire management to open her own business. She created a company called Fire Protection Solutions, which specialized in consulting and in assessing structures for inherent fire risk. Her expertise would allow companies to improve their structures, thereby reducing the risk of accidental damage by fire. Not long after, Hugh was laid off from Lockheed Martin and went to work full time as a fireworks technician. Soon he became a partner in Fireworks America, a nationwide pyrotechnic company based out of San Diego, causing him to move to Waukesha, Wisconsin, in 2004. Merideth decided she would move with him.

Both Hugh and Merideth were enjoying their lives together in Wisconsin when she received some unexpected news. In mid-2005, Merideth was notified by the IRR that she was being called to active duty for service in the Global War on Terror. Fifty-one years old at the time, she never thought she would be involved with the war; it had been eleven years since she had left the Army Reserve. Being the hardworking individual that she was, she never once complained.

Concerned about the inherent dangers of war, she and Hugh finally decided to get married. Although they had been together for fourteen years, they had been content not to get married until now. Without a marriage certificate, Hugh would have no connection to the military in the event something happened to her, no matter how long they had been together. As a spouse, Hugh would have access to all the privileges and resources the army could offer. So, on December 28, 2005, Hugh and Merideth were married. The ceremony happened very quickly, as neither Merideth nor Hugh wanted an extravagant event. Their plan was to make it official before she left; once she returned home, they would take the time to go on their honeymoon.

A few years had passed since she had ceased drilling with a reserve unit, so Merideth was sent to school to prepare for her upcoming deployment as part of the army's mobilization process. By 2006, the military had adopted a counterinsurgency strategy in Afghanistan. A key component of that strategy was the implementation of civil affairs in operations, which resulted in a shortage of civil affairs–trained personnel across the army. So when Merideth was completing the mobilization process, she was sent to the mobilized civil affairs course at the US Army John F. Kennedy Special Warfare Center and School in Fort Bragg, North Carolina. This course focused on how to win the hearts and minds of the Afghan people. Now newly trained, Merideth was assigned to the 364th Civil Affairs Brigade, headquartered in Portland, Oregon.

In February 2006, Merideth was given an opportunity to take leave prior to the deployment. Upon returning home, she expressed some dissatisfaction with her ability to quickly disassemble and reassemble her military firearm. In keeping with her attitude of never accepting anything less than her best, she had Hugh buy her a civilian model M-16 (AR-15). During her leave, instead of relaxing as many other soldiers were doing, she was practicing with her newly purchased rifle. She spent an entire weekend disassembling and reassembling her weapon. She became so proficient that she was eventually able to conduct the procedure while blindfolded. In the days prior to her departure, she spoke with many of her friends and family. Although she was the one going to a hostile and dangerous place, she would tell everyone else to be careful until she got back.

Finally, Afghanistan

On April 17, 2006, she deployed to Mehtarlam (150 kilometers east of the capital city, Kabul) and was assigned to a provincial reconstruction team (PRT). A PRT is an interim civil-military organization designed to operate in semipermissive environments, usually following open hostilities. The PRT is intended to improve stability in an area by helping build the host nation's legitimacy and effectiveness in providing security to its citizens and delivering essential government services.[6] Merideth and her team conducted a relief-in-place with a team that had just completed a year-long deployment in the area. This team was one of twenty-four that were operating in Afghanistan that year. Initially, Merideth was assigned to managing the Commander's Emergency Response Program (CERP), an integral part of the PRT's mission. Since a PRT is supposed to improve government services for its population, it needs to inject money into the local economy in order to spur growth and start projects that will build infrastructure. The CERP enabled local commanders in Afghanistan to respond to urgent, small-scale, humanitarian relief and reconstruction projects that immediately assisted the indigenous population and that the local population or government could sustain. The Department of Defense (DOD) defines as urgent any chronic or acute inadequacy of an essential good or service that in the judgment of the local commander calls for immediate action.[7]

As the CERP manager, Merideth was responsible for millions of dollars. She also had to track the progress and funding for all the civil projects in the province that both the PRT and the coalition maneuver commander were conducting to ensure that all the different organizations maintained synchronized effort. In addition to managing the CERP for the PRT, she also conducted humanitarian aid missions. Laghman Province was a particularly poor area, and the citizens needed assistance. Merideth once described the local situation to a friend: "We have a good relationship with the people here in the village and, of course, as everybody in Afghanistan they are in need."[8]

One of the projects that Merideth took extra interest in was lunchbox distribution to the young children of the city. She was always very interested in improving the lives of Afghan children: "We wanted to do a humanitarian drop here so we can help the kids out. We're giving them some backpacks for school. Most of the kids are in school, even if it's just a few hours a day."[9] The PRT was constructing a school for the children in the area to attend; as an incentive to increase attendance the team would conduct periodic missions to distribute lunchboxes filled with school supplies to all the children who were attending the school.

Between her duties and responsibilities, Merideth would spend time getting to know all the personnel on the base. She would often spend her evenings in front of her CHU (containerized housing unit), basically a portion of a trailer, conversing with other soldiers who lived near her. But Merideth was never fully satisfied with staying on the base and organizing paperwork. Within a couple of months of arriving in-country, the PRT became shorthanded because of a non-combat-related injury, and some of its personnel were transferred to other units. Since the team still had to travel to its objectives and make weekly logistical trips to Bagram Air Base along dangerous roads, it needed someone to fill the position of gunner. Merideth quickly volunteered for the position. Despite the increased danger of being a gunner (gunners had 40 percent of their bodies exposed outside the protection of the armored high-mobility multipurpose wheeled vehicle, or HMMWV), Merideth continually performed this duty. Since she was only 5'4" tall and she had to see over the steel shield at the front of the turret, she constructed a wooden box to stand on to provide additional height so she could see her surroundings; however, her new platform also left her more exposed to danger. Despite these additional dangers, Merideth loved being a gunner; not only did it give her an opportunity to get off the base, but it inspired many of the locals. Air force senior airman Brenda Patterson explains:

> For Afghans in this conservative tribal area, where most women wear burqas that cover everything, it must have been a bizarre sight: a gray-haired woman in a helmet on top of a HMMWV. . . . That's why SFC. Howard loved the turret; she wanted to give little girls dreams of their own."[10]

Merideth was getting into a great rhythm. Now she was able to do all the things she wanted to do. She was excited that she was not stuck in an office all day. In some of her correspondence with her husband, she wrote about how much she enjoyed this new job and was even thinking of extending her tour so she could stay longer. She felt that her actions were having a lasting impact on the local community.

Then, on September 8, 2006, the unimaginable happened. A supply run to Bagram Air Base, north of Kabul, occurred every month or two. On this trip, the soldiers picked up mail, ammunition, supplies, and three new HMMWVs with adjustable platforms for the gunner. For the first time, Howard would not need her wooden box. On that Friday morning, the convoy of five HMMWVs left the base. Staff Sergeant Robert

Joseph Paul and Howard were alone because they planned to pick up two other people at the US Embassy in Kabul. At Camp Phoenix, just outside Kabul, the soldiers dropped off one HMMWV with transmission problems and a second HMMWV pulling a trailer of ammunition. The other three vehicles made their way down Jalalabad Road, Kabul's suicide bomb alley. The convoy headed for the embassy. A Lexus SUV pulled up behind the third HMMWV. A blue Toyota Corolla followed the Lexus. Witnesses said the Corolla tried to pass the Lexus on the left. The Lexus blocked the Corolla and started trying to pass the convoy on the left but was blocked. The gunner on the third HMMWV told soldiers after the attack that he was focused on the Lexus, warning it to stop. At the same time, the blue Corolla moved up on the right. One soldier in the third HMMWV saw the back of the driver's head and his blue shirt. Another soldier noticed the brake lights. And they all watched as the car swerved into the second HMMWV, bounced off, and then swerved in again. Everything seemed slow, the soldiers said, slow enough to notice the driver's face as he pulled in the last time—his mustache, no beard. And then a loud explosion, a flash, and everything was on fire. The blast left a six-foot-wide crater in the road, killing at least eight Afghans.

The soldiers hoped for survivors in the second HMMWV, that somehow no one had died. But the medic never even got to open his bag. Howard and Paul, who did most things together on the base, who always referred to each other politely by rank and last name, were killed in the same instant.[11]

Before she left for Afghanistan, Merideth had updated her will with instructions not to bury her remains in the ground. Hugh honored this request by doing something special. After Sergeant 1st Class Merideth L. Howard received full military honors at her funeral ceremony, Hugh had her remains cremated. Then he had her ashes separated into two parts. The first half was sent to Corpus Christi, her hometown. The second half was sent to San Francisco, near the home where she spent most of her adult life. He enlisted the assistance of the Patriot Guard (a nonprofit civilian motorcycle group dedicated to honoring fallen soldiers) to escort her ashes to their destinations. Hugh used his connections at the fireworks manufacturing facility to have her ashes placed inside actual fireworks. In November 2006 he blasted her ashes over Corpus Christi Bay in a firework barrage. On December 29, 2006 (the day after their wedding anniversary), the second half of her remains were combined with her mother's and blasted over San Francisco Bay.

Although her life was cut short, she made a lasting impression on everyone she met. By living life to the fullest and always striving to be the best in every endeavor, she inspired those around her and brought out the best in others. Even after her passing, her impact is still felt, both here in South Texas and in eastern Afghanistan.

Notes

1. Melissa Addison, interview by Jenni Vinson, November 5, 2013.

2. Debbie Stevenson, interview by Lieutenant Colonel Richard Spainhour, November 5, 2013.

3. "California's War Dead," *Los Angeles Times*, accessed November 5, 2013, http://projects.latimes.com/wardead/search/?q=Howard.

4. R. Bridges, "Remembering Merideth Howard, the Oldest American Servicewoman Killed in Combat," interview by M. Ghost, Iraqi Bloggers Central, http://www.jarrarsupariver.blogspot.com/ (blog discontinued).

5. Hugh Hvolboll, interview by Jenni Vinson, 2013.

6. *PRT Playbook* (Fort Leavenworth, KS: Center for Army Lessons Learned, September 2007), 07.34.

7. *Commander's Guide to Money as a Weapon System* (Fort Leavenworth, KS: Center for Army Lessons Learned, April 2009), 09.27.

8. *Commander's Guide to Money.*

9. Bridges, "Remembering Merideth Howard."

10. Bridges.

11. K. Barker and J. Janega, "Merideth L. Howard," Iraq/Afghanistan War Heroes, accessed September 24, 2006, https://iraqwarheroes.org/howardm.htm.

16

Paving the Way for the Next Generation

JODY A. MARÍN

Arnold Gonzáles's mural *Mujeres a Través del Tiempo* memorializes the women pioneers of South Texas as fighters and survivors. These women consistently struggled against and overcame patriarchal, racial, and social oppressions to become leaders, innovators, and professionals, showing future generations of South Texas women how to create the changes needed to ensure the equality and professionalization of all women in South Texas.

Gonzáles begins the mural with the image of *la soldadera*, the epitome of strength, resilience, integrity, and feminism in early South Texas. During a time when women were considered properties of their fathers and husbands, women's participation in frontline infantry as revolutionary leaders, soldiers, ammunition smugglers, and nurses during the Mexican Revolution of 1910 transformed the image of women and what women could do. The strength of *las soldaderas* emboldened South Texas women to break from prescriptive and oppressive gender roles to create their own identity as leaders who served their communities. It is only fitting that *la soldadera*, with the dignity, respect, and integrity of a salute, welcomes *las mujeres* in the mural and pays homage to their respective struggles and successes.

The successes of *las mujeres* are also attributed to progressive education reform, which emphasized citizenship and democracy. South Texas

State Teachers College (now Texas A&M University–Kingsville), the first higher education institution in South Texas, was part of that educational movement. Founders of South Texas State Teachers College—the college's first president, Robert B. Cousins; Kingsville's longtime superintendent of schools J. N. Bigbee; owner of Kingsville's expansive King Ranch Robert J. Kleberg Jr.; and Texas senator A. E. Wood—envisioned an academic institution that would transform South Texas by creating access to higher education in rural areas of the region, graduating teachers dedicated to service, and growing a middle-class leadership, many of whom were women. In fact, Gonzáles's tribute is in many ways reminiscent of what Cousins envisioned for graduates.

Cousins foretold the importance of graduates of South Texas State Teachers College to future generations when he penned "A Message to the Students" in the first volume of *El Rancho*, the college's annual:

> In the years to come those who follow in your tracks will be interested to see the faces and finger prints that you have left here, and will be influenced by the traditions which you have begun. I am glad to believe that your foundation will bear safely the weight of a great superstructure. The strengthened purposes of the best of you, and the changing spirit of the rest of you give evidence of the presence of a wholesome atmosphere about the college which you yourselves have helped to create.[1]

What made South Texas State Teachers College a "great superstructure" were the ideological foundations on which it was built—democracy, patriotism, and philanthropy—which created a call to service for all college graduates. Cousins explained this call to service to future graduates: "In a few years we shall be out in the world men and women, shoulder to shoulder, helping the big world to carry its load. Your task is already laid out and is waiting for you. Arise and gird yourself, and repair to your place of service."[2] This chapter pays homage to the women who instilled a philanthropic call to service in students of South Texas State Teachers College (and its successive names) and those female graduates who answered it.

Female graduates fulfilled their philanthropy in various ways in the fields of their major discipline. For most female graduates of South Texas State Teachers College, later renamed the Texas College of Arts and Industries, the top two majors were English and education. Thus, most early female graduates of South Texas's first institution of higher learning became teachers in South Texas schools.

South Texas superintendents recruited their new teachers from the college largely because of their skill in teaching monolingual Spanish-speaking students, a large demographic in South Texas that often took two academic years to pass a grade level as a result of the language barrier and discrimination against Mexican Americans.[3] In fact, in Elsa, Texas, in the 1930s and 1940s, many Mexican American elementary students were often detained in the first and second grades for multiple years, making some "11 or 12 years-old and still in the first or second grade."[4] As a result, many Mexican American students stopped attending school because they felt discouraged at their lack of educational progress. In an attempt to close this educational gap, South Texas superintendents sought teachers who could work with these monolingual Spanish-speaking students. These new teachers were trained by Lila Baugh, South Texas State Teachers College professor of education, director of student teaching in the grades, and dean of women.

Lila Baugh

Baugh earned a bachelor of arts from Carlton College in Kentucky Town, Texas, and a master of education from the University of Texas at Austin. After earning her degrees, Baugh began her teaching career in Houston public schools, where she served as teacher and principal for nearly twenty years. In addition, Baugh coauthored five volumes of *New American Readers*, primary and secondary school readers that focused on the development of reading and vocabulary skills through patriotic- and Christian-themed stories. During her tenure with the Houston school district, Baugh met Robert B. Cousins, then superintendent of Houston public schools. Impressed with Baugh's teaching and administrative career and with the success of her educational series *New American Readers*, Cousins, who was appointed president of South Texas State Teachers College, asked Baugh to teach at the college. Baugh accepted and began developing a curriculum that she believed would shorten the time it took monolingual Spanish-speaking students to complete their grade level.[5] However, Baugh's curriculum was controversial and problematic because it called for the segregation and "Americanization" of monolingual Spanish-speaking students.

Baugh recognized that English-speaking children and non-English-speaking children did not have the same "control of the [English] vernacular." As such, Baugh, along with an Educational Survey Commission created by the Texas legislature, believed that both groups would progress better if they were segregated. However, Baugh and the Educational Survey Commission feared that segregation would create discrimination: "In some instances it has been used for the purpose of giving Mexican children a shorter school year, inferior building equipment, and poorly paid teachers." Nevertheless, Baugh and the commission ensured that the decision to segregate English-speaking and non-English-speaking children was based solely "on educational principles."[6]

Baugh's pedagogy centered on English-only instruction that emphasized personal hygiene and social behavior.[7] This "Americanization" approach has since been deemed patronizing, oppressive, and discriminatory toward non–English speakers. As such, to include Baugh in this anthology of South Texas revolutionary women is personally afflicting, but her exclusion would be to deny the historical linguistic, educational, and cultural oppressions suffered by Mexican American students during this time and the well-intentioned yet overtly discriminatory educational practices in our earliest years as a region and nation. Baugh's educational approach for these children was viewed as progressive and groundbreaking at the time and eventually influenced the college to create a doctoral program in bilingual education, the first of its kind in the nation.

The college, renamed the Texas College of Arts and Industries in 1929, memorialized Baugh upon her death in 1941. Editors of the college annual *El Rancho* wrote that Baugh's "untiring efforts were to unlock and make fruitful the latent powers of our student body," recognizing Baugh as one of the college's foremothers who instilled a philanthropic call to service in students.[8] In addition, the college built the Lila Baugh Hall, a residence hall for female students. Interestingly, the next influential South Texas woman to be discussed resided in Baugh Hall while a student at the Texas College of Arts and Industries.

Lola Lee Bonner

Lola Lee Bonner, a native of the small South Texas coastal township of Gregory, attended the Texas College of Arts and Industries from 1950 to 1953. During her time at the college, Bonner excelled in her studies and dedicated herself to service in the form of student government and student-run organizations. Bonner was the first female Student Council president at the college. In addition, she participated in the following student-run organizations, where she often served as an officer: Delta Theta Sorority, the Women's Recreational Association, the Health and Physical Education Club, the Forensic Society, and Pi Kappa Delta: National Honorary Forensic Society.[9] Participating and serving in these organizations prepared Bonner for her callings later in life as a lawyer, humanitarian, and philanthropist.

Upon earning a bachelor of science in health and physical education from the Texas College of Arts and Industries in 1953, Bonner enrolled in the law program at the University of Texas at Austin. She earned a bachelor of laws from the University of Texas in 1958 and became a member of the Texas State Bar, after which she moved to Rockport, Texas, to begin her private law practice. Bonner was a successful lawyer in South Texas who tried cases in local courtrooms, the Supreme Court of Texas, and the US Supreme Court. As exemplified by her time as a student at the Texas College of Arts and Industries, Bonner was passionate about a variety of issues and determined to make a difference by serving her community, where she became a trailblazer and "pioneer for women in the county."[10]

Bonner was the first in many of her community service roles. For example, she was the first female president of the Rockport-Fulton Area Chamber of Commerce and the Aransas County Bar Association, the first woman elected as chair of the Democratic Executive Committee, and the first woman elected to the First National Bank of Rockport's Board of Directors. In addition, Bonner served as a trustee for the nonprofit Margaret Sue Rust Foundation; served on the Board of Directors of Aransas County Medical Services, a nonprofit organization that provides ambulance services to the area; served on Texas's School Land Board; and founded the Texas Maritime Museum, the official maritime museum for the state of Texas. Moreover, Bonner actively raised funds for social and cultural programs, such as the Rockport Center for the Arts, the Aransas First land trust, and Aransas County Independent School District's nonprofit Education Foundation. For these selfless philanthropic acts of service Bonner was awarded the Distinguished Alumni Award from Texas A&I University (formerly South Texas State Teachers College and Texas College of Arts and Industries), the first woman to receive the award since its inauguration.[11]

Bonner was truly a pioneer for South Texas women. She used her intelligence and ambition to help others and serve her community. In so doing, she was the first woman in many areas to break through patriarchal restraints in South Texas and create new, progressive realities for South Texas women. As stated in the *Rockport Pilot* newspaper after her passing in 2008, Bonner "touched the lives of so many people in so many ways over the years"[12] that the fruits of her service to her community will continue as future South Texas women look to Bonner's legacy for inspiration to persevere and serve their community.

Norma Elia Cantú

Another alumna of Texas A&I University who has dedicated herself to the service of others is internationally renowned Chicana scholar, author, folklorist, and educator Dr. Norma Elia Cantú, professor of English and Latino studies. Cantú was born in 1947 and raised in the US-Mexico border town of Laredo, Texas. The oldest of eleven children, Cantú pursued a college degree out of high school but had to drop out after one year to help her family financially. During this one year of college, however, Cantú faced racism and classism from her educators. In "Centering the Margins: A Chicana in the English Classroom," Cantú explains how her English professor stopped giving her As on essays after learning she had graduated from a public high school instead of a private high school like the other A students in the class, who were Anglo.[13] Cantú, who was raised in a proud working-class monolingual Spanish-speaking home, also describes the linguistic terrorism enacted by her speech professor: "The speech professor became one of my tormentors. In his efforts to eradicate the heavy Spanish accent of our speech, he taunted and teased and made fun of our mispronounced 'sheet' and 'keys.' One day I ran out of his class crying; I swore I would not return."[14] Cantú did return, however; she was not ready to give up on her dream of becoming a teacher, a teacher who would embrace diversity, not scrutinize it.

After taking several years off to help her family, Cantú graduated cum laude from Texas A&I at Laredo (now Texas A&M International University) with a double major in English and political science. In 1973, Cantú was accepted into the English graduate program at Texas A&I University (formerly South Texas State Teachers College and Texas College of Arts and Industries), where she was awarded a teaching assistantship; her dream of becoming a teacher had come true. During her assistantship, Cantú found that she related to the mostly working-class students of Texas A&I: "My students at Texas A&I were similarly positioned. Sons and daughters from working-class communities in South Texas."[15] Cantú further explained, "To my Chicano and Chicana students I became a link to home. I recall one particularly homesick group of undergraduates from Laredo who came over one evening; we had baloney sandwiches and Kool-Aid for supper."[16] Cantú was not only an educator; she was a mentor, role model, and *comadre* (friend) to her students (the benefits of which I would personally experience). After graduating from Texas A&I University with a master of science in English, Cantú was accepted to the English doctoral program at the University of Nebraska–Lincoln, where she was awarded a teaching assistantship, a Ford Foundation Graduate Fellowship, a Fulbright-Hays Research Fellowship, and a Ford Foundation Chicano Dissertation Completion Grant. Cantú earned her doctor of philosophy in English in 1982 from the University of Nebraska–Lincoln.

While earning her doctorate, Cantú moved back to Laredo to teach at Laredo State University (formerly Texas A&I University at Laredo; currently Texas A&M International University), where she continued teaching until 2000, earning tenure as a full professor of English. Cantú then taught at the University of Texas at San Antonio and served as the graduate adviser for its English doctoral program until 2013. After a few years as full professor of Latino studies and English at the University of Missouri–Kansas City, Cantú returned to South Texas and, at the time of this writing, is the Murchison Professor in the Humanities at Trinity University in San Antonio, Texas. Regarding the breadth of her teaching career, Cantú has said, "Teaching and working in an academic setting is when I feel most alive. The educational environment is where I feel I have had the most impact."[17]

In addition to teaching, Cantú has authored many critical multigenre scholarly works that have significantly contributed to border studies, women's studies, cultural studies, feminist studies, Chicano literature, and folklore. Cantú's scholarship has earned her many academic honors, grants, and awards, including Fellow of the American Folklore Society, Exceptional Texas Woman, National Association of Chicana and Chicano Studies Scholar of the Year, Américo Paredes Prize, Distinguished Scholar Award from the Division on Chicana and Chicano Literature of the Modern Languages Association, Award of Merit from the Association of Women in Communications, Premio Aztlán, and Webb County Heritage Award for Publication. One of Cantú's most well-known and internationally acclaimed works is *Canícula: Snapshots of a Girlhood en la Frontera*, a "fictional autobioethnography," a memoir of Cantú's childhood in Laredo during the "dog days of summer."[18] As an undergraduate student at Texas A&M International University, I was first introduced to Cantú through this work. My second encounter with Cantú would be in person, and it would change the course of my life.

I met Cantú in spring 2000; it was the first semester of my junior year at Texas A&M International University in Laredo and my first semester as an English major. I was working behind the counter at FedEx, and one Saturday afternoon that spring, in walked this woman with long, straight black hair. She gave a slight smile and then went to fill out her airway bill. When she came to the counter and handed it to me, I recognized her name as the author of *Canícula*. I was so excited to meet her. I informed her that we had just read *Canícula* in my English class and that I had enjoyed it. While I processed her package, Cantú asked me about my educational plans. I told her I was getting a bachelor's degree in English, with hopes of teaching high school. She asked whether I had thought about getting a master's degree. When I informed her that I had not, she stated that I would have more opportunities with a master's degree and even more with a PhD. She then gave me her card and explained that she was the English graduate adviser at the University of Texas at San Antonio. She urged me to contact her if I had questions about the program. I thanked her and put her card in my pocket. A couple of years later, I graduated and began teaching at a high school in Laredo. Almost immediately I knew that this career path was not for me. I quit teaching and went back to school. During my first semester in my English master's program, my father lost his job, so my family and I moved back to our hometown of Alice, Texas, and I continued my English master's degree at Texas A&M University–Corpus Christi. During my last year there, I participated in the university's annual Author's Day workshop, for which Cantú was the guest author. She recognized me as soon as she saw me. She gave me a big smile and an *abrazo*. Then she went straight to it: "Have you thought about getting your PhD?" I smiled and told her no. She gave me her card again and urged me to email her about the University of Texas at San Antonio's English doctoral program. Again, I thanked her and put her card in my pocket. After I graduated with my master's degree, I struggled to make ends meet as an adjunct lecturer. Cantú's words came back to me—"you'll have more opportunities with a PhD"—so I applied to the University of Texas at San Antonio's English doctoral program and earned my PhD a few years later. I discuss my experiences with Cantú because she positively changed my life. I am a testament to Cantú's dedication to and mentorship of others, especially future generations of South Texas women.

Eva Jacqueline Longoria Bastón

Another alumna of the university (now Texas A&M University–Kingsville [TAMUK], formerly South Texas State Teachers College, Texas College of Arts and Industries, and Texas A&I University) dedicated to serving others is Eva Jacqueline Longoria Bastón, actress, director, producer, author, restaurateur, and philanthropic political activist. Best known for her award-winning role as Gabrielle Solis in ABC's television series *Desperate Housewives*, Longoria Bastón has now made a name for herself as a philanthropic political activist who has used her star power as a megaphone to bring attention to issues that impact Latino communities, such as education attainment, college readiness, entrepreneurship, agricultural labor laws, and immigration reform. In addition, she has created, funded, and advocated for numerous foundations that help women, children, parents, educators, and immigrants, specifically within Latino communities.

The youngest of four sisters, Longoria Bastón was born on March 15, 1975, in Corpus Christi, Texas, to working-class parents Enrique Longoria Jr. and Ella Eva Mireles Longoria. After high school, Longoria Bastón enrolled at TAMUK, where she earned a bachelor of science in kinesiology in 1997. During her tenure at TAMUK, Longoria Bastón was an exemplary student who showed a willingness to represent the best of the university. In fact, Longoria Bastón's long career of service began in 1996 when she won Miss Texas A&M University–Kingsville and continued when she won Miss Corpus Christi, Texas, in 1998. After an unsuccessful bid at Miss Texas, USA, Longoria Bastón moved to Los Angeles to pursue an acting career.

Upon her arrival in Los Angeles, Longoria Bastón won acting roles in small films and television shows. Then in 2001, she won the role of Isabella Braña in the popular soap opera *The Young and the Restless*. Her portrayal of Braña from 2001 to 2003 earned Longoria Bastón an American Latino Media Arts Award for outstanding actress in a daytime drama. Longoria Bastón left *The Young and the Restless* in 2003 to star in the short-lived television police drama *L.A. Dragnet*.

In 2004, Longoria Bastón won her most famous role to date as Gabrielle Solis in the television comedy *Desperate Housewives*. She starred alongside award-winning actresses Teri Hatcher, Felicity Huffman, Marcia Cross, Nicollette Sheridan, and fellow South Texan Ricardo Chavira. During her eight-year tenure as Solis on *Desperate Housewives*, Longoria Bastón received multiple Golden Globe nominations, Screen Actors Guild Awards, and a People's Choice Award for "Favorite Female TV Star." She was listed in *People*'s "50 Most Beautiful People," *People en Español*'s "50 Mas Bellos," and *Rolling Stone*'s "People of the Year" in 2009. In addition, she was named *Maxim*'s "#1 Hottest Woman in the World" two years in a row and celebrated as *Forbes*'s "Highest Paid TV Star" in 2011. While earning these awards and recognitions, Longoria Bastón created the film production company UnbeliEVAble Entertainment, which she uses to fund film and television projects that showcase women and Latino issues. In addition, Longoria Bastón earned a master of arts in Chicano studies from California State University, Northridge, in 2013 to better understand her historical subjectivity, identity, and culture as a Mexican American and to learn how to become a more active advocate for Latino communities. In fulfilling this philanthropic goal, Longoria Bastón has become a fierce advocate for the Latino community by joining the board of directors at the Mexican American Legal Defense and Educational Fund and the National Museum of the American Latino and working with the National Council of La Raza, the United Farm Workers, and the Dolores Huerta Foundation.[19] Longoria Bastón has also become a prominent and vocal member of the national Democratic Party. She was cochair of President Barack Obama's 2012 presidential campaign and campaigned nationwide for the Democratic presidential nominees in 2016 and 2020.

Additionally, Longoria Bastón has used her production company UnbeliEVAble Entertainment to bring attention to the Latino community. For example, one of the first projects produced by UnbeliEVAble Entertainment and directed by Longoria Bastón was *Latinos Living the American Dream* (2010), a documentary that showcases Latinos throughout the United States who are making a difference in their communities and inspiring Latinos to further their education, pursue careers, and enact positive change on a national and local scale. Another production of UnbeliEVAble Entertainment is *The Harvest / La Cosecha: The Story of the Children Who Feed America* (2011), an emotionally raw documentary that follows three US Latino child migrant laborers as they travel across the United States picking crops. *The Harvest / La Cosecha* follows twelve-year-old Zulema Lopez, fourteen-year-old Perla Sanchez, and sixteen-year-old Victor Huapilla as they travel with their families picking crops in Texas, Michigan, and Florida. In many ways Zulema, Perla, and Victor look and act like stereotypical US preteens and teens. For example, Zulema is always on her cell phone, never leaves home without makeup, and often defies her mother. Perla is seen taking pictures with her friends at school, playing on her laptop, and joking with her family. Victor is seen placing his younger sisters on their school bus and then later contributing to discussions in one of his high school classes. All seem like stereotypical US teens, but they're not. When not in school, "they face back breaking labor in 100-degree heat, physical hazards from pesticides, the emotional burden of helping their families through economic crises when work opportunities dry up, separation from their families and peer groups, and dwindling hope for their educational and economic advancement."[20] By documenting Zulema, Perla, and Victor's day-to-day struggles, *The Harvest* brings to the forefront the struggles of the four hundred thousand US child migrant laborers and the contradictions and exploitations built into the Fair Labor Standards Act, which states that there is no minimum wage requirement and no overtime pay, and that children can begin working in agriculture at any age (with parental/guardian consent) without hour regulations outside school hours.[21]

A more personal philanthropic endeavor for Longoria Bastón is Eva's Heroes, a San Antonio–based nonprofit organization that provides inclusive experiences for teens and young adults who have intellectual special needs. Eva's Heroes also provides family counseling, parenting workshops, and sibling support groups for their families. Eva's Heroes is especially personal to Longoria Bastón because of her older sister Lisa, who has intellectual special needs. The workshops and support programs offered by Eva's Heroes are a direct result of the experiences the Longorias have had as a family. Eva has stated, "I was extremely fortunate to grow up with an intellectually disabled sister. My mother became a special education teacher because of her, and therefore, I have been involved with all facets of this community since I could walk and talk."[22] Her experiences provide her with intimate insight into the intellectual special needs community and what the family and friends of these individuals go through. Longoria Bastón uses her star power to garner support and funds for this organization, the most successful of which is an annual celebrity Casino Night where all proceeds go directly to Eva's Heroes.

Longoria Bastón has also established the Eva Longoria Fund, a funding source within the California Community Foundation dedicated to improving the quality of life for children with illnesses from all racial and ethnic backgrounds and the Latino community; and the Eva Longoria Foundation, a nonprofit organization focused on helping Latinas attain higher education and become successful entrepreneurs. To explain the Eva Longoria Foundation's focus on Latinas, Longoria Bastón states, "The growing Latina population is an untapped resource in this country. If we give Latinas the tools to unlock their potential, we will see amazing results."[23] The Eva Longoria Foundation provides business literacy for Latina entrepreneurs. Specifically, the foundation provides workshops for Latinas on how to create a business plan, apply for a small business loan, keep financial records, and network to capitalize on assets. Longoria Bastón is not only educating Latinas on how to become successful business owners but is also funding them. The Eva Longoria Foundation Microloan Fund contributed $2 million to Latina small business owners.[24]

The Eva Longoria Foundation also helps Latinas attain higher education. In researching the educational trends of Latinas, Longoria Bastón became concerned with the "stop-out" rate of Latinas, meaning the high rate of Latinas who do not pursue a degree past a two-year college, thus limiting their career and financial opportunities. Longoria Bastón explains in her master's thesis, "Success Stems from Diversity: The Value of Latinas in STEM," that most Latinas begin their postsecondary education at a community college; however, STEM majors often encounter STEM course transferability issues from the community college to the four-year university or find that their community college courses have not prepared them for STEM major courses at a bachelor degree–granting institution, resulting in Latina students stopping their educational attainment at the community college.[25] The Eva Longoria Foundation helps improve educational opportunities for Latinas by supporting bridge programs from high school to college and from college to university that foster student retention, resulting in a higher percentage of four-year degrees and career paths for Latinas, some of which are in the STEM fields.

The Eva Longoria Foundation also supports the Parent Institute for Quality Education (PIQE), an organization that fosters collaboration between parents, educators, and their students to ensure a holistic approach to educational attainment. PIQE offers workshops regarding family financial literacy, professional development for teachers, and programs that focus on parent educational engagement, parent leadership, early childhood development, and enhancement in STEM fields. PIQE advocates for a focus on STEM courses and careers for women because of the gender gap in these fields.

According to the National Science Foundation, only 29 percent of positions in the STEM professions are held by women.[26] This is in large part because of the long-standing sexism against girls in STEM-affiliated educational courses. For example, girls have historically been underestimated and made to feel inferior in math and science courses in middle and high school and as a result are discouraged from taking advanced courses or majoring in these areas.[27] This sexism has deterred women from pursuing STEM professions, creating a lack of role models in the STEM workforce, including in secondary and postsecondary STEM classrooms.[28] As this anthology of powerful and intellectual women proves, women are *not* inferior to men in any capacity, including in STEM fields. So why are more women not entering STEM fields? After studying high school and college academic trends across the country, Catherine Riegle-Crumb, Chandra Muller, Barbara King, and Eric Grodsky found that women are academically matching their male counterparts in STEM courses; however, they are excelling in other areas as well.[29] Riegle-Crumb explains, "It's not that they [women] did poorly in high school math and science classes—it's that they did even *better* in English and have a comparative advantage . . . [they] are making a choice *for* something [else], not just *against* STEM majors and professions."[30] Although 29 percent of TAMUK female graduates earned STEM degrees from 2015 to 2020, the single standout major for women at TAMUK is communication science and disorders, which was the degree earned by our next alumna.

Jo Ann Briones

The communication science and disorders major at TAMUK specializes in speech-language pathology, communication therapy that focuses on speech, language, and swallowing disorders in patients ranging in age from infants to geriatrics. To understand why so many TAMUK female students choose this major, I interviewed Jo Ann Briones, a TAMUK alumna who earned a master of science in communication science and disorders in 2009 and is a practicing speech-language pathologist in South Texas. In the interest of full disclosure, Briones is also my sister, which made this interview convenient; however, I also interviewed Briones because I have observed for years how she approaches her profession and how she treats her patients. This exposure has given me exclusive insight into how she and her TAMUK cohorts serve their communities. I believe her story, and those of the women of service she represents, deserve to be heard, especially in the context of the other women in this anthology. Like Longoria Bastón, Briones is a present-day pioneer for South Texas philanthropic women.

Briones was first introduced to the speech-language pathology profession while employed at a child day care. Her employer, in addition to owning the day care, was a speech-language pathologist and would treat some of the day-care children. After sitting in on a few sessions, Briones became intrigued by the science of the profession and was drawn by the social aspect of working with a patient one on one. She decided speech-language pathology was the profession to which she wanted to dedicate herself, and she knew she wanted to remain in South Texas to practice it. Briones knew that those who lived in the more rural areas of South Texas needed the most help, not because they had more speech or language issues, but because they were often forgotten—unseen and unheard. To better serve bilingual and monolingual Spanish speakers in these rural areas, Briones first earned a bachelor of arts in Spanish from Texas State University and then earned a master of science in communication science and disorders from TAMUK in 2009.

Briones first began practicing as a speech-language pathologist in a South Texas speech-language rehabilitation center that specialized in treating children. She later began seeing patients in their homes in the more rural areas of South Texas. Although working with children was rewarding, Briones found her true calling in providing speech-language therapy to the geriatric population:

> Working with the geriatric population, especially those with dementia, a patient that has been bed-ridden for weeks or months or years—people don't realize that they were a pilot or somebody that raised 10 kids that are all professionals or a teacher for 50 years or a librarian. And I feel that as a therapist, I get to find out those things. I get to interact with them on that level, knowing these extra things about them; and I feel that sometimes we're the only ones that get to do that, whether you're a speech therapist, physical therapist, or occupational therapist, because as a nurse you don't have that time with a patient. But as a therapist, you're able to sit with somebody for thirty minutes or an hour and converse with them and laugh with them and hug them and talk with them and play with them and feed them. You get that human connection, and that's why I don't think I could do anything else.[31]

This human connection calls so many TAMUK female graduates to their philanthropic humanitarianism, to help those who have lost their voice.

These women, who treat their patients with respect and compassion, are paving the way for future generations of South Texan women. They are showing us that it is not enough to just earn a degree and enter a profession. It is important to help people in real, compassionate ways, to create positive change in yourself and in others, and to be of service to your community.

When shown the mural that is the subject of this book, Briones praised the progressiveness of its message but stated, "I hope graduates see the mural and think, 'Look what's happened so far,' because there's more to do. There is still change to come and advancement for the female student, for women in the workforce, and for educated women." Briones is all too right.

While more women than men are earning associate, bachelor's, and master's degrees, only 42 percent of those who earned a professional or doctorate degree in 2019 were women,[32] which means women are populating the workforce, but not leading it. However, this influx of women in the workforce has resulted in 41 percent of women being the sole or primary financial provider for their family, doubling since the 1960s.[33] Although this is undoubtedly a significant gain for women, unfortunately, most women still get paid less than men. On average, women earn eighty-one cents for every dollar a man earns, including women with doctorate degrees.[34] The wage gap is even more significant for women of color. According to the National Women's Law Center, African American women earn sixty-three cents for every dollar a man earns, while Hispanic women earn fifty-five cents for every dollar a man earns.[35] Furthermore, women of color are disproportionately denied tenure and promotion within academia, as detailed in the eye-opening *Presumed Incompetent: The Intersections of Race and Class for Women in Academia* (2012).

Briones is right—there is more to do. What has been accomplished by Baugh, Bonner, Cantú, Longoria Bastón, Briones, and the other women in these pages is only the beginning for South Texas women. As the soldadera and millennial South Texas woman salute each other's evolutionary accomplishments, they also wave in the next generation of women revolutionaries, pioneers, educators, politicians, and artists—all future leaders of South Texas and all called on to serve their communities. May they be inspired by the righteousness and selflessness of the women in these pages and pave new paths for those who will come after them, as the soldadera paved the way for the millennial South Texas woman.

Notes

1. *El Rancho* (Kingsville: South Texas State Teachers College, 1926).

2. *El Rancho*.

3. Cecilia A. Hunter and Leslie G. Hunter, *Texas A&M University–Kingsville* (Chicago: Arcadia, 2000), 51.

4. Miguel A. Guajardo and Francisco J. Guajardo, "The Impact of *Brown* on the Brown of South Texas: A Micropolitical Perspective on the Education of Mexican Americans in a South Texas Community," *American Educational Research Journal* 41, no. 3 (January 2004): 512, https://doi.org/10.3102/00028312041003501.

5. Hunter and Hunter, *Texas A&M University–Kingsville*, 50.

6. Hunter and Hunter, 50.

7. Hunter and Hunter, 51.

8. *El Rancho* (Kingsville: Texas College of Arts & Industries, 1941).

9. *El Rancho* (Kingsville: Texas College of Arts & Industries, 1953).

10. "Lola Bonner Passes Away; Pioneer for Women in the County," *Rockport Pilot*, February 13, 2008, accessed December 30, 2013, http://www.rockportpilot.com/people/article_e5ad7c0f-722c-550f-9a9c-298ceabde123.html.

11. "Lola Bonner Passes Away."

12. "Lola Bonner Passes Away."

13. Norma Cantú, "Centering the Margins: A Chicana in the English Classroom," in *Race in the College Classroom: Pedagogy and Politics*, ed. Bonnie Tusmith and Maureen T. Reddy (New Brunswick, NJ: Rutgers University Press, 2002), 231.

14. Cantú, 232.

15. Cantú, 230.

16. Cantú, 233.

17. Cantú, 236.

18. Norma E. Cantú, *Canícula: Snapshots of a Girlhood en la Frontera* (Albuquerque: University of New Mexico Press, 1995), xi.

19. "Eva Longoria Fund," California Community Foundation, accessed January 7, 2021, https://www.calfund.org/eva-longoria-fund/.

20. "Actor and Activist Eva Longoria Joins Congresswoman Lucille Roybal-Allard (CA-34) in a Renewed Push to Protect Child Farmworkers in the United States," Mexican American Legal Defense and Educational Fund, June 16, 2011, https://www.maldef.org/2011/06/actor-and-activist-eva-longoria-joins-congresswoman-lucille-roybal-allard-ca-34-in-a-renewed-push-to-protect-child-farmworkers-in-the-united-states/.

21. US Department of Labor, Wage and Hour Division, *Child Labor Requirements in Agricultural Occupations under the Fair Standards Act*, Child Labor Bulletin 102, November 2016, accessed December 28, 2020, http://www.dol .gov/whd/regs/compliance/childlabor102.pdf.

22. "Eva's Heroes," Eva's Heroes, accessed May 25, 2013, http://www.evash eroes.org/.

23. "Eva Longoria," Eva Longoria Foundation, accessed May 26, 2013, https:// evalongoriafoundation.org/leadership/.

24. "Our Programs," Eva Longoria Foundation, accessed January 4, 2021, https://evalongoriafoundation.org/our-programs/.

25. Eva Longoria, "Success Stems from Diversity: The Value of Latinas in STEM," (master's thesis, California State University, Northridge, 2008), 31–32.

26. Beethika Khan, Carol Robbins, and Abigail Okrent, "Science & Engineering Indicators: The State of US Science and Engineering 2020," US National Science Foundation, January 15, 2020, accessed January 4, 2021, https://ncses .nsf.gov/pubs/nsb20201/u-s-s-e-workforce.

27. Catherine Hill, Christianne Corbett, and Andresse St. Rose, *Why So Few? Women in Science, Technology, Engineering, and Mathematics* (Washington, DC: American Association of University Women, 2010), xiv, https://www.aauw .org/app/uploads/2020/03/why-so-few-research.pdf.

28. Hill, Corbett, and St. Rose, xiv–xvi.

29. Kay Randall, "Where the Girls Aren't," *UT News*, April 8, 2013, http:// www.utexas.edu/know/2013/04/08/where-the-girls-aren%E2%80%99t/.

30. Randall.

31. Jo Ann Briones, interview with the author, June 30, 2013.

32. US Department of Commerce, "Educational Attainment of the Population 18 Years and Over, by Age, Sex, Race, and Hispanic Origin: 2019," March 30, 2020, https://www.census.gov/content/census/en/data/tables/2019/demo/ educational-attainment/cps-detailed-tables.html.

33. Sarah Jane Glynn, "Breadwinning Mothers Continue to be the US Norm," Center for American Progress, May 10, 2019, https://www.americanprogress. org/issues/women/reports/2019/05/10/469739/breadwinning-mothers-contin ue-u-s-norm/.

34. *The Annual Report on the Economic Status of the Profession, 2018–19* (Washington, DC: American Association of University Professors, May 2019), https://www.aaup.org/report/annual-report-economic-status-profes sion-2018-19.

35. *The Wage Gap: The Who, How, Why, and What to Do* (Washington, DC: National Women's Law Center, October 2020),
https://nwlc.org/wp-content/uploads/2019/09/Wage-Gap-Who-how.pdf.

Epilogue

SUSAN L. ROBERSON

In *Telling to Live: Latina Feminist Testimonios*, the authors write of the importance of finding discursive space for women's stories, for the stories that reveal complex individual identities, common experiences among women, and the ways the complexities of culture impact their lives. The stories the Latina Feminist Group discover and construct about their own lives in *testimonios* and autobiographies counter the silences, the gaps in knowledge that have conspired against women's autonomy and empowerment. In doing so, they open an oppositional historical space in which women are agents of politics and change. If there is no history, only auto/biography, then telling the forgotten, the unknown, the uncelebrated lives of women counters and completes the histories that hegemonic society articulates about itself. Creating alternative biographies and histories, the Latina testimonios and the biographical sketches of *Women across Time* open discursive space for women and their stories, a space where a feminist standpoint or perspective frames the past.[1]

The biographies collected in *Women across Time / Mujeres a Través del Tiempo* reveal some of the complexities of identity that the *testimonios* explore—the ways that intersections between race, ethnicity, class, gender, language, location, and culture shape a sense of self. The biographies indicate how expectations for women's lives, shaped by class and culture, impacted the decisions women made and ignited their determination to create their own futures. Whether they came from the upper classes of money and privilege or from the working classes, the women featured here had to contend with expectations about the trajectory of their lives. These sketches indicate how women negotiated gender stereotypes and expectations, many balancing traditional roles as daughters, wives, and mothers with their more public lives. They demonstrate how these determined women confronted the gender politics of Austin and the academy, of the military and the art world. Set in South Texas, these stories inevitably tell about language, Spanish and English, and about racist attitudes at play in the borderlands. Traversing the border between Mexico and Texas, many of the women adopted a bilingual double consciousness that propelled them to careers in education or art that have disrupted and healed assumptions about cultural identity. These brief sketches also reveal how a South Texas politics of location, shaped by history, the semiarid terrain, and the people who claimed it as home influenced individual identity and purpose. Demonstrating the intersections of "family history, labor history, immigration history, women's history, and intellectual history" that Emma Pérez examines in *The Decolonial Imaginary*, these sketches imagine the social spaces where South Texas women forged identities and lives.[2] Although each sketch focuses on one woman, the collective multibiography reveals not only personal connections between women—the relations between the Kings, Klebergs, and Armstrongs, and the connections between "The Rebel," Jovita Idar, and Jovita González—but also the common experiences of living and finding a calling, a life's purpose, in the social spaces of South Texas.

Waving across time, *la soldadera* to the millennial graduate, the essays in this book remind us that women's lives, women's stories, women's issues matter not only for the particular and collective woman, but for the larger society. Using their talents, fortunes, and abilities, these women made important and lasting contributions to the fields of ranching, education, politics, the military, and the arts. They shared a sense of responsibility often learned from their mothers and fathers to do something with their talents and gifts. Telling their stories illustrates their shared sense of a calling that led them into careers of advocacy and caring for others. Indicating how one person can make a difference in the lives of others and in a regional politics of location, the stories gathered here inspire and point the way for others to become their better selves and to better the lives of others. That may be the most important legacy they leave for those who come after them, the legacy of inspiration.

The mural and the book begin with the figure of the unnamed *soldadera* saluting, waving to the unnamed college graduate across time who returns the salute. Let us now imagine a scene where the college graduate turns to the unseen women who figuratively stand off the edge of the mural and waves them into the story, the mural of *mujeres*. By waving across time and sending a shout of encouragement to young women wondering what to do with their talents, she figuratively joins the future to the past. Having surveyed the past, the mural and this book encourage a view to the future, a future that women will help shape.

Notes

1. The Latina Feminist Group, *Telling to Live: Latina Feminist Testimonios* (Durham, NC: Duke University Press, 2001), 1–5.

2. Emma Pérez, *The Decolonial Imaginary: Writing Chicanas into History* (Bloomington: Indiana University Press, 1999), 19.

Contributors

Shannon L. Baker is a professor of Mexican history. Throughout her career at Texas A&M University–Kingsville she has taught courses on Latin American history, Mexican history, and Mexican American history. She currently serves as associate vice president for student success.

A native of Kingsville, Texas, **Santa Contreras Barraza** is a contemporary Chicana/Tejana artist and founder of Barraza Fine Art, LLC, a gallery and studio committed to furthering the appreciation of the visual arts in the borderlands. She has a master of fine arts from the University of Texas and formerly taught at Texas A&M University–Kingsville. Her artwork has been widely exhibited in the United States, Europe, Mexico, and Argentina.

Veronica Nohemi Durán is a doctoral candidate in the history department at the University of Nebraska–Lincoln.

Adriana Garza-Flores is a South Texas native. She earned a master's degree in history and politics from Texas A&M University–Kingsville. She is currently the director of marketing and communications at Texas A&M University–Kingsville.

Manuel Flores is a professor of journalism and communications at Texas A&M University–Kingsville. He is an award-winning journalist for his work at the *Corpus Christi Caller-Times* and *Irving Daily News*. He has published three books, *Hispanics in Journalism: 200 Years of Spanish-Language Influence in U.S. Communications* (2008), *Chicanadas: The Adventures of Growing Up Mexican in South Texas* (2020), and

Cuentos Tejanos: Tales of Life in the Wild Horse Desert (2021). His new book *Hispanics in American Media* came out in fall 2021.

Born and raised in Kingsville, Texas, **Mary Jane Garza** now lives in Austin, Texas, after graduating from the University of Texas at Austin in 1986 with a degree in fine arts. She taught arts and crafts in public and private schools for the Texas Commission on the Arts, the Austin Arts Commission, Education Service Center Region 13, and several other nonprofit organizations for more than twenty years. In 2019 she was awarded a public arts commission from the city of Austin for the new Montopolis Recreation Center. She is also a freelance writer and has contributed articles to several publications including the *Austin Chronicle*, *Hispanic Magazine*, and *Austin American Statesman*. Carmen Lomas Garza is her sister.

Nirmal Goswami is Regents Professor of political science at Texas A&M University–Kingsville. His areas of interest include American politics, global political economy, and demographics. He has developed multiple initiatives with universities and nongovernmental organizations in Asia, Africa, and the South Pacific. Dr. Goswami has provided unique experiential learning and research opportunities in locations across the world, to students from a wide spectrum of academic backgrounds.

Mary Lee Grant has a PhD in history from Texas A&M University. She is a lecturer at the Hanoi University of Mining and Geology. She has written two books on ESL teaching, published by the Vietnamese National Publishing Company, and is the editor of *Artist in Exile*, a memoir by Vietnamese American movie star Kieu Chinh. She writes for the *Washington Post*.

Michelle Johnson Vela is a professor of Spanish who earned her PhD in Latin American literature from Indiana University in 2001. She has worked in the Department of Language and Literature at Texas A&M University–Kingsville for nineteen years. Her scholarly interests include Hispanic Caribbean literature, literature from the Southern Cone of Latin America, US Latino literature, and cultural studies.

Larry Knight received his PhD at Texas A&M in College Station. He has taught Texas history for over thirty years. His research focuses on San Antonio and South Texas in the nineteenth century.

Jody A. Marín is an associate professor of English and coordinator of freshman and sophomore English at Texas A&M University–Kingsville. Her fields of specialization include Chicano studies, and composition and rhetoric.

Octavio Quintanilla is the author of the poetry collection *If I Go Missing* (Slough Press, 2014) and served as the 2018–2020 Poet Laureate of San Antonio, Texas. He holds a PhD from the University of North Texas and teaches literature and creative writing in the MA/MFA program at Our Lady of the Lake University in San Antonio.

Sandra Rexroat was a longtime member of the Texas A&M University–Kingsville family, serving in several capacities including director of sponsored research and director of the South Texas Archives.

Susan L. Roberson is Regents Professor of English at Texas A&M University–Kingsville. Her works include *Antebellum American Women Writers and the Road: American Mobilities* and *Emerson in His Sermons: A Man-Made Self.* Her scholarly interests include nineteenth-century American literature and American travel writing.

Regents Professor of English Emeritus **David Sabrio** retired from Texas A&M University–Kingsville in 2014 after thirty years of service. He received his PhD in English from the University of South Carolina.

Lieutenant Colonel Richard P. Spainhour (US Army, Retired) served as the Texas A&M University–Kingsville professor of military science from 2010 to 2014. He retired from active duty in 2014 following almost twenty-four years of service and relocated to Austin, Texas, He works for a Fortune 20 health insurance company as an analytics manager.

Homero S. Vera has been a regional historian since 1997, when he started editing and publishing *El Mesteño*, a magazine about the history of the Mexican Americans of South Texas and northern Mexico. Homero was the former chief property officer and museum coordinator for the Kenedy Memorial Foundation in Sarita, Texas.

Jenni Vinson, a South Texas Mexican American, was educated at Texas A&I and Texas A&M University–Kingsville. She is currently employed by Alice High School, where she teaches and serves as chair of the English Department.

Pamela Wright is an assistant professor of English at Texas A&M University–Kingsville, where she teaches nineteenth- and twentieth-century British literature. She is former editor of *The Newsletter of the D. H. Lawrence Society of North America.* Her most recent publication, "One Woman's Song IS Another's: Sisterhood and Defying the Patriarchal Order in Jean Rhys's 'Let Them Call It Jazz,'" appeared in the *South Atlantic Review.* Her teaching and research interests include modern and contemporary British literature, particularly the works of D. H. Lawrence, World War I trench poetry, and disability theory.

Index

acting, 210–11
Afghanistan, 197–201
Alvarado, Francisco, 33
American G. I. Forum, 180, 184–85
American Home Missionary Society, 25
Annenberg, Walter, 131
Anzaldúa, Gloria, 156
Armstrong, Anne, 1, 3–5, 75, 125–32; ambassador to Britain, 130–31; awards and honors, 125–26, 128, 131–32; education, 125–27
Armstrong, Charlie, 127
Armstrong, John, 126
Armstrong, John III, 126–27
Armstrong, Tobin, 126–29, 131
Armstrong, Tom, 126
Armstrong Ranch, 5, 125–28
art, 5–6, 131, 154–57 (*see also* lotería, monitos)
Arte Publico Press, 87–88

Barker, Eugene, 82
Barnes, Ben, 119–20
Barraza, Santa, 154–55, 160, 162
Baugh, Lila, 204–05
Berlanga, David and Bertha Hinojosa, 92
bilingual education, 79, 84–85
biography, 2–3, 211
Bonner, Lola Lee, 206–07
Briones, Jo Ann, 215–17; education, 214–16
Briscoe, Dolph, 120–21
Briscoe, Janey, 121

Campbell, Phillip Pitt and Mary Helen Goff, 70, 72
Canales, Hipolito, 181
Canales, J. A. "Tony," 181
Cantú, Norma Elia, 207–10; education, 207–08
carrancistas, 16–17
Carranza, Venustiano, 11, 14, 16–18, 83
Casis, Lilia, 81, 82
Castañeda, Carlos, 82
Castro, Mauro, 146
Catholic Church, 42, 44–45, 47, 50–51, 62–65, 89, 119
Chamberlain, Hiram, 24–30, 34
Charles, Prince of Wales, 131
Cheney, Dick, 127
Chicano movement, 155–56, 209; artists, 155–56, 158–59, 161, 163; exhibits, 159
Cisneros, Sandra, 161
Civil War, 33, 48–49, 54
Clotilda García Collection, The, 188–89
conjunto music, 168; female performers, 168
Cortina Wars, 48
Cotera, Maria Eugenia, 86
Cousins, Robert B., 203–04
Cruz Blanca, 5, 16–19
Cruz, Isabel, 86
Cypher, John, 72, 74

De la Barra, Francisco, 16
Democratic Party, 126, 128–29
Department of Homeland Security, 107
Díaz, Porfirio, 15, 84

"Dirty Thirty, The," 119–20
Discrimination, 84, 88, 93, 96, 102, 104,
    132, 136–37, 168–69, 180–81, 184,
    204, 207 (*see also* sexism)
Dobie, J. Frank, 81–82, 88
Doddridge, Perry, 35

Earthman, James Bradshaw "Jim" III, 120
East, Arthur Lee, 57, 59
East, Sarita Kenedy, 1, 4, 51, 53–67;
    education, 59
education, 38, 81–82, 86, 92–93, 94,
    185–86, 204–06; higher education,
    104–07, 121–22, 143–45; STEM
    fields, 214–15; teaching, 6, 81–82,
    84–85, 91, 93–96, 104–05, 156, 158,
    180–81, 203–04, 208 (*see also* entries
    for individual women; bilingual
    education)
Eimer, Margaret (pseud. Eve Raleigh),
    83, 86–87
El Progresso, 15
El Radical, 15
Elisofon, Eliot, 74
Emerson, Ralph Waldo, 3
Equal Rights Amendment, 128, 187
Erwin, Frank C., 119
Escandon, Count José de, 43, 80, 180

Farenthold, Frances "Sissy" Tarlton,
    1, 3–4, 113–23; education, 115–16,
    Wells College, 121–22; "Women's
    Search for Peace," 121
federalists, 13, 17
feminist, 221
Ferber, Edna, 69, 71
fire risk assessment, 196
firefighting, 194
fireworks, 195
Flores, Enrique, 157
folklore, 79–83, 85–86, 88
Ford, Gerald, 128, 130
Frissell, Toni, 73–74

García, Clotilda, 1–2. 4, 7, 179–89;
    activism, 185–87, 188; awards and
    honors, 185, 189; education, 180

García, Hector, 2, 97, 121, 138, 154,
    180, 183–85
García, J. A., 180–81, 183–84
García, Jose G. and Faustina Perez, 180
García, Juliet, 4, 6, 101–8; awards and
    honors, 101, 106–08; education,
    102–04
García, Oscar, 103
García, Oscar and Paulita Rico
    Villarreal, 101–03
García, Xico, 180, 184
Garza, Carmen Lomas, 4–7, 153–63;
    art exhibits, 157, 159–60; awards,
    161; books, 161; education, 154–55;
    paintings, 160, 162
Garza, Maria Lomas, 154, 162
Gonzáles, Arnold, 1, 3, 91, 94–95, 99,
    202
González, Jacobo and Severina Guerra
    Barrera, 80
González, Jovita (Mrs. Jovita González
    Mireles), 4–6, 79–89, 94; education,
    81–82, 86; honors, 86; publications,
    82–83, 86–88
Gonzáles, Mary Alice Berlanga, 4, 6,
    91–99; awards and honors, 97–98;
    education, 92–93, 96; principal,
    96–98
Gorena, Javier, 157
Graves, Curtis, 117
Groves, Helen "Helenita" Kleberg, 69–72
Guerra, Carlos, 156

Halston (Roy Halston Frowick),
    130–31
Hardin, John Wesley, 126–27
Hazlitt, William, 3
Higareda, Sergio, 105
Hispanic, 108, 117, 217 (*see also* Latino
    and Mexican American)
Hopwood v. Texas, 144
horses, 126 (*see also* racing)
Howard, Frank and Mildred Elisabeth
    Hill, 192–93
Howard, Merideth, 2, 7, 192–201;
    education, 193
Huerta, Victoriano, 11, 16–17

humanitarian service, 198–99
Hvolboll, Hugh, 195–97, 200–01

Idar, Jovita, 12
immigration, 127
Irma Rangel School of Pharmacy,
147 (*see also* Texas A&M University
Health System College of Pharmacy)

John G. and Marie Stella Kenedy
Memorial Foundation, 63–65
Johnson, Belton "B," 69, 71–72
Johnson, Lyndon Baines, 71, 94, 119,
187
Johnson, Sarah Kleberg, 71
Juarez, Rumaldo, 145–46
Junta Revolucionaria, 15

Kahlo, Frida, 158–59
kenedeños, 60–62
Kenedy Ranch, 55, 59–62 (*see also* La
Parra Ranch)
Kenedy, John Gregory, 51, 57–58, 60
Kenedy, John Gregory, Jr., 51
Kenedy, Marie Stella Turcotte, 50, 58,
52
Kenedy, Mifflin, 1, 29, 32, 34–35,
47–51, 55–60
Kenedy, Petra de la Vela, 1, 4–5, 42,
85–51, 58, 62
kineños, 30, 38–39, 55
King, Henrietta, 1–2, 4–5, 23–39, 71,
154; education, 25–28
King, Richard, 2, 23, 29–36, 47–49,
55–56, 71, 153
King, Richard II, 32–35
King, Robert E. Lee, 33–35
King Ranch, 23, 30, 32, 34–36, 55, 60,
69, 71–74, 126, 135–36, 153–54, 203
King Ranch Stables, 72
Kleberg, Alice King, 23, 34–37, 71
Kleberg, Helen Campbell, 69–75, 126;
education, 70
Kleberg, Richard "Dick," 71
Kleberg, Robert, 36–38, 71
Kleberg, Robert J. Jr., 70–75, 203
Kleberg County, 32

La Croníca, 15
Laney, Pete, 144
language oppression, 170–71, 207
La Parra Ranch, 50, 56–58
Larkin, Henrietta Kleberg, 126
Larkin, John, 126
Las Víboras Ranch, 80
Latino/as, 170, 212–14 (*see also*
Mexican American)
law, 113–14, 116, 138, 206
League of United American Citizens
(LULAC), 85
Lebh Shomea House of Prayer, 63–64
Lee, Robert E., 31–32, 34
Legendre, Armant and Olive, 125
Limón, José, 86
Longoria, Eva (Mrs. Bastón), 174,
210–15; education, 211; philanthropic
organizations, 211–14
López, Jennifer, 165, 173
lotería, 154, 157, 162–63

Madero, Francisco, 11, 15–16
Magnon, Adolpho, 15, 17
Mauzy, Oscar, 120
McGovern, George, 129
medical field, 179–80; 183–84; medical
school, 181–82
memoir, 18
Mesa-Baines, Amalia, 158, 163
Mexican American, 6–7, 79, 81, 101–
05, 108, 136–38, 140, 142–44, 155–56,
159, 161, 165, 173, 182, 184–89, 204
Mexican American Legislative Caucus,
142, 144
Mexican American Youth Organization
(MAYO), 155–56
Mexican Revolution (1810–1821), 54
Mexican Revolution (1910–1917),
11–19, 80, 84, 202
Mexican War (with US), 45–47, 54,
79–80, 87
Mifflin Kenedy & Co., 47
military, 192, 194–201
Mireles, Edmundo "E. E.," 83–84,
85–87, 94
Mireles Papers, The, 80, 86

monitos, 154, 163
Montoya, Greg, 138
Mora, Pat, 161
museums, 159
Mutscher, Gus, 118–20

National Women's Political Caucus, 6
newspapers, 15 (*see also La Cronica, El Radical, El Progresso*)
Nixon, Richard, 128–29
Northway, J. K., 72
Nueces Strip, 45–46, 54, 87

Oblates of Mary Immaculates House of Prayer, 51
O'Donnell, James, 47

Pan American Council, 85
Patman, Bill, 120
patrón system, 55, 114
Peña, Amado, 155
Petra Vela Kenedy Center, 51
philanthropy, 6, 51, 53, 56, 58, 62, 63–67, 206–07, 210–11
photography, 70, 73
politics, 6, 70, 89, 92, 113–14, 116, 125–32, 135–41
portraits, 4

Quintanilla, Abraham Jr., 166–75
Quintanilla, Abraham III, 167
Quintanilla, Marcela, 166
Quintanilla, Selena (Mrs. Perez), 1, 2, 4–5, 165–75; albums, 173–74; awards, 168, 174
Quintanilla, Suzette, 167

racing, horse, 72
Raleigh, Eve (*see* Eimer, Margaret)
ranches, 42–46
ranching, 6, 43–44, 53, 55–56, 60–61, 71–73, 126–27
Rancho Los Laureles, 49–50
Rangel, Irma Lerma, 1, 3–4, 134–47; education, 135–37; Higher Education Committee, 142, 144; Irma

Rangel School Pharmacy
Rangel, Presiliano M, "P.M." and Herminia, 136–38
Rangel-Henderson, Minnie, 135–38, 140
Reagan, Ronald, 128, 131
religion, 24–28, 31, 37–38 (*see also* Catholic Church)
Renfro, William, 155–56
Republican Party, 125, 128–30, 132
Richards, Ann, 121
Rivera, José, 154–55
Rodríguez, Pedro, 155, 158
Rohmer, Harriet, 160–61

Sadler, Jerry, 120
Saldivar, Yolanda, 172
Santa Gertrudis cattle, 72, 126
Sarita Kenedy East Foundation, 63–64
Selena (movie), 165–66, 174–75
Selena Museum, 166
Selena y Los Dinos, 167–68
sexism, 6, 113, 115, 117–18, 168–70, 182, 186–87, 194, 214–15, 217
Sharp, Frank, 118–20
Sharpstown Stock Fraud Scandal, 118
Sheridan, Philip, 54
Smith, Preston, 118, 120
soldaderas, 2, 5, 12–13, 17–19, 202, 222–23
South Texas Border Initiative, 143, 145
South Texas State Teachers College, 203–05
Spanish American Genealogical Association, 188
Spanish language, 84, 129, 170–71, 207; instruction, 84–85, 204–05 (*see also* language oppression)
Spohn, Arthur, 50
steamboat business, 33–34, 56
Stillman, Charles, 47=49

Taft, William Howard, 36
Tarlton, Judge Benjamin D. Sr., 114–15
Tarlton Law Library, 115
Taylor, Elizabeth, 69

tejano/a, 79, 171

tejano music, 7, 165, 168–69, 171–72; female performers, 168

Texas A&M University Health System College of Pharmacy, 134, 145–47

Texas A&M University-Kingsville, 7, 136, 145–46, 160, 210, 215

Texas A&I University, 92, 94, 134–35, 137, 145, 154–55, 158, 163, 205–06, 208

Texas Constitution, 114

Texas Higher Education Commission, 142, 144

Texas Folklore Society, 81

Texas legislature, 114–20, 139–41

Texas Revolution, 54

Texas Southmost College, 101, 105–08

Texas Women's Political Caucus, 138–39, 187

"Top Ten Percent Rule," 144–45

Treaty of Guadalupe Hidalgo, 47

United States Army Reserves, 195–96

University of Texas – Brownsville, 101, 105–08

vaquero, 36, 49, 60, 153 (*see also* kineños and kenedeños)

Vela, Francisco, 42

Vela, José Gregorio and María Josefa Reséndez, 43–45

Vela, Lázaro and Maria Garcia Vela, 42–43

Vela, Nicodemas and Gertrude Ramirez, 43–44

Veleño Ranch, 43

Vidal, Adrian, 48, 50

Vidal, Luis, 45, 47, 49

Villa, Francisco "Pancho," 12, 17

Villegas, Don Joaquim and Valerianna, 13–14

Villegas, Leopold, 14

Villegas de Magnon, Leonor, 5, 12–19; *The Rebel*, 18; *La Rebelde*, 18

Walworth, James, 32

Watergate Scandal, 128–29

Wendorf, Richard, 3

Whittington, Harry, 127

Wissinger, Charles, 5

women's rights, 12, 88, 186–87

Yturria, Francisco, 48

Zapata, Emiliano, 12